THE SANCTIFIED

SALVATIONIST

SHOWMAN

NISHAN DER GARABEDIAN

also known as

JOE THE TURK

EDDIE **H**OGBOOD

CREST
BOOKS

Published by Crest Books

Crest Books
The Salvation Army National Headquarters
615 Slaters Lane
Alexandria, VA 22314
Phone: 703-684-5523

Lt. Colonel Lesa Davis, *Editor-in-Chief*
Caleb Louden, *Managing Editor*
Maryam Outlaw-Martin, *Editorial Assistant*
Andrea Martin, *Graphic Designer*

ISBN print: 978-1-946709-19-6

All photographs used are courtesy of The Salvation Army National Archives,
The Salvation Army Eastern Territorial Archives, The Salvation Army
Western Territorial Museum & Archives, and The Hobgood Collection.

CONTENTS

APPENDIX

ENDORSEMENTS

"What a character! Saturated and overflowing with the joy of the Lord; immune to the societal strictures of cultural convention or public propriety; motivated by God's love for folk on the margins; willing to test the boundaries of extremity to introduce people who are still lacking the ongoing transformative experience of forgiveness of sins to a relationship with Jesus; this guy leaves a gospel-shaped stamp on everything he touches! The subject of Hobgood's book, this Garabed fellow, is one-of-a-kind!"

Major Stephen Court
Author, armybarmy.com blogger, and editor of *The Journal of Aggressive Christianity*

"Buckle your seat belts! You are about to embark on an extraordinary journey through the life, ministry, and legacy of a man who truly became a legend in his own time. Eddie Hobgood's book delivers a well-researched, thorough, and compelling examination of one of The Salvation Army's early-day 'sanctified characters'—Nishan Der Garabedian, better known as Joe the Turk. Although some may know his name and anecdotal tales of his unconventional approaches to evangelism, few comprehend the depth and extent of Joe the Turk's impact on The Salvation Army's mission in the late nineteenth and early twentieth centuries. ... In this one volume the author chronicles the amazing history of Joe the Turk. His careful citing of quotes increases the historical value of the book. It is a must-read for all who want to better understand the heart and passion of The Salvation Army's mission."

Commissioner William W. Francis
The Salvation Army

"What an adventure! What a story! Tragedy, comedy, villains, and heroes all in one book! A special story about a special life. Joseph Garabed found The Salvation Army in San Francisco and was able to make a career of 'fighting for Jesus.' No one else has gone to jail as many times to proclaim their faith. Lt. Colonel Hobgood's extensive research and love for this story will allow you, the reader, to feel what Joe went through. Persecution and stubbornness pushed Joe forward in his fight. This book documents what happened, and how it changed The Salvation Army for us all."

Susan Mitchem
National Archivist

"Joe the Turk's story is an important one for The Salvation Army as an organization to tell, and for all of us as individuals to hear. Eddie Hobgood's book is an engaging reminder of the courage required to listen for, acknowledge, and follow our calling. In its early days, The Salvation Army was viewed by others as a nuisance organization filled with peace-disturbing individuals in strange uniforms, but thanks be to God, the organization boldly followed its calling to live out the Mission, even while enduring physical abuse. … May Joe's story be a lesson to us all to listen, to discern, and to fully embrace our calling—even when it's not easy or comfortable."

Derek D Alley, CFRE
Co-Founder & President of Arthur Alley Associated

"In this book, Eddie Hobgood has gone beyond playful impersonation and given us an inspiring and challenging read. For the Salvationist historian it will give ample data on this colorful historic character. For the missiologist it provides inspiration for the creative use of metaphor and cultural engagement to communicate the message of Jesus. For the deeply conservative it may even prompt a 'please never again, dear Lord' type of prayer, but for all who read and follow Jesus, it provides us with a moving and motivating narrative of a transformed life fully surrendered to Jesus, and for that I am deeply thankful."

Phil Wall, MBE MSc
Master Executive Coach

"Throughout church history, a cloud of witnesses has surrounded us. However, regrettably, over the past century, a comprehensive biography of Joseph Garabedian, also known as Joe The Turk, has been absent. Eddie Hobgood now fills this gap by presenting the essential biography of an Armenian immigrant who became a Salvation Army officer and pioneered bold methods of ministry, establishing himself as one of America's foremost evangelists. This is a must-read for Christians today to find inspiration to be fearless and innovative in sharing the Good News of Jesus Christ."

Dr-Reverend Haig Kherlopian
Pastor, Church for the Nations

"Through years of careful research, God has given Lt. Colonel Eddie Hobgood a strong love and respect for Joe the Turk. His account of this singular Salvation Army life will influence hearts to be deeply challenged about following Jesus. 'Joe's' sense of the importance of religious freedom, his commitment to justice, and willingness to pay the price for their cause is as vital to American history as it is to Salvation Army history. What could cause a person to be so selfless, enduring such persecution and heartbreak for decades and yet continue in evangelistic ministry? The same Spirit of Jesus who filled the apostles had entirely sanctified Staff-Captain Nishan Der Garabedian with God's love for the lost. ... We are indebted to Eddie for making our acquaintance with Joe the Turk. Reader, be encouraged through this creative, surrendered man, that you too can persevere in whatever kind of life Jesus has called you to."

Reverend Diane Ury
National Ambassador for Holiness

FOREWORD

Lt. Colonel Eddie Hobgood's *The Sanctified Salvationist Showman* is an action-packed thrill ride through the life of one of The Salvation Army's most colorful early-day pioneers. Staff-Captain Joseph Garabed, better known as Joe the Turk, was an irrepressible, larger-than life officer-evangelist gifted with a passion for souls and an eye for the theatric. Arrested at least fifty-two times, Joe never shied away from a controversy or a crowd. With his trademark vibrant umbrella and eye-catching uniform, Joe traveled across the United States, sharing the good news of Jesus with all.

Through these fast-paced pages, Lt. Colonel Hobgood traces the life and ministry of this Salvationist showman from his roots in historic Armenia to his wayward years in California, his miraculous conversion, and his imaginative ministry. Lt. Colonel Hobgood has done the Army and the world a great service by sharing the story of Joe the Turk.

Lyndon Buckingham
22nd General & International Leader
The Salvation Army

PREFACE

For as long as I can remember, Nishan Der Garabedian/Joe the Turk has been a household name at the Hobgood home. Like a distant cousin, he was a part of our family and often filled a seat at the dinner table in our conversations. While many kids grew up hearing stories of knights and princesses, we grew up hearing stories of the "Sanctified Salvationist Showman" and his many adventures. We sang "For Freedom," a song from the dramatic presentation of Joe's life, as we marched down the hallway of our home. While some kids drew with crayons and markers, we were stamping "Jesus Saves" on the walls, and halls, and towels! (Father's note: not literally!)

When my dad was asked to portray Joe many years ago, I'm not sure he knew the impact it would have on us all. Dressed from head to toe like the colorful showman, he began his portrayal of Joe in 1992. Joe's passion for showmanship immediately drew my dad to his life and story. Joe's bravery and persistence made him difficult to forget.

I always knew I liked Joe, but his story has come alive in this book. There are times when he fills the role of your noisy, annoying neighbor, and other times, you find yourself weeping as you walk through his experiences and words. He is seen painting in prison cells, holding open-air meetings, and sharing the story of God's pursuit of him with capacity crowds. He is the very definition of being sold out for Jesus, and we can all learn and grow from his brave example.

A note about my dad: he has worked relentlessly on this book. He has left no word or detail unturned as he poured himself into the life of this legendary saint. He struggled to decide what stories to share out of the hundreds that he discovered through countless hours of reading and research. The words that fill these pages are a pure act of love that is thirty-plus years in the making. Without his research, Joe's full story could have been lost forever. But now it will continue, and Joe's persistence and bravery will live on in our minds and hearts.

Joe has forever changed the lives of not only my dad but our entire family. Joe fought for the freedom to march—those open-air marches would eventually take place in a small North Carolina town and bring my dad to the knowledge of Jesus and the doorstep of The Salvation Army. Perhaps he would have gone sooner had he heard the Sanctified Salvationist Showman blaring his double-jointed cornet down the street!

We can all use a little color in our lives. We can all use a little Joe in our ministry. We can all use a little of his passion for proclaiming, "Jesus is Mighty to Save!" As Joe said himself, "I have never been afraid of dying for my faith. Even today, I consider it the highest honor to be thought worthy to suffer for my Lord and Master, Jesus ... even to die for Him! When I stop, and I consider the incredible pain and agony that Jesus suffered for me, what is a bruise or a broken bone? What is being stabbed or even shot at? No, I count it all joy to suffer for Him who gave His life for me, and if through my pain, one more person comes to know Jesus Christ as Lord, then everything, everything that has happened to me has been more than worth it."

– Annie Hobgood-Bridges

Dedication and Special Thanks

"We should no more waste our breath sighing for the return of the giants of the past unless, with equal fervor, we covet the Spirit by whose strength they subdued kingdoms, wrought righteousness, and waxed valiant in the fight. We cannot praise the total devotion of our fathers [and mothers] in the past and, at one and the same time, refuse to make a like dedication of ourselves in the present."

– Frederick Coutts, *Essentials of Christian Experience*

This book is dedicated to the glory of God and to The Salvation Army for changing the trajectory of my life. I learned of Joe the Turk when I was a nine-year-old junior soldier. Even though he had been dead three decades, I had no idea how intertwined my life would be with his. It is truly an honor to play a small role in bringing this hero of the faith's story to life through this more complete telling.

I must thank many people who have walked this journey with me over the years. My wife, Kathy, has been my biggest cheerleader, and I cannot thank her enough for the support she has given me throughout this entire process. To my daughters, Annie, and Ashley, thank you for believing in me and letting me talk incessantly about Joe.

I came to The Salvation Army through the open-air ministry, which is a huge theme of this book. The faithful corps officers, who, week after week, proclaimed the gospel in the open-airs—evangelistic out-of-doors meetings conducted widely in the beginning years of The Salvation Army—changed my life.[1] If there had been no open-air, I most assuredly would not have found The Salvation Army. I owe a debt of gratitude to Majors Wayne and Susan McHargue, who brought me to The Salvation Army through their ministry, and Majors Al and Bobbie Sue Smith, who loved me as their own son. Lt. Colonels John Roy and Arduth Jones supported my passion for the theater during my high school years, and Majors Fred and Miriam Musgrave modeled excellence for me as an officer. This book is my tribute to all the officers and soldiers who believed in this "street urchin" and loved me unconditionally—Lanier, Busby, Jewett, Delaney, Cooper, Canning, Bratcher, Jeffrey, Swyers, Mikles, Holz, Tritton, Friday, Garrett, Congleton, Street, and so many more! Stephen Dahlem, you believed I could write this book; thank you for the incredible gift of your friendship and encouragement all along the way.

Susan Mitchem, The Salvation Army's national archivist, has been beyond generous in sharing her time and making The Salvation Army's national archives available to me. She has responded to questions after hours and on weekends. She has fed me pictures and stories that have added to this book. We have become dear friends through this process. Thank you, Susan; you're the best!

Rob Jeffrey, The Salvation Army Eastern Territory's archivist in New York, has provided resources that have enhanced the telling of this story. Rob has been most helpful with acquiring photographs of Joe's personal belongings that are housed in West Nyack, New York.

I am also grateful to the Houston Public Library, which has a treasure trove of Salvation Army documents in The Milsaps Collection. John Milsaps played a key role in Joe's conversion and amassed an extensive collection of Salvation Army materials. At his death, he bequeathed those items to the Houston Public Library, which has safely maintained and preserved them in the Houston Metropolitan Research Center (HMRC). HMRC has, to my knowledge, the only surviving poster Joe used to advertise his meetings. The pristine copies of *The War Cry*—the official national publication of The Salvation Army in The United States—from the Pacific Coast Division, helped me study Joe's early involvement with The Salvation Army and find unique biographical details.

I want to thank Lt. Colonels Jim and Pat LaBossiere for letting me share Joe's life with their officers and cadets over the years. They, along with Lt. Colonels Raphael and Sandra Jackson, have provided me with lodging when in New York to conduct research. Their gift of hospitality has overwhelmed me. I am truly grateful to many across North America, the Caribbean, the United Kingdom, and Argentina who have let me share Joe's story.

Additionally, Commissioner William W. Francis, Lt. Colonel Kathy Hobgood, Major Margaret Kennell, and Annie Hobgood-Bridges reviewed the manuscript and gave important feedback during the editorial process. This took many hours, and their contributions were extremely helpful and vital. I owe you all a huge debt.

Before this book was even at the printers, Major Stephen Court began blogging on it and promoting it to those who are followers of his amazing column, *ArmyBarmy*, and *The Journal of Aggressive Christianity*. I am grateful for his enthusiastic support.

I must also acknowledge those who, toward the end of this writing, helped me understand more about Joe's Armenian heritage. Thank you to Reverend Father Hovnan Demerjian, Daniel Bazikian, Reverend Joseph Garabedian, and Dr. Reverend Haig Kherlopian for your support and vital wisdom. Dr. Haig interviewed me on his podcast about the book and Pastor Joe was especially helpful to me in getting Armenian history correct. Understanding the Armenian story and the impact it had on the life of Nishan, Joe, is of the utmost importance. To truly know Joe, we must know the history of Armenia.

I am giddily grateful that the General of The Salvation Army read the book and wrote the foreword. From the bottom of my heart, I thank you. I also wish to thank those who read the manuscript and wrote endorsements. On a personal level, this has meant so very much to me. You are all people whom I dearly admire.

Finally, I would like to express my gratitude to The Salvation Army National Headquarters (NHQ), and in particular, Crest Books, for publishing this work—Lt. Colonel Lesa Davis, Dr. Caleb Louden, Andrea Martin, and Maryam Outlaw-Martin. It only seems fitting since Joe was a National Headquarters officer most of his life that NHQ would publish the amazing story of his ministry and impact on The Salvation Army of the United States ... and beyond.

I have endeavored to be as accurate as possible with the stories contained herein. Because of the primitive nature of communication, as stories passed through numerous hands, they sometimes arrived at the end of their journey slightly different than they began. In those instances,

I have returned to the source material and especially to the words of Joe himself. Any inaccuracies are truly unintentional.

Thank you for your interest in this book. May the stories of this larger-than-life hero of the faith bless, challenge, move, and even entertain you.

INTRODUCTION

The story as follows was originally reported by *The Boston Traveler* in Boston, Massachusetts on December 11, 1923:

It was 1896, a warm June evening in Malden, Massachusetts and the Square was teeming with people. Thousands formed a solid mass from the Baptist church in the upper square all the way down to the old fire station to the south. Children by the score got to stay up an hour past their usual bedtime that night because something big was about to happen. The excitement in the streets was electric.

Dozens of police officers moved through the crowd, some on foot and others on horseback. This was no ordinary night. The city authorities had ordered that The Salvation Army, which held meetings in Malden Square every evening, could not beat their bass drum.

Feeling persecuted, The Salvation Army announced that at 8 a.m. they would beat the big bass drum as usual, and, not only that, but they would also have a special guest known across the country to do it.

Around 7:50 a.m., a dozen members of the Army appeared. With them was someone Malden had never seen before, an impressive figure named Joe the Turk. He was a massive man, 250 pounds and six feet tall, which made it easy for him to stand out in the crowd. He was dressed in bright red trousers and a matching coat, trimmed with gold braid. A red fez sat on his large head.

Everyone was eager to see "that man" get arrested. Joe certainly looked like he could take on the whole Malden police force by himself. The tension in the Square was intense. Everyone was waiting for 8 a.m. The sight of the bass drum with Joe behind it had the crowd all worked up, almost to a frenzy.

The people began to shout, "Bang it, Joe!" "Hit it so they hear it up to North Billerica." "Use a policeman as a drumstick."

After what seemed like an eternity, the clock on the Methodist church began to chime the hour of eight.

The crowd fell silent. "… five-six-seven-eight!" A mighty boom sounded as Joe hit the drum. He continued to pound it while a cornet blared and the Salvationists sang, "We will follow the Lamb."

For a moment, the police hesitated, but orders were orders, and they charged. "You'll follow me," shouted the Malden police captain, facing the towering Joe. Everyone in Malden Square went wild!

Every member of The Salvation Army group was arrested. However, within a few days, the old bass drum was beating again in Malden Square. The Salvation Army had won its case.

Stories like this, and countless others, drew me to this Salvationist soldier and raised many questions, such as, "Was he a Turk, or wasn't he? What attracted him to The Salvation Army? Why was he willing to rush headlong into danger for this ragtag band of evangelists? Where did his amazing uniforms come from?"

I am honored to share the story of one of the most significant refugees, immigrants, and American Salvationists to ever live. On this side of history, we have a unique perspective on Joe the Turk and the impact he had on The Salvation Army of the United States. I have endeavored to tell a more complete story. Gathered from hundreds of newspaper articles, Salvation Army periodicals, books, and personal documents, I have sought to bring this long-overdue story to print.

Joe went into communities where The Salvation Army was often struggling, mistreated, and misunderstood. By the time he left, people in the community knew him and what The Salvation Army was all about. Most importantly, they heard the gospel preached. Over the course of his ministry, thousands gave their lives to Christ.

While it is true that Joe was born in Turkey, he was not Turkish, but Armenian. The Turks conquered Armenia, but they did not fully assimilate the population into Turkish culture. As with other ethnic minorities, the Armenians were able to maintain their culture and religion. There came a day, however, when this was no longer the case, and the Armenian population was then persecuted and martyred. To understand Joe, we must understand the story of his people.

Joe's Armenian name was Nishan Der Garabedian. In the beginning years of my research, I had little understanding of the significance of his name. My wife and I attended a Salvation Army leaders conference, organized by Lt. Colonels Jim and Pat LaBossiere. The group had been at this retreat site before, and Jim and Pat were excited for us to meet the Turkish manager of the conference center's restaurant. They believed it would please him to know there was a famous "Turk" in The Salvation Army.

Upon being seated at our table, they introduced us to the manager. Jim shared some details about the presentation with him, paused, and asked me to tell him Joe's Turkish name. When I said, "Nishan Der Garabedian," the man bristled and curtly stated, "He is not Turkish. He is Armenian." And with that, all interest in our reason for being at the conference had disappeared. He abruptly excused himself to tend to something in the kitchen. I remember thinking, "How did he know Joe was an Armenian?" Joe's name has a significant meaning in the Armenian language. That he allowed himself to be called "Joe the Turk" is also noteworthy. From the very beginning, Joe was a showman, and I believe he realized the potential this appellation would have for ministry. It was not long after his commissioning as a Salvation Army officer, that he began wearing his Turkish/Armenian uniforms with all the trimmings. It certainly helped draw the crowds, and crowds were as the breath of life to him.

When Joe immigrated to the United States, he eventually ended up in California, a dangerous place at the time. He arrived in San Francisco about a year before the Salvationists. It took a few months to connect with them, but when he did, he wholeheartedly joined the salvation war.

Joe answered the call to become a Salvation Army officer and entered the training garrison, or training college, in San Francisco. Immediately, the leaders sent him to help a seasoned officer begin the work of the Army in Los Angeles. Commissioned as a lieutenant after six months, he spent the next few years traveling up and down the West Coast. He opened new corps and went into towns where the Army was most heavily opposed. He marched up and down the street, playing his cornet until arrested, thrown into jail, and ultimately, released. This typically meant the Army had won its constitutional right to preach, play, and pray in the streets.

A few years into his officership he received the notice to report to the eastern side of the country. Joe was appointed to National Headquarters and served as a traveling special (evangelist) and representative of the trade department, which sold Salvation Army uniforms, logo wear, office products, musical instruments, etc. He sold uniforms and all the extras that went with it, holding the appointment until his retirement. During his officership, he would travel the length and breadth of the United States.

Joe averaged campaigning in approximately one hundred cities a year, which would be more than 4,000 communities during his officership. I am not sure there is or has been any other officer with that kind of travel schedule.

Throughout the book, you will find lyrics to several of the songs Joe sang or played during his evangelistic campaigns or while in jail. These have been included because some have been lost to us, as The Salvation Army Songbook has been updated and lesser-used songs removed. Reading the lyrics of the songs sung by early-day Salvationists gives us a deeper understanding of their psyche and depth of commitment to carrying the gospel of Christ to all the world at any cost.

Once Joe began evangelizing under the auspices of National Headquarters, he quickly settled into a three-day campaign mode. Each campaign included open-air meetings, one at lunch for businesspeople and another in the late afternoon, focusing on the public. He would also conduct an open-air just before the evening meeting and then march the crowds to the Army hall.

On the first night, Joe would start at the beginning: his conversion, call to officership, and his arrests in San Francisco, Los Angeles, and Portland. He titled that night, "How I Shut Up the Hole in the Wall."

On the second night, he would tell the amazing story of how his sister Maritza Yoskatchian was converted. We are truly fortunate that in 1906, *The Daily Democrat and Standard* newspapers from Woodland, California recorded the story from one of Joe's meetings.

On the third night, Joe would present a sacred gospel concert using the latest technology to bring in the crowds. Between musical numbers, he would relay the story of the Armenian massacres by the Turks. It is a story of heartbreak and tragedy the United States government has only recognized in recent years. The final meeting would also be a night of show-and-tell. Joe would display a two-edged sword he brought back from Smyrna and his artistic masterpiece, his multi-colored umbrella.

You will also find that a section of this book is focused on Armenia. Why? Again, it is important for us to know the story of Armenia if we want to really know Joe. This story is also a testament to the bravery of The Salvation Army in the mid-1890s. The Army publicly condemned the injustice against innocent people and actively helped the victims of this dark period in history.

Joe had a real, life-changing encounter with Christ, and was so grateful to The Salvation Army for the new life he found and his adoption by this new family. He was determined to use whatever methods, however bizarre, to tell people about Jesus and keep his new family safe.

When Joe hit his stride, newspapers reported that hundreds, and sometimes even 20,000 to 30,000 people, crowded the squares, parks, and roads to see and hear him. In many towns, there was not a meeting hall large enough to accommodate the crowd that wanted to come inside to hear the sacred concert. Newspapers reported that hundreds of people were at times turned away at the door because there was not enough room for them inside.

At one point, Joe was the most recognized Salvation Army officer in America. Newspapers would quote him without any reference to who he was. It was just, "Joe the Turk said …"

The movie industry did not take off until after 1900. Prior to that, newspapers made celebrities. In every city into which he went, whether it was a positive or negative story, Joe made the papers. Newspapers across the country would carry those stories via the Associated Press. The accounts of his run-ins with the law were popular fare so that by the time he came to town, people already knew who he was.

After World War I, the unexpected success of the doughnut girls caused American soldiers to return home in love with The Salvation Army.[2] The Army experienced something it had rarely felt prior to the war—respect, admiration, and positive public opinion. As The Salvation Army became more highly regarded and accepted by society, Joe was a reminder of the old days, a time that was quickly ending. In the past, *The War Cry* celebrated and highlighted his arrests. The public looked forward to the latest write-up of his adventures. That image no longer fit in with the changing and now "respectable" Army. Joe was becoming a dinosaur.

Joseph Garabed died in his apartment in New York City on October 11, 1937. The Salvation Army gave Joe a beautiful funeral at its historic Centennial Memorial Temple in Lower Manhattan. His burial in The Salvation Army section at the Kensico Cemetery is not the end of his story.

Within these pages is the true story of the legend, the myth, and the man: Joe the Turk.

CHAPTER 1
LET'S START FROM THE VERY BEGINNING

On January 14, 1860, Nishan Der Garabedian was born in the ancient Anatolian town of Talas, located close to the geographical center of modern-day Turkey.[3] In the eleventh century, the Seljuk Turks conquered Armenia. Armenia was the first country to adopt Christianity as its national religion. Large numbers of Turks migrated to the region to live and brought with them the Muslim faith, which would, through the centuries, set them at odds with the Armenians. Through repeated invasions and takeovers, the Turkish sway extended over the surrounding small kingdoms and principalities until it seemed the Ottomans would swallow all of Europe. A series of military setbacks weakened the Sultan's Empire, but it still encompassed at least a dozen distinct nationalities within its borders when Nishan came on the scene.[4]

Racial pride was of the utmost importance to the Turks. Because of this, many of them failed to understand the significance of learning the languages or customs of the various nationalities under their control.[5] Ignorance of culture breeds mistrust and creates great societal divides. The Turks' inability to understand the Armenians in Turkey would lead to the devastation of an ethnic minority on a scale not yet seen in modern history.

In the multi-cultural capital city of Constantinople, individuals from diverse national backgrounds worked together during the day, only to retreat to separate ethnic neighborhoods at night. This eclectic mix of populations encompassed Arabs, Armenians, Kurds, Greeks, Jews, Albanians, Slavs, and various other ethnicities. In smaller Turkish communities, it was not unusual for people of various nationalities to interact, work, and socialize together. Their children, who knew little about racism and cultural divides, would go to school, play together, and become friends.[6]

Immigrants who left Armenia for fear of Iran invading its borders settled in Talas. Talas sits at the foot of Mount Erciyes, where summers are typically dry and hot, and winters are snowy and cold. Some of the earliest photographs of Talas show the town to be rocky and already ancient-looking by the time of Nishan Der Garabedian's arrival on the scene.

Nishan's father was a priest in the Apostolic (Orthodox) Armenian Church, which allowed its clergy to marry. Nishan's mother was described as a godly example of her Christian faith.[7] At the age of three, Nishan had his first taste of tragedy when his father died, leaving his mother penniless and with five young children to raise. During this time in Turkey, education was not free. As a result, Nishan's schooling was delayed. He occupied his days wandering the alleys and back roads of Talas, becoming a "street rat."[8]

When he did begin school, he encountered a harsh environment. Students could only speak Turkish, and disobeying teachers would cause swift and harsh punishment. After a couple of years in this setting, he stumbled upon a recently opened school in Talas, run by a group of American Congregational missionaries. Motivated by his insatiable curiosity, he entered the building and discovered tuition was free, giving him the opportunity to be an inaugural student.[9]

Running home, he told his siblings and friends about the new school, and before long, excited students filled the school. At an early age, Nishan exhibited leadership skills that would put him in good stead for the future.[10]

Studious in school during the day, Nishan was a star recruiter in the afternoons. He lined up his recruits and proudly marched them past his old, much-disliked school to the new school. Nishan's success at recruiting new students made the Turkish school notice they were losing kids to the school operated by the missionaries. An Armenian priest was sent to Nishan's home to persuade him to come back to the former school. However, the priest, impressed by Nishan's reading abilities and positive remarks about the school, advised him to stay where he was. Nishan and the priest became friends. When he graduated, the priest showed up in full religious regalia to show his support.[11]

On one occasion, Nishan and a group of friends hiked up a hill a couple of miles away from town to have a picnic. At the bottom of the hill, the children encountered a drunken man and his donkey. The man had a scatter-shot musket, and when he saw the crowd of children, he threatened to shoot them all. It is not known why, but the man followed through with his warning and hit Nishan directly in the chest. A neighbor witnessed the incident, stopped the drunken man, and took Nishan to his aunt's house on the man's donkey. A doctor was called to treat Nishan there. For fifteen days, he hovered between life and death. Nishan's assailant was placed in jail. When Nishan had recuperated from his injury, he learned the man was his family's only source of support. He walked two miles to the jail to carry the papers his mother had signed to have the man released.[12] Throughout his life, Nishan would find it difficult to hold a grudge when someone wronged him.

When Nishan was fourteen years old, tragedy struck again when his mother died. He moved in with his aunt for a short while. At the urging of his elder brother, who had become a wealthy businessman, Nishan moved to Constantinople. His brother took him into his household. He wanted Nishan to learn a trade, so he became a shoemaker's apprentice. He turned out to be quite proficient and skilled, thus filling his pockets with the currency of the day, Ottoman lira.[13] He became well known as an expert shoemaker, and so pleased was his brother with his skill set that he set him up in a stylish new shop.[14]

It was not long before Nishan developed the bad habit of squandering his weekly wages on riotous living. At about this same time, the Russo-Turkish War of 1877–1878 broke out. Thinking he would find a better life, Nishan sold his shop without obtaining his brother's permission. He took the money and left Constantinople for Tiflis (modern-day Tbilisi), which was under Russian rule.[15] In Tiflis, he found shelter in an Armenian refugee settlement and reestablished his shoe business. Soon after, he forgot the faith of his parents, finding the taste of alcohol and rowdy living to be more appealing than work. He soon ran out of money and friends and found himself very much like the Prodigal Son, destitute.[16]

One day, Nishan received a letter from his brother in Constantinople, asking him to come home. When he returned, he continued living a rough life until his brother could take it no longer.[17] Nishan's other brother, Simon, had immigrated to the United States earlier. He wrote many letters telling his younger brother how wonderful his new situation was. Wanting Nishan to have a fresh start in life, the wealthy brother in Constantinople, whose name is unknown, paid for his passage to North America.[18] At the age of twenty-one, Nishan began his journey to the United States.

***

In September of 1881, Nishan left Constantinople for America to stay with his brother, who was living in Worcester, Massachusetts. It so happened an Armenian priest was traveling to the United States, as well. The priest, who had traveled abroad before, became his unofficial guide and translator.

Their itinerary included a stop in Liverpool, England, where they would change ships and continue to the United States, but they arrived late and missed their connection to America. The pair had to stay in Liverpool for eight days until they could catch the next ship heading to their destination.

The first morning in England, Nishan and the priest were out walking and heard a brass band playing. Thinking it was the circus, it surprised them to see a group in black military uniforms being harassed by a bunch of ruffians. One of the female marchers wore a large black bonnet with a red ribbon across the front. The priest, who spoke English, read the words, and said they were some sort of religious group. He was quite distressed to see the crowd throwing things at them.

During the early days of The Salvation Army, the marchers faced the most villainous persecution and acts of cruelty. People hurled stones, bad eggs, bottles, decayed fruit, and vegetables at the Salvationists regularly. The rear guard for the Army usually received the lion's share of the punishment. These Christian soldiers would return home from the mobs they encountered beaten, bruised, cut, bleeding, and with broken bones. Nevertheless, they continued their nightly march to the meeting hall. The morning Nishan and the Armenian priest saw the Salvationists was no exception.[19]

They followed the soldiers into an old theater and sat in the front. The uniformed marchers, who he later discovered were Salvation Army soldiers, went onto the platform and sat. While Nishan did not speak English, he could tell when the Salvationists were praying, and he sensed by their countenance they were good people.[20]

During the service, one man got excited and jumped off the platform, landing directly in front of Nishan. The priest leaned over and said to him, "Stay still. What they are excited about is good, and I will explain it to you when we are outside."

Deeply moved by the experience of that morning, Nishan attended all eight nights of meetings. He was also upset by the belligerents that harassed the Salvationists every time they marched, so much so that he picked up a big stick and marched at the end of the procession. After knocking down a few of the antagonists and threatening the others, the troublemakers backed down. Nishan also had a large pipe of tobacco in his mouth that let the crowd know he was not a member of The Salvation Army, which further encouraged them to stay clear.[21]

Even though he could not understand what they were saying or singing, each evening, Nishan played the part of a layman police officer. He brought up the rear of the march with his stick and his big pipe of tobacco.[22] This was a foretelling of things to come.

Nishan felt the Salvationists were good people who were being persecuted because of their faith.[23] Given the history of his people, the Armenians, who faced persecution and death for their Christian faith, he could easily draw this conclusion. While there were periods of peace between the Armenians and the Ottoman rulers, their coexistence was anything but peaceful. Nishan would have seen his relatives treated as second-class citizens. He knew the history of religious persecution they suffered. These two realities may have been the reason he protected the Salvationists so passionately.

Because of this experience, he fell in love with the Sallys (Salvationists) and began to have second thoughts about going to America. He believed he could earn a living using his skills as a shoemaker and make England his new home.[24]

Nishan asked the priest to inform the Salvation Army captain about his plans to stay in Liverpool, join them as a soldier, and serve as their body-guard. The captain was thrilled by the news and promised that some of his soldiers would teach Nishan how to speak English.[25]

The priest was not happy with this turn of events and persuaded Nishan to continue his journey to the United States.[26] After eight days in Liverpool, the duo boarded a ship and set off for America.

Nishan had a large supply of Turkish tobacco and cigars in his baggage. Having learned about the Army's teaching against the usage of tobacco, he determined to give it up and dispersed it among the other passengers of the ship.[27] Nearly ten days later, Nishan and the priest landed in New York City where they parted ways.

***

When Nishan was in Constantinople and Tiflis, he heard many wonderful stories about America, of how it was a land untarnished by sin and distrust. He believed it to be a place where everyone was friendly, gentle, cultured, and kind.[28] He also believed every citizen in the United States was a Christian, and because of that, wanted to live there.[29]

Nishan quickly learned that everything he had heard and hoped about his new home was not entirely true. Upon landing, one of those "Christian" people offered to retrieve his luggage. All Nishan had to do was give him the claim receipt, and someone would deliver his baggage directly to his brother's home. Awed by this Christian kindness, it would be days before he realized he had been hoodwinked, his luggage stolen. He had nothing but the clothes on his back with which to begin his new life.[30]

***

When Nishan arrived on the shores of the United States in October of 1881, he determined he would make a new name for himself—literally. His Armenian name is very significant and even borderline prophetic. *Nishan* means "sign," "message," or "miracle." *Der* was a title of honor given to priests, used much like the English word "Father." It was placed before the last name when referring to a member of the clergy's family.

The surname *Garabedian* is the combination of two ideas: *Garabed*, meaning "Good news bearer" (a reference to John the Baptist), and *-ian*, meaning "belonging to the family of." When put together, Nishan Der Garabedian's literal translation means, "the child of a priest who is a sign, a miracle, a good news bearer."

When Nishan arrived in New York, he Americanized his name. He took John as his first name, in reference to John the Baptist, and shortened his last name to Garabed. He would go by John Garabed for several years, and, as his life unfolded in America, he would more than fulfill the name given to him at birth by his parents.[31]

***

John left New York City and lived in Worcester, Massachusetts, with his brother Simon for a year. While he was there, he began to learn English, preparing himself for his future endeavors. But he grew restless and, longing for adventure, turned his sights toward the Wild West. The frontier was calling him! So, he left his brother's home for the unknown and dangerous West Coast. Working odd jobs along the way allowed him to earn enough money to keep moving toward the Pacific until he landed in California.

CHAPTER 2
WEST COAST CALLING

In short order, John found himself in the Wild West. He ended his trek in San Francisco, then commonly known as the Barbary Coast. The Barbary Coast was a North African coastline that stretched from modern-day Morocco to Libya, a region teeming with slave traders and pirates who menaced villages lining the Mediterranean shores. San Francisco received this name because of its widespread anarchy and criminality. The authorities struggled to maintain law and order in the city due to the influx of gangs and the resulting corruption and chaos.[32] From the 1860s up to the time of the 1906 Earthquake, gang violence, brothels, illegal drugs, and saloons characterized the city. The law was all but nonexistent. Police officers would only patrol the streets with a partner and rarely a night passed without a murder.[33]

In his book, *Sketch of Life in the Golden State*, Colonel Albert S. Evans (United States military) says this about San Francisco, "Speak of the deeper depth, the lower hell, the maelstrom of vice and iniquity—from whence those who once fairly enter escape no more forever—and they will point triumphantly to the Barbary Coast, strewn from end to end with the wrecks of humanity, and challenge you to match it anywhere outside of the lake of fire and brimstone."

Upon arriving, John Garabed effortlessly integrated into the San Francisco scene, embracing all its vices. Standing six feet tall and weighing almost two hundred and fifty pounds, he was described as a "Walking Terror; a man the average hoodlum would not dare get on the wrong side of." So strong of body and emotion was John Garabed, he could clear out a crowded barroom in no time at all. Once, his best friend angered him, and a drunken John Garabed beat him to within an inch of his life. Those who knew him said his "brute strength was from the devil, and the devil lived in John Garabed."[34]

***

John found work doing odd jobs during the day and spent his evenings drinking the night away. One night, while imbibing with a coworker from Ireland, he had a conversation that changed his life. He would not realize the importance of the event until sometime later. His Irish friend asked him what his full name was, to which he replied, "John Garabed." The Irishman countered, "You don't look like a John Garabed to me. You look like a 'Joe,' and since you're from Turkey, I'm going to call you 'Joe the Turk.'"[35]

One can never know exactly why he embraced this moniker, which based on the history of Turks and Armenians, could be uncomfortable, to say the least. History would recall he used it to full effect over the years, turning an ignorant—or, at best, seemingly innocent remark—into the impetus for living a colorful and eventful life. The name "Joe the Turk" would empower him to serve Christ in the future in ways "John Garabed" may never have been able to.

While *The War Cry* would at times recognize him as "John Garabed," as early as 1886, it also, along with everyone else, began referring to him as "Joe the Turk." Throughout his lengthy career, newspapers and Salvation Army periodicals were careful to use his legal last name, Garabed. They often reminded readers that while Joe was born in Turkey, he was an Armenian by birth.

One evening, as Joe walked along the street, he heard a drum and saw a couple of lit torches. Inquiring as to what it was all about, he found that it was The Salvation Army, who had just arrived in San Francisco. Remembering his time in Liverpool with the Salvationists, Joe wanted to see them, so he followed the light and the sound of the drum. Later, someone would write a song about his conversion based on his testimony of following the light and the drum of The Salvation Army. It was printed in *The War Cry*.[36]

I Followed the Drum and the Light
Joe the Turk
Tune: "Have you been to Jesus for the cleansing power?"

1. As my soul in darkness wandered to and fro,
   I was roused by the beat of the drum,
   And the flaring torches showed the way to go,
   While the drum and the light said, "come."

Chorus:
Yes, I did! Yes, I did!
Yes, I followed the drum and the light.
And my great Redeemer gave me liberty,
When I followed the drum and the light.

2. O the drum to Jesus now is calling all,
   And proclaiming Him able to save,
   When the light of Calv'ry on the drum doth fall,
   Sounding freedom to every slave.

3. O, the invitation to the Cross obey.
   Come and follow the drum and the light,
   Let the blood of Jesus wash your sins away,
   Then for others enlist in the fight.

4. Well we know that to our pride and flesh and blood,
   It is trying to follow the drum,
   But the Savior wants you in the light of God,
   With it after the lost now come.[37]

Joe noticed a man in a uniform that looked like what the Salvationists in Liverpool had worn. He had been thinking about them since he arrived in America. Attending the meeting that evening, he spoke to the officer afterwards, and told him about his experiences in Liverpool. Joe frequented the meetings enough to know the officers and soldiers by name, but he did not get converted ... yet.[38]

About this time, Joe began working at a company that smelted lead. Historical records show the only smelting company in San Francisco to be The Selby Smelting Company, which in 1879 became the Pacific Refinery & Bullion Exchange (PRBE). In addition to lead, the PRBE processed gold and silver.

Joe met a soldier of The Salvation Army named John Milsaps there, whom he had seen every night at the Army meetings. While Joe had given away all his tobacco products during his transatlantic journey, he did not leave his love for them there. Joe could not easily resist his pipe and tobacco. At every opportunity, he enjoyed a smoke break. Milsaps would follow him on these breaks with an apple, trying to persuade him to eat it rather than smoke his pipe. Milsaps would then press Joe to accept Christ as his personal Savior from sin, but to no avail.[39]

Joe decided to put Milsaps to the test to see if he was anything like the Salvationists he had met in Liverpool and to find out if he really practiced what he preached. When the boss was around, everyone gave one hundred percent and Joe wanted to know if Milsaps worked just as hard when his supervisor was not there. To Joe's surprise, he did. In addition, Milsaps would arrive each morning with his Bible and songbooks and lead devotions before the men began their workday.[40]

Joe and Milsaps were living in the same boarding house with about thirty other men. Joe would watch to see if Milsaps would pray over his food in front of the other men—a further test. Once again, to his surprise, he did.

The men had thirty minutes to eat dinner, and Joe used a good portion of that time smoking. Even at the boarding house, Milsaps would continue to chastise him over his addiction to smoking and plead with him to follow Jesus. This made Joe uncomfortable and even put his heart under conviction. He didn't want to deal with how he was beginning to feel, so he started avoiding the Salvationists.[41]

After a couple of months, Joe left the white lead workshop and began working at a gunpowder factory. He continued to feel the weight and burden of his sin and knew if he died in an explosion, his soul would be eternally doomed. When this job only lasted two weeks, he went back to what he knew best and had excelled in while in Turkey and Russia; he opened a shoe shop at 48 Sacramento Street.[42]

Joe's shoe shop was located next door to Finnegan's Saloon. In taking up his old trade, he continued his old habit of smoking. He had also, by now, developed quite a thirst for whiskey and beer. Growing tired of leaving his shop to walk next door to the saloon to quench his thirst, he cut a hole in the wall between the two sellers. This allowed him the convenience of having his beer delivered through the opening without ever having to leave his shoe shop.[43] This act would give his little business the nickname of "the Hole in the Wall." Joe moved his work bench near the service window and acquired a whistle that he blew whenever he wanted a fresh drink. Mrs. Finnegan, the proprietor of the saloon, knew what the whistle meant, and at its sound, provided the alcohol Joe now so deeply craved and spent his earnings on.[44]

The Shanghai Game

"The Shanghai Game," a deadly con, was prevalent in San Francisco during this time, ensnaring numerous unsuspecting men. Ships that pulled into the harbor needed sailors, but laborers were proving difficult to find. Criminals invented "shanghaiing" to kidnap and drug able-bodied men whom they would sell to the ships' captains. Once caught in the web, they found themselves bound for Asia before they knew what was happening.[45]

Joe was an eyewitness to this practice, as he could see into the saloon through his hole in the wall. The game worked like this: prospectors who found precious nuggets in the gold mines would stop by the saloon for a celebratory drink before boarding their trains or ships to trade the gold for money. Unknown to the prospector, there was a trapdoor at the bar, which opened, causing the unsuspecting man to fall onto a cushioned spot below where the captain and first mate of a ship in need of sailors would be waiting. When a strong miner who looked like a potential candidate came in, he was encouraged to drink enough to dull his senses. Before he knew it, the floor opened, swallowing him. By the time he came to, he was on a boat bound for China. His treasures became the property of the saloon hostess and her cohorts in crime.[46]

Joe also witnessed another swindle executed inside Finnegan's Saloon. This con spoke to the depravity of the city and the lawlessness that reigned supreme. When an unsuspecting miner came into the saloon with a pack full of gold, Mrs. Finnegan would bring over a bottle of whisky and encourage him to keep drinking until he was drunk. When he was suitably inebriated and made it known he was ready to leave, the hostess hit him from behind with a big club. She then would call her two sons, Bill and Ned, who would carry the victim outside. Taking the unconscious prey's gold, Mrs. Finnegan called the police. Law enforcement officers, who were in on the fraud and received a cut of the spoils, would take the man to jail, charge him with public drunkenness, and sentence him to six months of hard labor.[47]

It was to this environment The Salvation Army would come in 1883.

***

When The Salvation Army arrived in San Francisco, it was met with great hostility. There was no city harder on the Salvationists than the city by the bay. When the Army held a meeting on the street corner, a menacing mob would gather around them and throw rocks, vegetables, or anything they could use as missiles to hurt them and try to break up their meeting. The police would stand back and laugh at the fun the crowd was having at the Army's expense.[48]

The Army was conducting an open-air meeting one Sunday afternoon, when Joe happened by. He saw ruffians throw mud at his friend John Milsaps. This angered him, and he threatened to go after them if they did not settle down. One of the thugs did not take Joe at his word or heed his threat, so Joe knocked him down, causing the others to back off. Because of this incident, Joe became the unofficial guardian angel of The Salvation Army once again. From that point forward, he rarely came home at night from an open-air meeting without a bruise, blackened eye, cut lip, or swollen head.[49]

One evening, someone in the mob threw a handful of mud into the face of a young Salvation Army lassie as she knelt and prayed. In recounting the story, Joe explained, "Those people [the Salvationists] were not doing any harm. And when that man ran out and threw a handful of mud in the face of that nice young woman who was kneeling there praying, I just got a piece of lead pipe and sailed in."[50] Joe took out six men.

The turning point in Joe's life happened one evening at an open-air meeting held in front of Finnegan's Saloon. Most new recruits were given the job of beating the bass drum. That night, a new recruit wholeheartedly performed the task. Suddenly, a drunk came staggering out of the saloon with a whiskey bottle in his hand. He swung it around his head, letting it fly, full force, into the face of the drummer, and break into a hundred pieces. When recounting this story, Joe commented that the result "was too hideous to describe."

The man fell into a heap on top of his drum. The mob broke out into hysterical laughter. But then the man began to feel around on the ground for his drumstick. He found it and slowly resumed beating the drum, encouraging the Salvationists to keep on singing. "Who were these people who could not be defeated, who could not be stopped from spreading their message of eternal love and redemption?" asked Joe. He fell down on his knees and prayed. His conversion was so intense, he was oblivious to the crowd's insults, rock-throwing, and spitting. He only knew Jesus Christ had come into his heart and he was a new man.[51]

Joe went to work the next day at his shoe shop and found that someone had broken in. The burglars destroyed equipment and furniture and stole his work tools. His "friends," who were angry at him for converting, did this. Undeterred, he put his shop back together, and it became not only a shoe shop but a salvation shop. Joe repaired the soles of customers' shoes and their spiritual souls, too.[52]

Conversions abounded in Joe's shoe shop, not only because of his preaching but because of the dramatic change that had taken place in his life. The quality with which Joe made and repaired shoes changed with his conversion. He began using top-quality leather on every pair of shoes he repaired and created. From then on, he hammered with tiny brass tacks into the soles of those shoes the shape of an 'S,' which he testified stood for: "Saved from Sin," "Saved and Satisfied," "Salvation Soldier," and "Solid Soles!"[53]

Joe's friend, John Milsaps, had become an officer by this time and was appointed as commander of the San Francisco #1 Corps. Joe was a faithful soldier, but would not join in the evening march of witness. After much coaxing, he finally agreed to march, but his first time out was unsuccessful. He was so nervous and worried about what his friends would say that before he had marched two blocks, he turned around and went back to the barracks.

The next night, before the open-air march began, Captain Milsaps strapped the bass drum on Joe, making it more difficult to run away. Somehow, Joe's "fighting buddies" knew he was going to march that night and gave him a warm reception. Rocks were flying, and one hit Joe in the head, causing a large gash. Blood was everywhere, so much so it filled his boots. His first thoughts were to run away, but strapped to the big bass drum, he knew he would not get far. He decided to make a stand and let whatever was going to happen, happen.[54] As he marched, his shoes made a squishing noise because the blood flowed down his face and body to his feet.

Looking back on his time in San Francisco years later, Joe would write:

> When we had the only corps in California, which was San Francisco #1, and when I got saved, in those days it was very bitter persecution days for the Army. Police and people were against us, and when we went to open-airs in those days, we never knew whether we would return alive, where we have been every night mobbed in the open-airs and in the buildings, and many times I was arrested for having meetings on the street.[55]

> Even when I was a soldier for three years, where I had my place of business, the mobs have broken in my shop eight times, when I was carrying on the meeting and such, stolen much goods each time, and many nights I returned from the meeting with broken head, and black eyes, and many knife wounds and stabs and bruises of all kind. Every day something happened, thank the dear Lord he was with us.[56]

People did not understand our work, and we had no police protection then, as we have now. Nobody dared to murder us outright, but we once had our uniforms slit with knives as we knelt in prayer; a ripper tried slashing my lip, and five times we were shot at. But, as you see, I was hard to kill.[57]

***

While not mentioned by name, The Pacific Coast Division *War Cry*, September 1884, lists recent converts who made up the San Francisco #1 Corps. An Armenian is among the group, which is an all but certain reference to Joe. Therefore, the report gives us a date with which to note his association with The Salvation Army and the age of his conversion, at twenty-four.

The February 1885 Pacific Coast Division *War Cry* mentions Joe by name for the first time, referring to him as an Armenian shoemaker. According to the article, Joe had three pairs of shoes stolen. When sharing the account of what happened with an officer, he said, "Told him he took my shoes. Something here (pointing to his heart) he not take—salvation. Jesus makes me happy all the day. Change my heart. Make it new. Hallelujah."

From the beginning, The Salvation Army was cognizant of Joe's Armenian heritage. Throughout his officership, it would be respectful of that fact.

There is no further mention of Joe until the October 1886 edition of The Pacific Coast Division *War Cry*, which wrote:

Night after night we are heard and seen on the streets; a converted Turk with a cornet in his hand playing the tune:

Are you washed in the Blood?

In the soul-cleansing Blood of the Lamb?"

When Joe joined The Salvation Army as a soldier, he received the rank of sergeant and the assignment of doorkeeper or bouncer at the

Army barracks.[58] One evening, a Frenchman came to the indoor meeting and stabbed Joe in the arm with a knife. Two weeks later, the same Frenchman appeared at the open-air meeting and, when they gave the invitation to accept Christ, he knelt at the drum and was converted.[59] This pleased Joe, and he later said his knife wound had not been in vain because of the Frenchman's conversion.

Mobs continued to abuse officers and soldiers for their own entertainment every day. Joe remained faithful and stood at his post night after night, despite the mobs abusing him and leaving him bruised and swollen. This went on for almost two and a half years. If Joe missed a meeting at the corps, it was only because he had been so badly beaten or attacked the night before.[60]

Very quickly, he earned the nickname of Happy Joe because his joy at having found Jesus as his Savior was so evident. A police officer who knew the old Joe watched him after his conversion for two years and remarked to him one day, "I believe you have salvation if ever a man had." This police officer pledged to watch over the Salvationists because he saw the change in people's lives after having met the Army.[61]

After his conversion, Joe continued to struggle with his addiction to tobacco. He even sold it at his shoe shop. As he was walking past a hotel one evening, he overheard two men commenting about how he (Joe) had joined The Salvation Army but continued to smoke his pipe. So distressed that his witness did not appear genuine to those around him, at that very moment he promised God he would not touch tobacco again. He immediately sold all the tobacco and cigar products in his shop at a two-thirds discount, taking a loss, but regaining his testimony.[62]

**

Joe's shoe shop, the Hole in the Wall, was located at the lower end of Sacramento Street. It was close to the waterfront and right in the middle of the most dangerous section of San Francisco. Its close neighbors comprised saloons and brothels. The shop now seemed out of place, but one would know it was a shoemaker's shop by the sign hanging over the entrance and the bundles of leather placed like haystacks outside the front door.

After his conversion, the shop got a new name: the Hallelujah Shoe Shop. As people passed by, Joe would preach the gospel to his customers and pedestrians without shame.[63] Joe would come to work each day in a red guernsey, which the Salvationists wore on the march, to give further testimony to his conversion.

He placed signs outside of his shop that read: "California for Jesus!", "Are you saved?", and "Where will you spend eternity?"[64] He had a seven-foot-high boot constructed out of wood and painted it the colors of The Salvation Army flag—yellow, red, and blue. On the top of the boot flew The Salvation Army flag.

Joe then engaged a hat maker to create a hat as tall as a person. He painted on the hat the question, "Is salvation in your hat or in your soul?"

The final gospel advertisement used four-foot-high brass letters nailed onto the sidewalk in front of his shop. They read, "Stranger, are you saved?" Day after day, thousands of people would pass by the Hallelujah Shoe Shop and look down to read the words. It received all kinds of reactions, from laughter to frowns. While others merely passed by, still others paused to consider the words.[65]

One day, a lady came into Joe's shop, ranting and raving about "all these religious goings on." However, as she continued to walk up and down the sidewalk in front of the shop, she pondered the question of her own salvation. Totally frustrated, she came back to the shop days later. Utterly convicted of her need for a savior, she left the Hallelujah Shoe Shop a new person in Christ.[66]

When they were not busy, soldiers from the San Francisco #1 Corps would hang out at Joe's place. Often, a customer would come into the shop to have work done on their shoes. While the work was taking place, Joe and the other soldiers would preach and testify to the customer. The testimony of those who shared what Christ had done in their own lives resulted in the conversion of many people.

The January 15, 1887, Pacific Coast Division *War Cry* chronicles the account of one gentleman who came into the shop under deep conviction. An impromptu salvation meeting ensued, resulting in the man weeping and giving his heart to Jesus. The man confessed he had been watching the men at the Hallelujah Shoe Shop and was impressed by their earnestness and sincerity. Their faithful witness brought him into a personal relationship with Christ.

Weeks later, Mrs. Finnegan called out to Joe through the hole in the wall and asked him why he was not drinking anymore. He replied he had become a Christian and joined The Salvation Army and no longer needed the alcohol. He promptly closed the hole in the wall with a Salvation Army almanac.[67]

Later, a leader of The Salvation Army operations in California, Major Edward Fielding, approached Joe and told him he was looking for a man with unshakable faith, someone hard to kill, to help him open the work of the Army in Los Angeles. He believed Joe would make a fine officer. By this time in his experience with The Salvation Army, people had pelted Joe with garbage, rotten fruit and vegetables, rocks, and stones. He was stabbed in the eye with an iron walking cane and hit with such force by a rock that it broke his nose.[68] He prayed about the proposal and accepted the call to officership.

Prior to entering the training garrison, which was in the Tenderloin District of San Francisco—a historically difficult section of San Francisco and the heart of Salvation Army ministry for decades—Joe gave his best handmade shoes to his corps officers and auctioned off everything else. He did keep some tools, which he stored away in the attic of the Oakland 1, California Corps ... in case things did not work out. Within two days of this monumental decision, Joe was ready to begin his training to become a Salvation Army officer.[69]

On April 24, 1887, Happy Joe became a cadet and closed his shoe shop for good, never to look back and never to collect his shoemaking tools.[70] Rather than train in an academic setting, The Salvation Army gave Joe on-the-job training and sent him to Los Angeles to help open the Army's work there.

The War Cry reported:

> Something's missing on Sacramento Street, San Francisco.
> The Hallelujah Shoe Shop is now closed; the Blood and
> Fire flag that was wont to float in the breeze outside is gone.

What has become of Joe? Well, Joe has shut up shop, and gone to Los Angeles to preach the gospel to the orange-blossom sinners down there. About the last thing Ye Editor heard, as the 'Santa Rosa' was swinging out into the stream, off the seawall, getting ready to steam through the Golden Gate, was 'Joe's irrepressible cornet.'[71]

CHAPTER 3
MARCHING ORDERS

The next few years would find Joe traveling around the Pacific Coast Division with a team of Salvation Army officers or paired with another cadet. Although he had been arrested as a soldier in San Francisco, the arrests as an "enlisted" man would set him on a path he would boldly and bravely take for the rest of his officership.

On April 24, 1887, Cadet Joe and Captain George Rutherford descended upon Los Angeles to open the work of The Salvation Army. In 1880, the population of Los Angeles was under 12,000 people, but by the end of the decade it would increase to 38,000 residents.[72] The price of a train ticket from Kansas to Los Angeles dropped to just one dollar because of a rate war between the two main railways. This caused a surge in both visitors and people choosing to settle there permanently. Los Angeles was rapidly growing with modern conveniences like a fire department, theater, post office, synagogue, church, high school, cathedral, newspaper, telephone company, horse-drawn streetcars, banks and electric streetlights.[73]

Into this more civilized city, Cadet Joe and Captain George Rutherford "opened fire," meaning they started the ministry and work of the Army in the community. The initial foray into Los Angeles was difficult. On their first day there, Joe and Captain Rutherford were marching down the street when a mob started chasing them. The people had heard that The Salvation Army was coming to invade the city, and they became incredibly unhappy when they discovered the advance party consisted of only two soldiers. Hoping to escape unharmed, the duo took off running, rounded a street corner, and saw a grocer's shop with its doors open. Inside the shop, the door of the cellar was open. They ran inside, jumped down the hole, and pulled the lid shut. The grocer did not let on that the pair were inside, and the mob ran by, unaware of what the fast-thinking duo had done. They hid in the cellar until it got dark, and when they came out, Captain Rutherford asked what they would do next after this narrow escape. Joe was unfazed and told the captain they would hold an open-air meeting the next day.[74]

When Joe woke up the following morning, he found the captain missing in action. He brushed off his uniform, went back to the street corner, and blew his cornet. Immediately, the police arrested him and placed him in jail. There he found himself among thirty men in various stages of intoxication. They were sleeping, snoring, groaning, and doing time for public drunkenness.[75]

Joe remained incarcerated for seven days, waiting for his trial. During those days, he got possession of his cornet and permission from the police to talk to his fellow prisoners. Joe stepped out into the corridor of the jail and played recognizable tunes. He chose songs such as "Marching Through Georgia" and other popular melodies the prisoners could not help but listen to. After getting their attention, he suggested they all form a line and march around the corridor. From time to time, he would stop the march and talk to them about their souls. Then he would sing a song, putting salvation words to a popular tune his fellow prisoners would have heard in a saloon. He then encouraged them to sing while they continued to march.[76]

> *March on! March on!*
> *We bring the jubilee!*
> *Fight on! Fight on!*
> *Salvation makes us free!*
> *We'll shout our Savior's praises over every land and sea,*
> *as we go marching to Glory!*
> – *The Salvation Army Songbook*

The enthusiasm was catching. Before the prisoners knew what was going on, Joe had every one of them down on their knees as he prayed with them, then up again marching and singing. When the music-making ended, many of them continued to pray. Joe led them all to a relationship with Christ.[77]

After seven days of jail time, Joe told the story of his arrest in court. While sharing his jail experience, he became so overwhelmed with emotion that he fell to his knees and began praying in the middle of the courtroom.

His petitions for blessings included his lawyer, the police officer who arrested him, and finally, the judge who sat on the bench.[78]

Deeply moved, the judge's eyes moistened. He took out his handkerchief, softly saying something about the excellent work of a man who would try to convert drunks and even pray for his persecutors. With that declaration, he pronounced Joe discharged. As Joe left the courtroom, the judge held out his hand and, with tears in his eyes, told him to continue his good work. The magistrate declared that as long as he was the judge in Los Angeles, The Salvation Army would always have the right to preach and play music in the streets. This incident changed the overall acceptance of the Army in Los Angeles.[79]

Soon, Captain Rutherford returned with reinforcements, and the crew set up camp in an orange grove. On May 6, a big circus-style tent reached Los Angeles by rail and was taken to the corner of Temple and Fort Streets. The crew worked hard, and by evening, the gray and white striped canvas chapel was glistening in the moonlight.[80]

Now that the tent was ready, the next challenge was to find seats and lanterns without having to pay, as there was no money in the budget for the new opening. After praying about the situation, the Salvationists were amazed by how quickly God answered their prayers. A man who had heard about their challenge sent enough wood to build the seats and a platform. He threw in enough cash to buy the nails needed for the construction. Another person donated eight lanterns and a can of oil for fuel.[81] God had wonderfully supplied their needs.

Volunteers were found to help the Salvationists build the seats. On May 7, just before midnight, everything was ready for the first meeting the next afternoon. The group of nine Salvationists lined up and, at 2:30 p.m., Sunday, May 8, stepped off on the march, announcing The Salvation Army's official presence in Los Angeles.[82]

The blaring of cornets and the marchers in militaristic uniforms quickly captured the attention of the crowd. During the open-air service, people listened respectfully to the testimonies of the Salvationists. At the conclusion of the open-air, the leader invited the listeners to the tent, a ten-minute walk. The crowd followed and quickly filled the tent up, resulting in standing room only. Another testimony service began, allowing the congregation to share their witness. The meeting concluded with Major Fielding, the group's leader, telling the history of The Salvation Army and its intention to serve the lost and needy of the city.[83]

Another march and meeting took place that evening, with comparable results. The sale of Salvation Army songbooks and *The War Cry* allowed the congregation to take part in the service. With the singing of the doxology "Praise God from Whom All Blessings Flow," the night ended. The day was an overwhelming success.[84]

Marches and meetings continued, and in less than a month, thirty junior soldiers were enrolled in the ranks.[85] Cadet Joe and Captain George Rutherford began conducting meetings for prisoners in the local jail. That July, the Army found a home, a building that would replace the big tent.[86] After three months in Los Angeles, Joe received farewell orders and left behind sixty new Salvation Army soldiers.[87]

During the next months, Joe, with other cadets, began a triangular tour of the area around Los Angeles. They held evangelistic meetings and solidified the work of The Salvation Army in these communities.

Joe began his first foray outside of Los Angeles when he was appointed to San Bernardino on July 6, 1887. *The War Cry* records these words from Happy Joe, "Lick the old Devil in San Bernardino. Fight till I die, never run away. Salvation in the heart, if I had salvation in the head, been knocked out long ago, got salvation in the heart, can't take it out."[88]

San Bernardino proved to be a difficult place for the Army. The press and the people were against it. Wrongdoers continued to taunt and harass the soldiers of salvation as they publicly proclaimed the name of Jesus.

Joe would only be in San Bernardino for two and a half weeks before being appointed to his next challenge. The following two appointments would be short as well.

On July 24, 1887, Cadet Joe was farewelled again and sent to Santa Ana to co-command the corps. The response of the public was more accepting than it was in San Bernardino. Open-air meetings and *War Cry* sales yielded good crowds that followed the duo back to the barracks for indoor meetings. The public response was positive.[89] Attendance briefly dropped when members of The Church of Jesus Christ of Latter-Day Saints arrived in town. Eventually, the crowds returned to the open-air and indoor public meetings.

In early September, Joe arrived in Pomona, and although he only spent two weeks there, he described the fight as hard. Despite the difficulties, a donor gave a tract of land to the Army on which to build a barracks. Joe characterized the population of Pomona as filled with good people. The work of the Army flourished.

***

In the middle of September 1887, not only was Joe sent back to San Bernardino for a second time, but his field training also came to an end. He received his promotion to the rank of lieutenant, and in less than two months, Joe enrolled seventeen converts and fifteen new soldiers. This group of evangelists marched every night on the streets.[90] During this tour of duty in San Bernardino, someone challenged Joe to a duel. This so rattled him he swore out a warrant for the challenger's arrest, but the police could not find the man because he had skipped town. The press was on Joe's side in this matter and felt he was totally within his rights to ask the authorities to get involved.[91]

The support of the press, however, did not last, as *The Daily Courier*, the San Bernardino newspaper, printed this article on September 27, 1887. It was clear the community was still not accepting of the unusual methods of worship and evangelism practiced by the Salvationists:

> "… the salvation meetings in the public streets are demoralizing in their effect. Now, we do not say this is the fault of the Salvationists. It is the fault of the hoodlums, but these screaming, farcical Salvationists afford the hoodlums an opportunity for the display of their deviltry, which they are not slow to embrace. We witnessed the meeting in front of the White House on Sunday night.[92] The Salvationists, with Joe the Turk in their midst, blared and blew instrumentally and vocally. They knelt and prayed, or went through the form of praying, surrounded by most of the rough element of San

Bernardino. The performance to an observer of sensibility was one of a dreary, disgusting drivel. Such a fantastic and ridiculous style of worship will, we fear, repel rather than attract. The offensive—it seemed so to one familiar with reverential worship—we might almost say the blasphemous invocations to the Savior were shocking in their vulgar, and evidently perfunctory familiarity. There was not a ray of spiritual fire in all their prayerful pyrotechnics. They were coarse, common-place, automatic in their allusions to the Deity. They prayed, it seemed to us by the yard; prayed with about as much heart and soul as we see in the gyrations of the puppets on the stage. Their praying and piety resembled very much the style of writing characteristic of some country editors—up in Oregon, of course—they were so mechanical. Still, all this is no reason why they should be pelted with bread or stones or salivated tobacco; no reason why half-inebriated roughs should go out before them, rub against them, and dance the hoodlum's fling for the amusement of the mob—no reason, whatever. Again, we noticed several boys ranging from ten to fifteen years of age who were actually devilish in their antics. One of them has 'gallows' depicted in every lineament of his features. This little wretch and his older companions should have been locked up for the night. If these Salvation Army meetings are legal, it is the plain duty of the police to arrest the roughs and toughs who so brutally obstruct them. If there is any way to prohibit these demoralizing parades, prohibit them at once, for their effect is very bad, in that it only scandalizes what some of us at least … believe are sacred things."

Joe's second arrest, and first as a commissioned officer, occurred one evening in San Bernardino when, during an evangelistic meeting, a young man with a history of disruptive behavior caused a disturbance. Joe, harkening back to his old job as a bouncer at the San Francisco #1 Corps, ejected the man from the meeting. Joe's actions prompted the troublemaker to file a complaint with the authorities, claiming Joe grabbed him by the collar and forcefully ejected him from the building. The next morning, Joe was arrested for assault and battery. The police threw him into the dirtiest cell in the jailhouse. He was placed under a $200 bond, the equivalent of more than $3,000 in 2024. The case was tried in front of the district attorney and was promptly dismissed.[93]

The San Bernardino Times seemed to have become an ally of the Army by this time and had this to say about the matter:

> … the arrest of this man (Joe) was an outrage, and it is about time the persecution of these Salvation Army people was stopped. They have a right to hold their meetings in peace, and if every young hoodlum who creates a disturbance there were soundly thrashed, it would be no more than they deserved.[94]

After four months in San Bernardino, Joe received his appointment to the San Francisco #2 Corps, which was also the home of the training garrison. The February 9, 1888, edition of *The San Bernardino Times* records the following:

> Since the departure of Joe the Turk, the renowned Salvation Army manipulator on the cornet, the Army seems inclined to sink into oblivion. They rallied on Tuesday evening and went around as usual to serenade the city … but were hardly recognizable and played the bass drum and cymbals. After several ineffectual attempts to strike the proper chord, the musicians finally gave up the idea of serenading for that evening and slowly and sadly went their way to the barracks, there to kneel before the mourner's bench and bewail the loss of Joe, the departed soul, and life of The Salvation Army.

***

During the summer of 1888, Joe, with a group of officers, toured various towns in California, calling their travels The Summer Campaign. The group was met with mixed reviews. In Maryville, the Salvationists encountered a gentle crowd. Despite charging admission for the evening meetings, they had good attendances. Joe delighted the audience with several musical numbers, one of which was entitled, "Sugar Bowl," whose lyrics have been lost to us, and "The Palace of the King."[95]

The Palace of the King
Fanny Crosby

1. 'Tis a goodly pleasant land that we pilgrims journey thro',
And our Father's constant blessings fall around us like the dew;
But its sunshine and its beauty to our hearts no joy can bring,
Like the splendors that await us in the palace of the King.
In this goodly pleasant land only strangers now are we,
For we seek a better country, and 'tis where we long to be;
Yes, we long to swell the anthem that forevermore shall ring,
From the pure in heart made perfect in the palace of the King.

Refrain:
O the palace of the King, royal palace of the King;
Where our Father in His mercy all the ransomed ones will bring;
Where our sorrows and our trials like a dream will pass away,
And our souls shall dwell forever in the realms of endless day.

2. Our Redeemer is the King; what a sacrifice He made,
When He purchased our redemption, and His blood the ransom paid;
In His cross shall be our glory, to that blessed cross we'll cling,
Till we reach the gates that open, to the palace of the King.
We shall see Him by and by, hallelujah to His name!
Thro' the blood of His atonement, life eternal we may claim;
We shall cast our crown before Him and our songs of vict'ry sing,
When we enter in triumphant to the palace of the King.

***

The group's second stop was Nevada City, and it is here that we read the first account of Joe dressing in his Turkish/Armenian costume. His unique uniform garnered much attention, especially from the children in attendance.[96]

After marching to the open-air, Joe gave his testimony of how he met The Salvation Army in Liverpool, England. The officer leading the meeting asked him to end his testimony as it had lasted too long. It would continue at the next night's open-air gathering.[97] Joe struggled with speaking concisely in his meetings, and during his life, some of his services lasted past midnight.

Grass Valley was the next stop on the itinerary, and Joe drew a great crowd by singing the chorus, "We Are All Here." *The War Cry* said of his testimony, "The Spirit of the Lord was with Joe in wonderful power, and the people laughed, cried, and laughed again as he went on to tell of God's wonderful dealings with him."[98] In the coming years, other newspapers would echo these sentiments. Some would write about his broken English and how it added to the levity of Joe's performances, sometimes unintentionally, and endeared him to his audience.

Upon arriving in Sacramento, the little band of witnesses were pleasantly surprised to discover a beautiful Army barracks where they could hold their meetings. During their time here, Joe was accused of getting rich off The Salvation Army in the newspaper. His reply: "Well, there's no denying the fact, we are all getting rich in grace."[99]

The reception given to the summer campaigners was not as warm in Woodland. Violent opposition came after the Army, hooting, hollering, and throwing rocks, potatoes, apples … anything they could turn into a projectile. Of the twenty-six soldiers who lined up for the march, half of them were women. This fact did not exempt them from the pelting received. The next morning, Joe met with the chief of police and asked for protection from the mob. The request was granted and that evening, the open-air meeting happened without incident. Joe sang a song in Armenian, and the campaign in Woodland ended successfully.[100]

When the group arrived in Napa City and began marching down the street, approximately one thousand people clamored to see the Salvationists. Joe sang a song in his native tongue and shared the story of his life prior to coming to the United States. The barracks were full the next night as Joe continued his story. He talked about living with his brother in Worcester, Massachusetts, and his conversion in San Francisco. He was fast becoming the headliner of the group and, even at this early stage in his officership, drew sizable crowds.[101]

In Alameda, Joe told the story of how he almost drowned in Nevada City. *The War Cry's* report from Nevada City did not mention this incident, but the people who traveled with Joe confirmed it. Joe fell into a hole filled with water that was at least ten feet deep. How did that happen?

During the gold rush of the late 1840s, fortune hunters dug holes and mines across the landscape of Nevada City. These men never filled the holes back in with dirt and rocks. The craters would fill up with water during the rainy season. Because landscaping was not a customary practice in many Western towns, people were not aware of the depth of what appeared to be a simple mud hole. It was into one of these water-filled cavities that Joe sank. Speaking about the incident, Joe said, "The devil thought he had fixed me that time, and would have no more trouble with me, but the Lord saved me."[102] He would also refer to this dousing as the time he got baptized.

The next-to-last stop on the campaign was Oakland. Here, Joe again used his vocal skills to witness. He sang a song entitled, "I'll (We'll) Never Give In."[103]

I'll Never Give In
Composer Unknown

1. Thank God, I'm saved and washed in Jesus' Blood,
And cleansed from every sin;
So now I'll fight, I'll fight for Thee, my Lord,
And never will give in.

Chorus:
Oh, no, no, no! We never will give in;
No, never, no, never;
We'll fight through thick and thin;
For the Savior He has cleansed us,
He has pardoned all our sin,
And we'll never, no, never,
We never will give in.

2. My comrades, let us boldly take our stand
Against the powers of sin;
Be soldiers brave to get poor sinners saved,
And never to give in.

3. We want no cowards in our Army brave,
We want true-hearted men,
Who'll boldly fight, and that with all their might,
And never to give in.

4. The Savior never did a battle lose,
He never did give in,
But on the Cross He shed His precious Blood,
That sinners He might win.

The last stop of the Summer Campaign would be Petaluma. *The War Cry* reported that even though Joe was still learning the English language, he possessed the ability to command the crowd. It stated, "Joe the Turk testified in his peculiar English, and every little while as he went on with his narrative, a ripple of laughter would spread over the audience, and kept the people in a good humor."

While in Petaluma, one campaigner, Mrs. Major Fielding, needed to have her shoes repaired. She gave them to Joe, who, after making the repairs, hammered small brass tacks into the bottoms of her uniform shoes, forming the shape of an 'S.'[104]

The tour ended, and the group returned to San Francisco #2 (Joe's appointment) for a praise and report meeting.[105] The Summer Campaign was an enormous success.

Joe remained at the San Francisco #2 Corps through the end of the year. In January 1889, he reported to his new appointment in Petaluma for a month. In that short period, he made quite an impression on the city. The press reported:

> The Salvation Army people have moved into the skating rink, and now the mellifluous sounds of the Saved Turk's key bugle ring out on the circumambulating air of Western Avenue to the

great delight of the denizens of that locality. One blast upon his bugle horn will bring a thousand sinners to repent—or drive them out of town.[106]

While the article may have been written with a bit of sarcasm, just a few days later, the same paper would offer this editorial:

East Los Angeles has a progressive congregation which has made a move in the right direction and placed itself in advance of all other religious societies that we have any account of on the Pacific Coast. This congregation has inserted in the *Tribune* of that city a five-inch advertisement and a cut [pencil sketch] of the church, the location of the edifice, and the name of its pastor, with the hours of sermon service, Sabbath-school, prayer, and social meetings. There is also added, in display type, a welcome to the public to attend. It is a good two-to-one proposition that this church will be well attended. We prefer printer's ink to the horns of The Salvation Army—even with a 'saved Turk' in the lead—as a means of bringing sinners to church.[107]

Headquarters Warriors

In February, Joe was assigned to the headquarters staff, not as an appointment, but to travel with the group around the Pacific Coast Division for one year. Along the way, they would stop a man from committing murder when Joe grabbed him by the collar and led him to the Army hall. The man knelt at the altar, cried for mercy, and found salvation.[108]

Joe delighted audiences at each port of call by sharing his story of coming to America and how he closed up the hole in the wall of his shoe shop that led into Finnegan's Saloon.

In one town along the way, a saloonkeeper tried to shut the open-air meeting down because it was hurting his business. Saloon and bar owners were often unhappy when the Army meetings resulted in men getting converted, as often they would stop drinking, leaving fewer people to frequent their establishments. In some locations, the owners would hire hoodlums to intentionally break up the open-air meetings. This saloon-keeper attacked Joe and wrestled him to the ground. In the scuffle, Joe lost his cornet mouthpiece and a bass drumstick.[109]

A most notable event during this tour of the division was the arrests of the Headquarters Warriors in East Portland. The account of the ordeal would quickly become a standard story they shared in their meetings. The ones arrested called themselves the Prison Brigade. Joe would talk about these incidents for the rest of his life and especially relished sharing about his encounter with the judge.

Joe the Turk with multiple Salvation Army officers and some of their family members.

CHAPTER 4

TOOLS OF THE TRADE

Joe's adventures would reach America's readers and beyond through Salvation Army publications. He was quickly becoming as much of a celebrity outside of The Salvation Army as he was within. One periodical declared, "Joe the Turk is one of the best-known characters in the country."[110] During his officership, people repeated this accolade.

The Salvation Army on the West Coast had not cornered the market on persecution as, across the country, Salvationists were being arrested and denied their constitutional right to assemble in public. This inspired Joe to spend the next thirty-five years of his officership crisscrossing the country to assist where the fighting was the hardest. Along his journey, he would continue to speak to people about their souls—inside the Army hall, at an open-air, or simply walking down the street.

In September 1890, Joe received an appointment to The Salvation Army National Headquarters in New York City as a traveling special. This meant his full-time ministry position would be to conduct evangelistic meetings across the country. He would keep this appointment and an additional responsibility that came later until his retirement in 1925.

In every community in which he appeared, the press was there to cover the story, positive or negative. Often, their news columns were borderline obsessive about his appearance and the tools of his trade. Besides his passion, these unusual items got him noticed and would become a strong reason why crowds came out in droves to see and hear him.

***

It may not have been obvious to John Garabed, when an off-the-cuff comment bestowed upon him the moniker of "Joe the Turk," that his name would become an important tool of his evangelistic work. When one considers the historical animosity between Armenians and Turks, it is even more surprising he would embrace this nickname.

The hostile relationship between these two people groups dates back to the eleventh century, when the Seljuk Turks invaded Armenia and killed tens of thousands of its citizens, almost decimating the entire population. The Armenians were a subjugated people and fell victim to discrimination and periods of great oppression.[111] This would continue through the end of World War I until Armenia once again regained its independence and recognition as a country.

The world was very aware of this history, particularly the aggressions exacted upon the Armenians. In the mid to late 1800s, these acts earned the Turks a reputation as barbarians, and "the terrible Turks" as a nickname.

The sensational way the press covered the subject only perpetuated this worldview. The average small-town American citizen would get both excited and terrified to meet a true citizen of Turkey. The intricate nuances of what that entailed for Joe would not be immediately understood, as the press often billed him as "a real, live Turk!"

As the conflict between the Turks and Armenians escalated, newspapers and *The War Cry* would often point out that, while Joe was born in Turkey, he was, in fact, an Armenian, an ethnicity persecuted by the Turks. When the stories of the massacres of the late 1890s and those committed under the cover of World War I were reported, many people would turn up to Joe's meetings just to hear the true-life accounts he would give of those atrocities, and to see not only an actual weapon used by the Turks but photographs taken of the victims as well.

In Springfield, Missouri, the crowd rushed in from all sides to see Joe the Turk. One man in the group said he had not seen such a crowd since P.T. Barnum's circus had come to town.[112] During his officership, Joe was continually known as "a real, live Turk," a citizen of Constantinople. He sometimes even used this terminology on the publicity posters he sent out ahead of his visits to communities.

When announcing Joe's visit, *The Cincinnati Enquirer* wrote, "Joe, the tamed Turk, who has been with the Army several years, has lost all his bloodthirstiness for everyone except the devil."[113]

There was also no way anyone could have known there would rise in

Europe an Ottoman wrestler named Youssuf Ishmaelo, whose stage name was "The Terrible Turk." He was one of the strongest men of his day. Described as a modern-day Hercules, he took the wrestling world by storm, beginning in 1894. Youssuf toured the United States in 1898 and created a sensation, wrestling before a sold-out crowd at Madison Square Garden and almost killing his opponent. This incident only increased his reputation as a "terror."[114]

When Joe was conducting an evangelistic campaign in La Grande, Oregon, "The Terrible Turk" was in town at the same time. He and Joe met, and during their conversation, the wrestler shared with Joe that people had asked him if he would pray and sing for them. Youssuf would reply, "I am not Joe the Turk. I am a wrestler, not a preacher. I cannot pray or preach."[115]

Youssuf told Joe his crowd had been taken away from him because of the evangelistic meetings, and he would be leaving the following morning for the next city on his itinerary. Joe persuaded Youssuf to come to the meeting that night, but The Terrible Turk did not receive Christ, although he said he enjoyed the service.[116]

***

The Salvationists were known for their dark, militaristic uniforms and caps, and the women, their coal-scuttle bonnets. Colors other than black and dark blue were not typically associated with the Army, except for red shirts and blouses worn in the very early days by new converts. Salvation Army uniforms did not attract attention using bright colors or exotic fabrics.

Joe's first uniform was the typical dark uniform of a soldier and officer and one he would don from time to time during his officership. The first picture seen of him was in a biographical sketch of his life in The Pacific Coast Division *War Cry* published in November 1886. It is a pencil drawing, and he is wearing the traditional uniform with two badges pinned on his left chest area. He is seen sporting the fully developed mustache that Armenians and Turks were known for. This was one of his trademarks, only growing more prominent with age. It was a fashion feature he kept his entire life.

His uniform eventually changed from the usual Salvation Army attire to a traditional Turkish/Armenian style, which the press would refer to as his "Turkish costume," even comparing it to the dress of a Turkish Sultan.

The November 1886 edition of the Pacific Coast Division War Cry carried Joe's story. This is the first drawing we have of Joe. At this time, he was going by the name of John. Photo courtesy of The Salvation Army National Archives.

The Boston Post wrote, "He was garbed in the splendor of a sultan. Scarlet his coat and Turkish breeches, gold his epaulets, and scarlet and gold his gaiters. On his head, a scarlet fez decorated with a gold crescent and sword. Above it are characters: 'YAARAH ALLAH,' which means, 'O, Lord, Our God.'"[117]

One newspaper informed its readers Joe would "appear in full war uniform, such as is now being used by Turkish soldiers ..."[118]

As for his looks, he was described as "a handsome, strapping young fellow, a native of Turkey, and he speaks the English tongue quite fluently."[119] Another described him in this manner, "Joe is rather good-looking, with a swarthy skin and coal-black eyes ... clad in a Turkish red costume, embroidered with tinsel and gold, his head topped with the traditional fez, his feet encased in blue shoes, upon the sole of each was the word, 'Salvation.'"[120]

Every visit to a town seemed to have begun with a description of his clothing. He was compared to "oriental diplomats found in Washington, D.C.," to a "pasha of high station," and a "potentate adorned with the robes of royalty."[121,122,123]

In addition to his attire, the press just as often wrote about Joe's physical size. One periodical described him in this manner: "Of magnificent physique, with keen piercing brown eyes, his well-formed head surmounted by a quantity of iron gray hair, Joe the Turk would command attention anywhere. He stands six feet high and weighs 240 pounds. His muscles are as hard as nails …"[124]

For all the adjectives used to help the public understand Joe the phenomenon, one of the best descriptions comes from his time in Abilene, Texas:

> He is noted for his talent and eccentricities. He appears on the streets in dazzling regalia, and at night, he uses an electrical umbrella with Salvation mottoes. He is a talented musician, and he and his saxophone are inseparable. But all his varied talents, his attractions, and peculiarities are used to the glory of God and the salvation of men, with the result that many thousands who would otherwise not have listened to a Salvation Army open-air service, have heard the story of Jesus from his lips, and on the last great day, many from the north, east, west, and south of this great country will arise to call him blessed.[125]

***

In the early days of his officership, the reviews about Joe's musical abilities were less than flattering, but as time went on, he began to gain notoriety as a competent musician. One periodical wrote, "His specialty is music, and he has the reputation of being able to play almost all known musical instruments, as well as having invented a few new ones."[126] What those new instruments might have been is not known. However, he took a cornet and made it an instrument to be reckoned with.

There is nothing in the interviews Joe gave through the years about his upbringing to explain how he became such a virtuoso on so many instruments. The only clue given is from an interview where he mentions that the instruments he plays are done so "by ear."[127]

The Double-Jointed Cornet

The second time *The War Cry* wrote about Joe, he was accompanying the Salvationists on the street corners of San Francisco with a cornet.[128] It is unknown how he developed the design for his famous double-jointed cornet, which could double the volume of the sound with a simple lever. One account described it as a "four-forte cornet" and indicated it was so loud that those around him had to put their fingers in their ears to lessen its volume.[129]

The Charlotte Observer described how his competence on the cornet drew crowds around him.

Joe the Turk, posed with his famous cornet, pictured in The Salvation Army American War Cry, May 5, 1894. Photo courtesy of The Salvation Army National Archives.

'It's Joe, the Turk,' shouted the soldiers, as the distinguished visitor climbed upon the chair and touched the pretty silver cornet to his mouth and made ready to give a solo. Everybody was attentive as the Turk blew the first blast on his horn. It was evident from that moment that Joe knew what he was doing, the note was clear, gentle, and sweet. The crowd circled close, hardly giving the performer elbow room, and grew larger every minute. The blazing red color of the Turk's uniform and the call of his cornet attracted the curious from every direction. Men and women climbed on steps and goods boxes and mounted the high places in the streets so that they could see Joe. For a time, the sidewalks were blocked, and the police officers had to threaten [to] use their billies [clubs] to clear the ways.[130]

His double-jointed cornet was his trademark instrument and constant companion when on the march. He served time in jail with it, held crowds spellbound when its "mellifluous sounds filled the air," and stopped busy pedestrians in their tracks with its "clarion bugle-call."[131,132] The case in which he safely stored and carried it was also a weapon of spiritual warfare, as on the outside was a sign that read, "Salvation or Damnation."[133]

***

Joe's cornet was not his only instrument of war. The saxophone and clarinet were soon added to his arsenal. Adolphe Sax, a Belgian instrument maker, invented the saxophone in the 1840s, and in the 1890s, the saxophone made its way to America.[134] Within five years of its arrival, Joe began using it to significant effect in his ministry. The saxophone became popular in jazz clubs in cities like New York, Chicago, and New Orleans, but it took longer to reach smaller communities out West. This gave Joe an advantage, allowing him to introduce it to a large segment of the American population. Because of its uniqueness, he was able to draw great crowds when he played it, and one newspaper described him as "a saxophone artist. Artist is correct, for he certainly knows all there is to know about the instrument he so sweetly plays."[135]

Although Joe was not the first to introduce the saxophone to America, newspapers credited him with that achievement in their

Joe and his saxophone in Lockland, Ohio. He is next to a selection of mottoes sold by Joe as he traversed the United States.

articles and interviews with him. While it was true Joe was the first to bring the saxophone to many parts of the country, he was slow to correct the error; it only added to his mystique.[136]

The Turkish drum was another instrument often mentioned in the papers, with descriptions of his proficiency and how he delighted the crowds with it. Joe used the unique drumsticks with a regular Army bass drum. One newspaper wrote that his presentation with a Turkish drumstick was "a marvelous performance."[137] While there are no detailed narratives or photographs to give more information, Joe possessed a Turkish drumstick called a davul. The davul would have been approximately sixteen inches long and made from wood. The tip of the stick was more bulbous and three inches in circumference. This would create a deep, booming sound when it hit the middle of the drum. He would also have used a thin rod about twenty-four inches in length to strike the opposite side of the drum and create a counter rhythm. This technique would have been foreign and incredibly interesting to his audiences.

***

The press would refer to Joe's command of many languages for several years. He could speak or sing in eight different tongues.[138] Growing up in Talas, he most likely interacted with many nationalities. He lived near people from Greece, Saudi Arabia, Israel, and Samaria, to name a few. It stands to reason, then, that children of his time would play together in the streets and learn bits and pieces of each other's native tongues.

During Joe's time in San Francisco, he may have heard Chinese and even Japanese. He was intelligent and languages came easily to him. In his concerts, he would sing and teach the audience songs and choruses in various languages. In rural settings, the songs he sang, especially those in Armenian, were well received.

Joe's Jolly Brolly

The first mention of Joe's jolly brolly, or umbrella, was in 1891. Simply described as a "variously colored umbrella on which was inscribed

Salvation Army quotations," it quickly became part of his appearance.[139] Newspapers questioned why a man would carry an opened umbrella when it was not raining, while others were quite taken by it and the gospel messages and paintings of famous Salvation Army personalities upon it. The early Army was always looking for ways to attract attention, and Joe was firing on all cylinders with his gospel umbrella.

In 1901, Joe gave an interview in which he shared his reason for utilizing an umbrella, "Joe the Turk has preached the gospel in almost every country in the world, and the famous Turk says that to ensure himself a royal welcome in almost any nation where he goes to preach, it is only necessary to raise his gospel umbrella."[140]

To understand Joe's statement, one only must look at the significance of umbrellas over time. Umbrellas date back to primitive times when our earliest ancestors figured out how to create coverings of leaves and other natural materials to keep rain off their heads. As civilization progressed, so too did the evolution and significance of umbrellas.[141]

In the Egyptian Empire, attendants kept the pharaohs' heads shaded from the blistering desert sun with royal umbrellas. They were a significant part of royal processions and

Joe in his traditional Salvation Army uniform and the first iteration of his umbrella, which, as time passed, would become more ornate and fantastical. Photo courtesy of The Salvation Army National Archives.

a symbol of great power and majesty. [142]

During the rise of Middle Eastern cultures, umbrellas became symbols for royal and political favor. When someone received an umbrella as a gift, it often meant they had personal ties to the pasha, sultan, or caliph. [143]

Growing up in Turkey, Joe would have undoubtedly witnessed examples of royalty and clergy walking beneath magnificent umbrellas carried by servants or attendants. Joe's shoe shop was located close to Chinatown, and he experienced Asian cultures on his visits there. In this section of the city, he would have seen umbrellas transformed into beautifully decorated pieces of art.

It is fair to assume these facts about umbrellas played a part in Joe adding it to his weaponry of spiritual warfare. From the day he first carried it, it received extra coverage in *The War Cry* and other press.

One incarnation of his umbrella was described as "made in stripes of yellow, red, and blue, with the following scripture texts painted on it, 'Jesus is the Drunkard's Friend,' 'Prodigal, Come Home,' 'Sinner, stop and think!' 'Where will you spend eternity?' 'No cross, no crown,' 'Jesus waits to save,' 'God is love.'"[144]

Joe was holding an evangelistic meeting in Elgin, Illinois, when Barnum and Bailey's Circus arrived and paraded through town. Seeing the animals and wagons, he realized this would be a wonderful opportunity to advertise salvation. He grabbed his consecrated umbrella and took off after the procession. Because of this unique method of advertising, a great crowd assembled for the evening meeting. The sides of the tent, used for the evangelistic services, had to be removed to accommodate them all.[145]

The press was enamored with his "prop," and when covering the Grand Continental Congress of 1892, where five thousand Salvationists descended upon New York City, the press reported, "Joe the Turk, with his many-colored umbrella, twenty feet in circumference and covered with startling scripture quotations, was there in all the glory of his Turkish National costume."[146] One suspects the newspaper a tad guilty of hyperbole regarding the measurements of the umbrella.

The next day, the same newspaper would continue its obsession with Joe's umbrella:

Each section of this umbrella is of flaming red, blue, or yellow
silk, the colors of The Army. And upon each section is a motto
in gold letters placed there by Joe himself with the skill of a
sign painter … That umbrella will attract a crowd anywhere. If
Joe makes his appearance upon the streets of New York with
it raised, he will need a whole police reserve to keep the crowd
from smothering him.[147]

In 1896, Joe wrote in *The War Cry* that his umbrella, "which has done
so much service for God and the Army," had been stolen. He wrote that
he hoped whoever took it would get converted when they looked at the
mottoes on it.[148] Months later, Joe replaced the missing umbrella and
informed the readers of *The War Cry* he had created a new, improved
umbrella that featured a portrait of General William Booth.[149]

In 1896, the nation was shocked when Ballington and Maude Booth,
Commanders of The Salvation Army of the United States, resigned and
formed The Volunteers of America. Receiving orders from International
Headquarters to vacate their positions for a new assignment, the Booths
decided to step down from The Salvation Army rather than leave the
country they had fallen in love with. Joe, with other Army luminaries, did
their best to persuade the Booths to reconsider, but to no avail.

Joe felt a deep kinship with the Booths and was devastated by the event.
He could not fathom how or why the Booths could turn their backs on
the movement created by their own family. Even deeper, Joe could not
comprehend how they could break the covenant they made with God to
serve Him all their days through the vehicle of The Salvation Army.

This continued to eat at him. He wrote about it in *The War Cry* and also
wrote a personal letter to the Booths requesting they explain themselves to
him and those they had turned their backs on. Later in the year, Joe was
home in New York City and visited the offices of The Volunteers of America
with the intent of speaking to the Booths in person about their desertion.
They welcomed him with open arms into Ballington's office until they discovered the real reason for his visit. The story was initially reported by the
New York Herald and later spread to California through the Associated Press,
where it was published in *The Los Angeles Herald* and other newspapers:

THE SALVATION ARMY WAR

Perils of a Friendly Call at Rival Headquarters.

The gentle heart of Joe the Turk, otherwise and less generally known as Ensign Joseph Garabed

of The Salvation Army is filled with righteous indignation. The objects of his anger are members of the rival movement known as the American Volunteers, whom he accuses of uncharitable and unchristian treatment that was uncalled for and unmerited.

Joe, the Turk has, besides his Salvation Army uniform, an inseparable companion in the shape of an enormous umbrella, rainbow-hued as to color and ornamented with words of warning to the unrighteous. In addition to such sermons-in-brief as "Jesus is Mighty to Save," "Heaven is real and so is hell," "No cross, no crown," the umbrella is decorated with pictures of General Booth, the founder of The Salvation Army, and Mrs. Booth, his deceased wife.

This umbrella, Joe the Turk has been in the habit of carrying high in the air when the Army marches out, in order that sidewalk spectators may read the flaming texts and be duly impressed thereby.

When the secession of Ballington Booth from the ranks of The Army took place, Joe the Turk and his umbrella remained with the parent organization. He did not, however, entertain any unkind feelings towards his late leader, and as soon as an opportunity offered, Joe furled his umbrella and marched over to the headquarters of the Volunteers to pay his respects to Ballington Booth and wish him Godspeed in his new work. Both Joe and the umbrella were received with open arms.

Looking at this warm reception in the light of later events, Joe, the Turk, says he is inclined to think that the Volunteers expected to find another seceder from the ranks of the parent body.

"Come in and see Mrs. Booth," said Commander Ballington,
heartily. Joe went in, leaving in the outer office his famous
umbrella, open, and with the General's picture turned from
the wall, in order that it might show the seceders, like Barbara
Frietchie's flag, that 'one heart was loyal yet."[150]

The interview with Mrs. Booth was not prolonged. Joe the Turk
thinks that the warmth of the welcome accorded him began to
wane when it was discovered that he was not a seceder.

When Joe the Turk reached the outer office, he found that
vandals had been at work upon the sacred umbrella. Over the
venerable features of General Booth someone had pasted a
picture of Ballington Booth, while in another section of the silk
a text had been obliterated by a life-like representation of Major
Patty Watkins, a leading officer in the Volunteer army.

Joe the Turk regarded the work with dismay and demanded an
explanation of this unbrotherly treatment of a comrade's much-
prized weapon of war. His protestations, he declared, were met
by smiles and assurances that no one there had been guilty of
the outrage. But the matter did not rest there. Joe the Turk has
had a photograph made of the ruined umbrella and intends to
begin a war of reprisal by offering the photographs for sale.[151]

Joe's next notable adventure with his traveling companion happened in
1898 while visiting Washington, D.C., and playing the part of a tourist. He
arrived in full Army regalia, accompanied by his sacred umbrella, carried
in its oil-skin case. When Joe entered the Senate Chamber, thinking the
umbrella case could be a bomb, the security guard became alarmed and
demanded that Joe open the case. The Spanish-American War had just
concluded, so security at the Capital was on high alert.

The commotion around Joe caused a small crowd of politicians to gather.
When Joe reluctantly opened the case, the first thing visible was the

portrait of General William Booth. When the senators saw the painting, they remembered the time General William Booth had prayed in their chamber and were satisfied, concluding that the umbrella was harmless. [152]

With each incarnation of the umbrella, it grew in adornment and wonder. Joe added a bell on the handle, like one on a bicycle, and would ring it in time to the music while he marched. He later added battery-operated lights to the bottom of each umbrella rib, which could be turned on and off by a switch. In the late 1800s, batteries had become more portable and less conspicuous. Attached by a cable, Joe's batteries rested in his uniform pocket. He flipped the switch on and off as needed.[153] Journalists called it "the only thing of its kind in the world and that he invented it. The umbrella is carried before him by a color bearer … and serves the purpose of making the Turk an extremely attractive personality wherever he goes."[154]

After Joe added these final adornments, he didn't bring his umbrella out until the last night of his meetings, using it as part of his sacred concert. He would talk it up during the first few days, which only added to its mystique. The press assisted in creating suspense by

Joe displaying his famous gospel umbrella. This photo was found on the outside back cover of the last version of songbooks he sold. The umbrella has a fringe of electrical lights and is crowned with a miniature Statue of Liberty. Photo courtesy of The Salvation Army National Archives.

printing: "Tonight, he will conduct a service of interest called 'Unveiling the Electric Umbrella,' which is conducted only once in each city."[155]

The lights around the bottom were not the only fixtures that lit up. In 1912, Joe added a miniature Statue of Liberty with an electric light in the torch, which the press declared "was enlightening the world."[156]

When Joe was Promoted to Glory, one newspaper that carried the story referred, even then, to his umbrella, calling it his trademark.[157]

***

"For the word of God is alive and active. Sharper than any double-edged sword, it penetrates even to dividing soul and spirit, joints, and marrow; it judges the thoughts and attitudes of the heart." – Hebrews 4:12 (NIV)

"To the angel of the church in Pergamum write: These are the words of him who has the sharp, double-edged sword." – Revelation 2:12 (NIV)

Swords have been used for as long as there have been armies, although their effectiveness was diminished by the advent of firearms. Today, most swords are ornamental. When the extermination of Armenians in Turkey began in the mid-1890s and again under the cover of World War I, ordinary citizens were relieved of all weapons, leaving them defenseless against any attack.

When Joe returned from a successful visit to Smyrna, he brought back with him a two-edged sword he claimed was an actual weapon used by the Turks on his kinsmen. This relic of war was promoted as a part of his sacred concert. He not only unveiled his umbrella but also displayed the two-edged sword referenced in the Bible.[158]

Photos of Joe picture him with a sword in his hand or hanging by his side. He would bring the sword out in between one of his musical numbers and talk about the massacres perpetrated against the Armenians in Turkey. He also showed actual photographs of victims placed on display after their deaths. These were quite gruesome, showing the inhumane treatment of Armenians in Turkey.

In one city, Joe described, in detail, the tragedy that had befallen the

Armenian Christians. He picked up the sword, illustrating its deadly use. Unknown to him, there were two women in the audience who were survivors of the massacres. The Armenian refugees had witnessed their husbands and family members murdered by a sword like the one Joe was wielding. The memory of the experience deeply distressed them. They were overcome with emotion to the point of fainting.[159] One woman cried out, "I lost all my family and relatives in Adana, Turkey; my husband and children were killed in cold blood! The total number of my relatives killed was thirty-two!"[160] This unsolicited testimony only heightened the tension and deepened the sorrow of the American people toward the Armenian refugees and those still trapped in Turkey.

Joe experienced personal loss when the Turks murdered one of his brothers and his nephew and burned their business to the ground. This forced his sister to flee to Greece to stay alive.

As painful as it might have been for Joe to display the sword, he understood the importance of telling this story to anyone who would listen.

***

Joe produced at least four songbooks during his officership. These were more like booklets, as they were typically sixteen pages, held together with two staples punched into the middle fold. The contents were similar in each one; only the cover and price changed with each new addition.

The earliest cover was a pencil sketch of Joe holding his cornet, and his umbrella opened in front of him. Of him, it said, "All the way from Constantinople." It listed Ballington Booth as the National Commander, which dates the booklet before 1896. The professionally printed booklet sold for five cents.

The inside cover contained a picture of Joe surrounded by a great crowd of businesspeople in Harrisburg, Illinois, who had gathered for a mid-day open-air meeting. The rest of the page described Joe's position as a traveling trade agent and made it known he would assist anyone who wanted to subscribe to any Salvation Army periodical.

The following nine pages contained songs used in his evangelistic meetings. The songs ranged from "The Holy City" to "Some Mother's Boy is Homeless Tonight."

Some Mother's Boy is Homeless Tonight
Composer Unknown

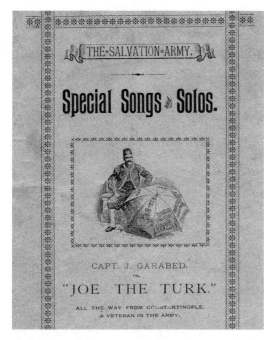

The cover of Joe's first songbook.

1. Out in the cold world
   and far away home
   Some mother's boy is
   wandering all alone
   With no one to guide him
   or keep his footsteps right.
   Some mother's boy is
   homeless tonight.

Chorus:
Bring back to me
my wandering boy.
For there is no other who's
bound to give me joy
Tell him that his mother
with faded cheeks and hair,
Is at the old home
awaiting him there.

2. Out in the hallway, there stands a vacant chair
   An old pair of shoes that he used to wear.
   Empty is the cradle he used to love so well.
   Oh, how I miss him no tongue can tell!

3. Well I remember those parting words he said
   We'll meet up yonder where tears are never shed.
   In that land of sunshine away from toil and care
   When life is over, I'll meet you up there.

On the final page of that section was a copy of a letter Joe received from a police officer:

"Dear Sir:

Kindly pray for me and ask the brothers and sisters to pray for my wife and myself. You put the question to me last night when I arrested you; you told me you were not afraid of me, for God would keep and protect you, and on the way to Station No. 2 you asked me where I was going to spend my eternity. That question has bothered me so I could not rest, and I left duty and came to the Army meeting at No. 1 corps last night, and when I saw you stand up for Jesus I quietly walked out and said, 'To Hell with whiskey! To Jesus I must go and be saved!'

By God helping me, I must and will, with your aid, seek salvation, and may God dwell with those who have found Jesus! I have been a drunkard, and always drank since I was eleven years old, and now I am very sorry and ashamed of myself, for I am a disgrace to all.

By God's help I want to spend eternity in Heaven and not in Hell. Kindly pray for me and my family that I may follow Jesus the rest of my life.

I do not want my name known, as I am a disgrace to all."
— Policeman, Sec. 2

The following page was a cautionary tale of a man on trial for the murder of his wife. Rather than offer a defense, he admitted to the murder but accused every person in the courtroom of being as guilty as he was; they were complicit in legalizing alcohol in the community. That action, he contended, contributed to his addiction, which led him to murder his wife. Long before Prohibition, The Salvation Army was an outspoken opponent of alcohol.

The final page of the songbook contained the Supreme Court of Wisconsin's position on Joe's illegal arrest. Joe would use this many times when defending himself in court. A portion of it reads:

The people do not hold rights as important and as well-settled as the right to assemble and have public parades and processions with music and banners and shoutings and songs in support of any laudable or lawful cause, subject to the power of any public officer to contradict or prevail therein. Our government is a government of laws and not of men, and these principles, well established by the Courts of the 14th Amendment to the Constitution of the United States, have become part of the supreme law of the land, so that no official body or lawful authority can deny to any person the equal protection of the laws. It is plain that the ordinance in question is illegal and void.

The inside back cover was another large advertisement for the Trade and Supplies Department.

The outside back cover was a story, with a photo promoting Joe's latest invention: "The only illuminated umbrella in the world—invented by Joe the Turk. The public is encouraged to not miss the opportunity to see this unique and original piece of work."

***

In the summer of 1893, Joe's latest method of leaving a lasting impression truly left a *lasting impression*. In 1866, rubber stamps were invented in the United States. However, it took Joe twenty-seven years to discover their usefulness for ministry. He had an India-ink rubber stamp created with the

An advertisement for The Trade and Supplies Department. This particular one was found on the inside of Joe's songbook entitled, Special Songs and Solos.

words, "Jesus is Mighty to Save" on it, and thus began an indelible method of ministry people would either appreciate or abhor.

The first mention of the rubber stamp comes from evangelistic meetings Joe conducted in Sioux Falls, South Dakota. A man who had backslid into sin came to the evening meeting. Joe was careful to stamp the man's hand before the service began. The man repeatedly looked at the words on his hand during the service. In the end, he fell to his knees and rededicated his life to Christ. The following night, he joined in the open-air march.[161]

Joe's stamp captured the attention of one of The Salvation Army's magazines, The Officer, which extolled his sense of enterprise and originality. "He leaves his impress wherever he goes, on the collars of gentlemen or on the neat white aprons of the young women. Recently paying a visit to the Territorial Headquarters, New York, his motto was to be seen everywhere, on the compositor's aprons and on the walls, ceiling, and floors, wherever he had gone, his mark was left."[162]

Once, when conducting evangelistic meetings, Joe was housed at an elderly widow's home. While the woman was a friend of The Salvation Army, she was not a professing Christian. After Joe left her home, she was shocked to go into the guest room and see "Jesus is Mighty to Save" stamped on the wallpaper, mirror, carpet, doors, and even on the ceiling. The woman was understandably quite upset. However, all during the day, the words kept running through her mind. She could not eat or sleep that night. The following morning, she knelt beside her bed and proved the words that "Jesus is mighty to save." Later, Joe received a letter from the woman, telling him of her conversion and asking if he could return to her home and decorate the rest of it with his stamp.[163]

As Joe crossed the country, and billeted with officers in their quarters, he promptly went to work stamping the entire house, towels, napkins, curtains, and anything he could "lay his hands on." In one quarters, he sat on the floor with a pile of linens, stamping each piece with indelible ink. And in yet another home, he took the bib off a baby, stamped it, and then tied it once again around the child's neck. Speaking of Joe and his stamp, someone once said, "After Joe has gone, we will be able to say truly that he, being dead, yet speaketh."[164]

***

On September 1, 1890, Joe joined The Salvation Army's National Headquarters in New York City and was given the rank of staff-captain. Six years later, he had an additional assignment, which he performed with almost equal enthusiasm to soul-winning. Traveling Trade Special was his new title and Joe lost little time in promoting the department he now represented. On his travels, he added an extra trunk to his already extensive cache of evangelism supplies and musical instruments.

In the monthly columns he wrote for *The War Cry*, highlighting his adventures, Joe advertised the items he sold on behalf of the trade department. He also promoted his unique ability to measure anyone properly for a uniform that would fit perfectly. He assured his readers their uniform would not have to be altered when it arrived.

The trade's news publication highlighted Joe's skillfulness:

> As our comrades are aware Staff-Captain Garabed has
> been touring the country ... acting in the capacity of Trade
> Agent. On the uniform line, particularly, Joe the Turk
> is an expert. His measurements are always correct, and
> alterations are never necessary when this comrade takes an
> order for both men and women. If he is visiting your corps,
> do not hesitate to let him line your soldiers up for uniform.
> You may be sure that they will be well-looked after and a
> perfect fitting be the result.[165]

In the articles written for *The War Cry*, Joe encouraged Salvationists to purchase uniforms to signify they were out-and-out for Jesus and show the world [they were] loyal blood-and-fire soldiers.[166,167]

In addition to visiting corps, Joe attended camp meetings around the country and hawked the trade department's wares to the attendees.

A group of Methodists established the Glyndon Park Campground, near Baltimore, Maryland, in 1868. Evangelical meetings were held under a big tent, and people flocked to the summer services. Some of the attendees stayed for weeks and camped out in tents of their own.

At the turn of the twentieth century, The Salvation Army began holding camp-meetings there as well. In 1904, the attendance reached three thousand for the evening meetings. Joe was there with his trade tent, dressed in his unique uniform, selling souvenirs and mottoes, such as modern ink pens, songbooks, Salvation Army badges (pins), and plaques containing words such as: "As for me and my house we will serve the Lord," "He Faileth Not," and "Mighty to Save."

The Baltimore Sun, which reported on the event, observed that because of the enormous crowds, food was proving difficult to find unless someone had packed their own lunch. However, it observed about the situation, "The only things that seemed inexhaustible were the enthusiasm and the mottoes and souvenirs of Joe the Turk."[168]

CHAPTER 5
ARRESTED DEVELOPMENTS

Joe the Turk
Author Unknown

His name is Joe, and he is a Turk,
Engaged every day in Salvation work,
He's been hit on the head with brick and stone,
But that doesn't stop his vocal trombone.
Joe, Joe, Joe the Turk,
Whose pulpit is boxes and streets his kirk.
Some say he's sensational, much too free,
A seeker for great notoriety,
Some think it suspicious, that pagan man,
Should flop, go to work on the Christian Plan.
Joe, Joe, Joe the Turk,
Oh, he is a fighter with a hymn for dirk.
Though jibed by the boy and jailed by police,
He bobs up serenely as slippery as grease,
Insists on his rights, takes a stubborn stand,
And gets what is granted a minstrel band.
Joe, Joe, Joe the Turk,
When once he gets started there's never a shirk.
Suppose what they say of the Turk is true,
There's nothing very wrong about it, think you?
So let him go on from goal to goal,
His labor is grand if he saves one soul.
Joe, Joe, Joe the Turk,
Let him go on with Salvation work.
The USA War Cry May 12, 1894

St. John Ervine, in his seminal biography of William Booth, *God's Soldier*, described the savagery with which the early Salvationists were treated by their foes. Groups of rowdies parodied the Salvationists by forming a Skeleton Army, carrying flags emblazoned with skulls and crossbones and mocking them with exaggerated prayers and singing. Pub owners saw some of their most profitable clientele converted and give up drinking. This infuriated them enough for them to hire members of the Skeleton Army to beat the Salvationists as they marched and preached on the streets. Religious leaders who had never set foot inside of a Salvation Army meeting, nor met a Salvationist face to face, condemned the Army from their pulpits and wrote articles to the newspapers denouncing the religious heretics.

William Booth was not impervious to these attacks and one evening when his son Bramwell showed him a vicious and exceptionally cruel newspaper attack, the General replied, "Bramwell, fifty years hence it will matter very little indeed how these people treated us; it will matter a great deal how we dealt with the work of God."[169]

As The Salvation Army spread across the world, so too, the violence exacted upon them. Officers and soldiers were placed in prison, attacked, beaten, and mistreated in criminal ways that regularly went unpunished. Not only were they beaten in the open-air, but many were followed to their homes and places of works to be assaulted or have their property destroyed.[170]

When The Salvation Army unofficially arrived in America, the Shirley family held the first American open-air to little notice. Subsequent open-airs were held at an area called Five Points, which was an intersection of five slum streets. The first attempt did not induce violence, only taunts and snide remarks. Coming back to that same location later in the day, the Salvationists were met with further verbal abuse as well as mud and garbage. As The Salvation Army spread across the United States over the coming months and years, Booth's soldiers were treated more harshly.[171]

Between 1880 and 1896, at least five Salvationists were martyred; a number of them were shot at, hit with bricks, and had bones broken for no other reason than preaching and testifying about Jesus in the streets. In the Chicago #3 Corps, a mob rushed inside the Army hall, overturned the wood stove, ran out, and locked the door in an attempt to burn the building with Salvationists trapped inside. It was not uncommon for these

Christian soldiers to be struck by stones, bricks, glass bottles, pears, apples, tomatoes, rotten eggs, garbage, small dead animals, or horse manure.[172]

But it wasn't just violence—these Christian soldiers also faced legal challenges. Laws meant to keep peace were twisted to restrict the Salvationist's right to gather, speak publicly, or march. Officers and soldiers were frequently arrested on weak charges like disturbing the peace or blocking traffic. In court, the Army's legitimacy as a religious and charitable group was repeatedly questioned.

On top of physical assaults and legal battles, Sallys faced social rejection. The unique uniforms and public marches were mocked in newspapers and cartoons. The Salvationists were portrayed as fanatics and ridiculed publicly in order to undermine their influence. Socially, they were often shunned and sometimes even fired from their jobs because they had aligned themselves with this "crude and crass" Army.

During the first three decades of his officership, Joe was arrested fifty-two times. This does not include his frequent arrests as a soldier at the San Francisco #1 Corps. His last arrest happened in 1917 at Athol, Massachusetts. In the latter part of his officership, Joe produced a large poster to advertise his

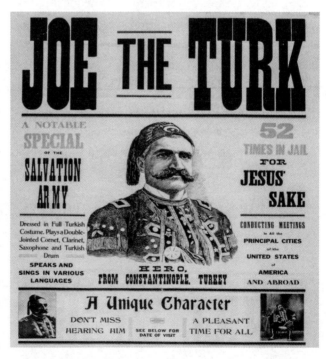

Joe used this poster to send ahead of his upcoming campaign sites. Photo courtesy of the Houston Texas Public Library.

evangelistic campaigns, highlighting his fifty-two arrests. In the appendix of this book is a list of all fifty-two arrests, with a brief description of each incident.

Speculation arose that Joe allowed himself to be arrested for the notoriety it brought. While this is a fair assumption, a deeper study of his arrests reveals he often endured harsh treatment under appalling conditions in jail. There were easier ways to attain celebrity, which he had already achieved through his unique uniforms and the various accouterments he surrounded himself with.

While he often sought capture and incarceration, it was his ultimate goal that the Army would have its constitutional right to assemble, play music, march, preach, and pray on American streets.

Malls, movie theaters, and theme parks had not yet come on the scene. People spent a great deal of time outdoors walking on Main Street and gathering with family and friends in the local parks. These outdoor settings were perfect evangelization spots, and Joe would not allow anyone to deny the Army its right to proclaim the name of Jesus in the open-air.

The January 10, 1910 edition of the *Daily Arkansas Gazette* offered this comment: "Joe the Turk, probably the most arrested man The Salvation Army or any other religious order has ever produced, is in Little Rock for the purpose of conducting a revival of three days' duration."

The following accounts are some of his more notorious run-ins with the law.

***

On February 4, 1888, Joe began his appointment at the San Francisco #2 Corps as its assistant officer. This corps also served as the training garrison, making Joe a member of the staff. When the cadets were on the march, Joe led the way, playing his cornet in his right hand and waving an American flag in his left.

The attitude toward the Army had not significantly changed since his previous time in San Francisco. Upon his return, he had a knife drawn on him, as well as a revolver. Undaunted, the Salvationists continued marching, playing, and preaching in the streets, particularly in the most dangerous sections of the city.

On Thursday, May 24, 1888, Joe led a group of officers, cadets, and soldiers in a march that took them onto Market Street, one of the principal thoroughfares of San Francisco. The police arrested them during an open-air meeting and took them to the Folsom Street Police Station. As the Salvationists made their way to jail, they waved their flags, sang, and played their instruments. A mob of approximately two thousand people followed alongside them, yelling, cursing, and throwing anything that could be used to hurt them.[173]

Locked into one cell, they continued singing and playing in their confinement. The police, who considered Joe the ringleader, thought they could stop the noise by removing him from the group and placing him alone in a dark cell. There was a drunken man in the communal cell. When he realized they had locked him up with the Sallys, he began to beg to be moved to a new cell. The man made such a racket that he was removed and put into the dark cell with Joe. When he discovered Joe the Turk was his cellmate, he hauled off and hit him with such intensity it knocked Joe to the floor. The police again removed the man and placed him in a different cell from all the Salvationists.[174]

The next day, the trial of the Salvationists commenced at the city hall, where witnesses for the prosecution claimed they were restaurant owners and the Army had been disturbing the peace, resulting in lost customers. When the defense cross-examined them, they found that the restaurant owners were saloonkeepers. So many of their customers had come to the open-air meetings, gotten saved, and quit drinking that their saloons were almost empty. The judge sided with The Salvation Army and dismissed the case, stating they had the right to march and play in the streets.[175]

Later that month, the Salvationists planned an evangelistic campaign for the entire city of San Francisco. They selected Joe to lead one of the three marching brigades. As the Salvationists left their barracks and made their way down the streets, the mob attacked, throwing bricks, rocks, and anything they could hurl to injure the Salvationists. During the barrage, they hit Joe in the face with a stone, but he continued with the march and the open-air meeting. It was not the first time, nor would it be the last time he was injured for proclaiming the gospel in the streets. Joe would bear the marks of this abuse with him until the end of his life. Newspaper articles written about him over time would offer commentary about the scars and marks on his face and head.

One afternoon, Joe was strolling down Market Street when a quartet of police officers stopped him and said they had something to tell him. Half-expecting to be arrested, he was pleasantly surprised when the officers told him that the police currently felt there was no point in arresting the Salvationists, as the courts would not convict them. The police officers believed this was because of the love of God in the hearts of the Sallys.[176]

Los Angeles Rewind

Joe spent much of 1888 and 1889 serving in corps and traveling with a small group of officers and lay members. They conducted evangelistic meetings around the Pacific Coast Division. Following both victories and defeats, Joe found himself again in Los Angeles during the spring of 1890. Despite making headway a few years earlier, the Army continued to face persecution in the city. On the evening of April 18, while out on the open-air march, the police arrested the Sallys, but immediately released them upon their promise not to march again.

The next evening, the Salvationists made up their minds to march again and informed the police they would play and sing for Jesus in the streets. This night, Joe was carrying The Salvation Army flag and leading the procession. A crowd of about two hundred followed along the march as the evangelists prayed to avoid arrest. The Salvationists exercised caution, but eventually, the drummer and timbrelists could not contain their holy joy and played. At that moment, the police swooped in, and much to the delight of the crowd that had begun to cheer and applaud, they apprehended the Salvationists. The police arrested everyone and charged them with disturbing the peace, setting bail at five dollars per person. Today, that would be $175 each. The weary warriors marched back to their barracks "with silent instruments and drooping flag."[177]

The following night, the little band was back on the streets with only a concertina to accompany them. When they reached their open-air location,

Joe stood on a chair and preached. The crowd jeered and catcalled during the entire open-air. When the meeting was over, and the Salvationists marched back to the barracks, hundreds of spectators followed alongside them, harassing, and yelling insults. The police did not intervene.[178]

Days later, the court heard and overturned the case against the Army. The crusaders could march and make music freely on the streets once again.[179]

Word continued to spread quickly about the sanctified Salvation Army Turk. At a masked ball in Nevada City, California, one participant came dressed as Joe. When *The War Cry* reported the story, the editor asked if the imposter was willing to share Joe's jail time as well.[180]

Once the case against the Army was settled in Los Angeles, the opposition decreased, but it did not go away. As the public got to know and understand the heart of The Salvation Army and saw the results of its work with those who were slaves to alcohol, they slowly became more accepting and supportive.

Thousands of people often packed the parade route. The Salvationists faithfully marched, prayed, and preached on the streets, leading to the conversion of many people, even in some of the roughest elements in the city. Joe would drop to his knees in front of a saloon door and fervently pray. While his earnestness and petitions touched many onlookers, the owners of the bars and saloons were not impressed. Men gave their lives to Christ in the open-air meetings. They gave up their thirst for alcohol, resulting in them taking better care of their families. When the saloon owners saw their profits slipping and clientele decreasing, they would often hire ruffians to instigate trouble and break up the open-air meetings. Occasionally, the police would side with the rabble-rousers and harass the Army. As time went on, this began to change … but not everywhere.

Portland Arrests

In the October 15, 1889 edition of The Pacific Coast Division *War Cry*, the editor decried public officials who abused their use of power in creating unjust laws. He wrote, "Arresting and jailing Salvationists is a matter of such frequent occurrence that it threatens to become monotonous, but whether it be so or not, as a reflex of current Salvation Army history, it is expected of *The War Cry* to chronicle events as they occur."

East Portland enacted an ordinance stating any public parade—except for funerals, marches, or processions using music—would require permission from the city government.[181] Upon the release of this ordinance, four Salvationists marched without this permission and were promptly arrested. The next day, six Salvationists without clearance marched and met the same fate. Despite the dismissal of the cases, the fight for the right to march, play music, and preach in open-air meetings in East Portland was far from over.

On the third night of the conflict, Joe and the group he was traveling around the division with marched with two tambourines, two drums, and three cornets. When they arrived at the open-air spot, the city marshal was waiting for them. He motioned with his finger for them to follow. Leading the brave little band through the streets, the cornetists played, "Never Run Away."[182]

Never Run Away
William Pearson

1.To save the world is our desire,
For enemies we pray.
We'll never tire, we'll stand the fire,
And never, never run away.

Chorus:
We're marching on to conquer all,
Before our God the world shall fall.
We'll face the foe, to battle go.
And never, never run away.
What, never run away?
No, never run away.
What, never run away?
No, never run away.
We'll face the foe, to battle go,
And never, never run away.

2. Sin's greatest strongholds we'll attack,
Our Captain we'll obey.
The foe shall yet be driven back,
We'll never, never run away.

3. We'll onward march, with flag unfurled.
Our King shall have the sway.
He lived and died to save the world.
We'll never, never run away.
                    – *The Salvation Army Songbook*

Marching the Salvationists to jail, the marshal became a victim of friendly fire. An egg meant for one of the Sallys hit him in the back of the head.[183]

When the authorities arrived at the jail, they released two women Salvationists on their own recognizance but kept the five men. Once in their cell, the musicians continued playing their instruments until the other jailers confiscated them. When offered release if they posted a ten-dollar bond, all the men refused and prepared to stay incarcerated for the entire duration. The jail was twenty-five feet by ten feet and contained three cells with a one-man bunk in each cell described as "not to be fit for anyone to sleep on." They chose to sleep on the floor. The women returned with enough blankets for each of them. Using blocks of wood for pillows and their coats for extra warmth, they survived the cold nights of incarceration.[184]

The group appeared before a judge in Portland two days later. A previous case had been tried in the same court, and the Salvationists were released; this time, that was not the case. The prisoners returned to East Portland, and four of the five were fined twenty dollars each. The judge, when giving Joe his sentence, was upset when Joe shouted, "Praise the Lord!" The judge promptly raised his fine to fifty dollars. Joe refused to pay the fine and had to serve one day in jail for every two dollars of the fine. Twenty-five days later, he left his jail cell.[185]

The prisoners were allowed outside for exercise only twice a week. While the police force was kind to the Salvationists, they were also strict and continued to deny them adequate resources to manage the coldness of the jail cell at night.[186]

Due to the city's injunction against the Army freely marching in the streets, the judge ruled no group would be allowed to march from that point onward, an unintended byproduct of the arrests.[187] This declaration did not go down well with the public.

On Sunday afternoon, October 27, people came running from everywhere as the sounds of Salvation Army music filled the air. The crowd was certain they were going to witness the arrest of the Salvationists again. However, the Army band played on the porch of their barracks instead, which did not violate the ordinance.[188]

When the Salvationists discovered the governor of Oregon resided in Portland, Mrs. Adjutant Parker, one of the original seven arrested, went to see him and explained the Army's difficulties. She hoped he would overrule the judge and set the prisoners free. He did not, and they had to serve their required time.[189]

After completing their time, the four male Salvationists who were arrested with Joe were released. Joe was the only one remaining, but he was not idle. A painter arrested for public drunkenness was placed in Joe's cell. The painter was allowed to keep his paints, and before the night was over, the duo had painted mottoes over all the walls that read: "Burning Hell for the Wicked," "Get Ready for the Judgement Day!", "What Will You Do in Eternity?", "Follow the Lamb!", "Sinner Repent!", and "Death is on Your Track!"[190]

Joe's evangelistic fervor yielded results during this time, as he led ten people to salvation. Ironically, the first convert was a shoemaker from San Francisco who was clueless about religious matters. When he inquired about who this Jesus person was, Joe shared the gospel story, and the man knelt in the jail cell and gave his heart to Christ.[191]

After reading the words that were painted on the walls, one of the men knelt and prayed. The second conversion happened after a man read the words, "Are you saved from sin?" A third man, who had been instrumental in getting the prohibition to march passed, was placed in jail for public drunkenness and was inconsolable by what he had done. Joe told him about Jesus, prayed with him, and he was gloriously saved. Similar scenarios were repeated seven more times during Joe's imprisonment.[192]

Once all the Salvationist prisoners were released, they titled themselves the Prison Brigade. When they shared their ordeal with future congregations, they often wore their jail clothes.[193]

Leaving East Portland and knowing a similar ordinance had recently been passed there, the Prison Brigade made the short trek to Portland. The group decided to march before the evening meeting with just two timbrels. Things seemed fine until they were approaching the barracks. Just before they entered the building, they were stopped by three police officers and informed they were under arrest. As the group marched to jail, they sang and announced the meeting that was taking place later that evening. The police ordered them to stop singing and talking. Joe marched with his cornet under his arm, and with each step, the crowd that followed them to the jail grew larger. In this instance, no eggs or missiles were thrown at the Salvationists, but they were relieved of their penknives.[194]

Joe, dressed in his Turkish garb, in Portland, Oregon during a return visit to the city a few years after his initial arrest. Photo courtesy of The Salvation Army National Archives.

The jail in Portland was approximately thirty feet by forty feet and only had two windows. To the Prison Brigade's dismay, hundreds of cockroaches were crawling all over walls, which had not seen a fresh coat of paint in years. Immediately, the women began a praise meeting in their cells. After the impromptu service, a sympathetic citizen paid the ladies' bail, resulting in their release. Before leaving, the women wrote their names on the jailhouse walls as a reminder to the police officers they were being prayed for by the Salvationists. The jailbirds were surprised at the next day's trial to learn no complaint had been sworn out, and they were free to leave.[195]

The Prison Brigade returned to Portland for a second series of meetings. They were arrested and marched to jail again. After posting bail, everyone was released.[196]

A year after the event, Joe received a letter from a friend in Portland. The friend reported that the judge who had sentenced him to jail had been converted. He was now attending The Salvation Army corps and indirectly credited Joe for his new faith in Christ.[197] Joe carried the letter with him to prove the claim of the judge's conversion. It read:

> I write you today to let you know that the power of God has been wonderfully displayed in the salvation of the police judge who sentenced Adjutant Parker, Captain Loney, and others over a year ago, to the East Portland city jail for marching the streets for Jesus, and giving 'Joe, the Turk,' 15 days extra for saying 'Praise the Lord' in the courtroom. A few days since, this same judge had returned home from his office, but was too drunk to get up the steps into the house, and was lying prostrate when a Christian man, passing, offered to assist him, and called him brother.
>
> The kind word and the ringing of the church bell nearby at the time

Joe arrested in East Portland, Oregon for open-air work. Behind him is a picture of himself hanging on the wall. Photo courtesy of The Salvation Army National Archives.

so enraged him that he went into the house raving like one possessed of the devil. A short time afterwards he found his way down into the basement of his house to get some stove wood, and in as miraculous a manner as Saul of Tarsus, there was the conscious presence of a Supernatural Being, and like Saul, he cried out: 'Who art Thou?' The answer came, 'I am Jesus, who is ready to save you.' Falling on his knees, he cried for mercy. Soon after, he rushed up to his wife's room and told her that he had met the Lord! This frightened his wife; she thought he had become crazy. But she was soon convinced of his sanity when he asked her to pray for him and fell on his knees, asking God for Christ's sake to forgive all his sins.

In the end, the judge was gloriously saved, started attending church, and testified to everyone about the saving power of Jesus. He attributed his conviction to the prayers of The Salvation Army and said from that time forward the Army would find in him a firm friend.

The judge sent this message: "God bless Joe, the Turk! I wish I could see him. Hallelujah to the Lamb forever!"[198]

**

In Portage, Wisconsin, the police arrested Joe for violating a city ordinance, specifically naming The Salvation Army as a group prohibited from parading on the streets and playing musical instruments. The ordinance stipulated the mayor had to grant prior approval before any group could march.[199] The Army could march on Tuesday and Thursday evenings, but at no other time. Joe arrived on a different night of the week to begin his evangelistic campaign. A soldier of the corps erroneously informed him he could march every night while conducting his unique meetings.[200]

Unaware of the ordinance, Joe led the Salvationists on a march down Main Street, and then to the open-air spot. Catching the town by surprise, it was not long before a great crowd gathered to hear what the unusual visitor had to say.

Suddenly, the marshal appeared and informed Joe he did not have permission to be on the streets. Joe told him their meeting would end soon, and then they would march back to the barracks. The marshal left and returned minutes later with a deputy. They grabbed Joe's arms and dragged him through the streets to jail. According to Joe's account in *The War Cry*, he believed the marshal needed help because he thought Joe was too much for one person to manage.[201]

The two law enforcement officers continued to pull Joe through the streets, but when they got near the corps building, they suddenly let him go. Joe quickly went to the barracks door, blew his cornet as a victory call, and invited the crowd that had been following him to the meeting that night.[202]

The next evening, because of the sensationalism of the previous night, the Army hall was packed to the doors. The corps officer led the open-air march, and Joe stayed behind at the barracks. When everyone had left for the open-air, the marshal and his deputy arrived at the corps and ordered Joe to follow them back to jail. Joe refused, stating he was not doing anything illegal. He suggested the sheriff apprehend the marching Salvationists instead.[203]

The duo took off after the Salvationists, and, finding them, tackled the female captain to the ground. Seeing what had happened, the assistant corps officer turned and marched a contingent of soldiers in a different direction. By this time, Joe could not restrain himself from involvement. He followed closely behind the marshal, and when he saw the captain attacked, he fell in line with the splinter group led by the assistant officer.

The public officials did not know how to manage all the confusion. Joe pulled out his cornet and played to signify solidarity with the captain, whom he believed had been arrested. When the marshal heard the music, he left the captain and went after Joe, placing him under arrest and leading him off to jail.[204]

The marshal put Joe in a tiny cell in which a huge fire was blazing, raising the temperature to an almost unbearable degree. In *The War Cry*, Joe wrote about the incident. He told his readers he thought jail cells were called coolers, but his cell was better described as a sweatbox.[205]

Business leaders in the community who witnessed the spectacle came to Joe's defense. One gentleman, enraged by the Salvationists' poor treatment, paid the one-hundred-dollar bail, allowing Joe to make it to the 9:00 p.m. meeting at the Army hall.[206]

Monday morning, Joe stood before the judge. He did not think he could get a fair trial in Portage, so he requested a change of venue; it was denied. He was also refused a public defender. Despite public support for the Army, no lawyer would represent Joe due to fear of retaliation by the marshal and judge. Describing himself as a lamb among wolves, Joe felt the presence of the Lord with him even though he was alone, just as the Bible's Daniel had in the den of lions.[207]

At Joe's trial, the court found him guilty and imposed a fine of five dollars, along with court costs totaling $18.85. He told the court he would not pay the fine and instead selected the second option of twenty days in jail. Before they took him from the courtroom and returned him to jail, he informed the judge he would appeal the decision. He secured the services of a lawyer from Madison who had represented him before. Joe remained in jail for five days until his lawyer could arrive. He did not waste those days and was allowed to have his cornet back. Since the officials denied him the right to do so in the streets, Joe played and preached to his fellow inmates.[208]

When Joe's lawyer appeared before the judge, he cited cases the Army had won through appeals to various state supreme courts. He listed examples: Michigan, Illinois, and Kansas. The lawyer argued it was apparent the ordinance in question specifically targeted The Salvation Army. As compelling as the defense was, the judge would not dismiss the case and passed it up to the Wisconsin Supreme Court.[209]

The business leaders of Portage, outraged by Joe's jailing, called for his release in a telegram to the governor. While Joe never saw the governor's response, he was immediately released.[210]

***

On Tuesday night, July 4, 1893, Joe led a group of Salvationists in a march down the streets of Saratoga, New York. Because the local authorities were not supportive of the Army's outdoor ministry, they arrested the group of Salvationists. Bail was posted, the prisoners released and forbidden to march again. Joe marched the next night, refusing to heed the warning. The police showed up and dragged him to jail.[211] He was released the following morning, but the group of Salvationists went out again that evening. This time they marched without instruments and without incident.

Emboldened by this, they marched again, this time singing and playing. Three police officers grabbed the captain, lieutenant, and a soldier, all females, and led them to jail. As they entered the facility, they heard Joe singing. He and a candidate for officership had been arrested earlier for the same offense as the women. As they got closer, they heard Joe singing "We Will Never Give In."[212]

We Will Never Give In

1. God is keeping his soldiers fighting,
Evermore we shall conquerors be.
All the hosts of Hell are uniting,
But we're sure to have victory.
Though to beat us they've been trying,
Our colors still are flying,
And our flag shall wave forever,
For we never will give in.

Chorus:
No, we never, never, never will give in.
No, we won't! No, we won't!
No, we never, never, never will give in.
For we mean to have the victory for ever.

2. We will follow our conquering Savior,
From before him Hell's legions shall fly.
Our battalions never shall waver,
They're determined to conquer or die.
From holiness and Heaven
We never will be driven.
We will stand our ground for ever,
For we never will give in.
3. With salvation for every nation,
To the ends of the earth we will go,
With a free and full salvation,
All the power of the cross we'll show.
We'll tear Hell's throne to pieces,

And win the world for Jesus,
We'll be conquerors forever,
For we never will give in.
                    – The Salvation Army Songbook

The Salvationists were placed in cells directly across from each other. Kneeling and asking God to intervene in their cases, they sang and prayed, and thanked God they were worthy to suffer for His sake. As they held their prayer meeting, the words and songs were heard through the windows of the jail. Slowly, a crowd gathered to listen to the prayer meeting by the incarcerated Sallys. The group standing outside of the jail became indignant about the situation and cried out, "Shame!" "Outrage!" "Disgrace!" Within a couple of hours, the prisoners were removed from their cages and placed before the judge. They all pled not guilty and were placed under a two-hundred-dollar bail. The candidate produced his bail, but the rest did not and were sent back to their cells.[213]

The jailbirds wasted no time in adorning the walls of their temporary prison with gospel slogans and Scripture verses. A nine-year-old girl, arrested for petty theft, was placed in the women's cell. The authorities had already convicted her and sentenced her to reform school. The women talked and prayed with her, and in the end, she gave her heart to Jesus. As evidence her conversion was genuine, the young girl gave a full confession to the Salvationists, something she had refused to do for the police.[214]

The prisoners went to court the next day, but the judge postponed their case until the following week. He offered bail to the women under the condition that they would not take part in any marches until Joe's case was resolved. They refused, and standing in solidarity with Joe, were returned to their cells to spend the weekend behind bars.[215]

Joe's case went to trial the following week. He asked for a public defender, but none was assigned. He pled his own case, citing Psalm 98, which he believed proved his right to play his cornet in the streets. Joe explained the typical methods used by The Salvation Army in the open-air. His plea failed to impress the jury, so they continued his trial to the following afternoon. By the time of his hearing, he had acquired a lawyer. Five hundred people filled the courtroom to witness the case. The jury found him guilty but asked the judge to suspend the sentence. Joe was ordered to either pay a fifteen-dollar fine or spend fifteen days in jail. Even though he refused to pay the fine, friends of the Army stepped forward and paid it on his behalf. They honorably discharged the women after they had served five days in jail.[216]

Not satisfied with the results, Joe appealed to a group of prominent Saratoga lawyers, who were supportive of the Army's right to march. They took the case to the county court, which ruled in favor of The Salvation Army. Joe was honorably discharged and moved on to his next engagement.[217]

Weeks later, Joe learned P.T. Barnum's circus was in Saratoga, so he went back and used the opportunity to make a statement. He harnessed two donkeys to a small wagon decorated with American flags and gospel messages, and then the captain and lieutenant rode in it and displayed Joe's spectacular umbrella. Joe also attached large banners printed with messages of salvation to the sides of the wagon. The Salvation Army soldiers walked alongside, wearing American flag sashes. Joe accompanied them in full Turkish regalia.[218]

As the circus procession passed by on the main thoroughfare, the salvation entourage pulled in behind them and joined the parade. They marched all the way to the circus grounds without being stopped or arrested.

Shortly after the parade, the officials in Saratoga passed an ordinance prohibiting anyone from marching on the streets without a permit from the chief of police. However, by this time, the Army had made its mark and its point.[219]

Joe wrote in his *War Cry* travelogue, "Praise the Lord we are still alive! Chastened but not killed, as sorrowful yet always rejoicing (under all circumstances), having nothing, yet possessing all things (2 Corinthians 6:4-10)."

***

Joe arrived in Lowell, Massachusetts, on February 4, 1894, and conducted his first night of street and indoor meetings with no trouble. The next evening, along with a group of soldiers, he and two other musicians stood in the middle of a principal street and played.[220] A crowd of one thousand gathered around the open-air ring, prohibiting the horse-drawn streetcars from moving along the roadway.[221] When the police showed up and ordered the Salvationists to move, they did, but once again, the crowd created a blockade for vehicles. When told to move again, Joe refused, and the police promptly arrested the trio of musicians. Frank Fox, John Fox, and Officer Brady were the police officers who led them to jail.[222] The last name of two of the police officers would prove useful to Joe as he spoke out against his arrest in the coming days.

Newspapers across the country carried the story, and it garnered continued attention as the case progressed.[223]

The following day, the courtroom was packed to the doors. When Officer Fox gave his testimony, he informed the court he and the other police officers had been assigned to follow the Army for their protection. It was only when the Sallys created an obstruction in the road that they asked the marchers to hold their meeting elsewhere. Only when Joe continually refused did they act and arrest them all.[224] The prisoners were fined three dollars. They refused to pay and asked that their case be heard by a higher court. Later, a friend of the Army paid the fine, and the prisoners were released.[225]

The next day, knowing the arrests of the previous day would bring in a sizable crowd, the Army rented one of the largest meeting spaces in town. According to the local paper, *The Lowell Sun*, Joe vowed to remain in Lowell and fight the charge. He canceled his next two engagements.

Even before the Army appeared on the streets that evening, a crowd of approximately four hundred had already gathered. There were ten Salvationists compared to more than fifty ruffians, who were excited by the prospect of making mischief at the expense of the Sallys. The pranksters joined hands and cleared the road ahead of the Army. As the Salvationists advanced down the street, the mob moved with them.[226]

As Joe addressed the people during the evening meeting, he contradicted the testimony of Officer Fox and told the crowd the Army had been followed to catch them doing wrong. He described the situation, saying, "It looked very much like a Fox hunting a Turkey."[227]

The local newspaper, which had initially been on the side of the Army, came to the defense of the police department. While gathering laughs, Joe's statement was seen by the paper as an arrogant taunt.[228] As public support for the Army faded, some people grew bolder and attacked the Salvationists whenever they were out marching. Although the police were supposed to be providing protection, they were missing in action whenever the abuse occurred.

Joe had a large sign created of a turkey with its feathers spread and little foxes snarling at it. The sign read, "Keep your eyes on the Foxes," referring to two of the arresting officers, Frank and John Fox. The crowd was not happy with this depiction of its police force, but Joe did not back down.[229]

While there were those who criticized Joe's portrayal of the police officers, others sided with the Army regarding the unlawful arrests. The leader of The Salvation Army in Massachusetts, Major Brewer, appealed to the governor to require law enforcement to give the Army greater protection across the state. Major Brewer delivered this address to a large crowd who rallied to support The Salvation Army in Lowell:

> "The greater body of citizens, even in Lowell, are highly
> indignant at the arrest, and one only needs to take a glance

A poster Joe had created by a local artist to demonstrate against his unlawful arrest in Lowell, Massachusetts. Photo courtesy of The Salvation Army National Archives.

at the columns of the press to find an expression of their indignation. There was great excitement at the trial. Joe was condemned, appealed his case, and thousands are anxiously looking forward to the outcome.

It is well known that The Salvation Army has thousands of enemies throughout the State, and these are trying to make their hatred felt through these arrests, but it is the worst thing they could do. It will only arouse the people who hate and detest tyranny and will crush it with mighty force."

The major shared an incident the Army was facing in Somerville, Massachusetts at that same time:

Suppose we want to hold a big meeting in Somerville some Sunday, and I wish to march one hundred soldiers through the streets. We must pay fifty cents apiece for every one of the one-hundred soldiers for the privilege to have them march in God's work. We haven't the money to pay in the first place. Many who go on these nights have not even a 10th part of fifty cents in their pockets and are simply depending upon the next day's work for the fifty cents they expect to have. It isn't right to oblige us, and we do not propose to pay for saving the souls of men and women.

He mentioned other towns where persecutions followed the warriors and ended his speech with:

It seems to me, and fair-minded people are thinking so everywhere in the state, that this persecution of us by a few in the smaller cities and in the towns of Massachusetts has gone past the limit. It is time we had full privileges in every part of the state as in Boston, and I believe the representatives of the people of the state will see that we have it.[230]

The press reported there was standing room only at the great rally in Lowell, even with a ten-cent admission charged. The crowd expected Joe to launch into a tirade against the police department, but he disappointed them by not doing so. He did, however, share his experiences of arrest and imprisonment in places throughout the country. The local paper reported that even though Joe's incidents were educational and moving, some accounts were also humorous.[231]

Following the rally, to avoid persecution accusations, the police made a concerted effort to protect the Army. Now, when they marched, the police kept people from throwing objects such as bricks, fruit, and snow-balls at them.[232]

A resident of Lowell sent in a joke about the matter to the local paper, their words unsympathetic to the plight of the Army:

> **Skinner:** Can you tell me when Joe the Turk looked the most like a rooster after eating his dinner?
>
> **Sniffins:** No, I can't tell you.
>
> **Skinner:** When he got arrested.
>
> **Sniffins:** How do you make that out?
>
> **Skinner:** He had his 'corn-et.'[233]

Joe stayed in Lowell, leading open-air marches and speaking in the city's largest meeting spaces. Hundreds crowded into the daily gatherings. To the dismay of the police department, Joe did not stop using his controversial artwork.

When one newspaper turned against the Army, *The Lowell Mail* picked up the cause and continued to present the Army's side of the argument. *The Mail* asked its readers why other preachers who had come to town with their gospel wagons and drew great crowds had avoided arrest. It also expressed outrage when the Army received a bill to cover the charges of their protection in the open-air at a rate of $2.75 per day. Even though the Army did not request the protection or agree with the charges, it paid the bill and did not publicly complain.[234]

Letters to the editor of *The Lowell Mail* were written in defense of the Army. These letters also criticized the police department for allowing common criminals to get away with what were more pressing criminal acts. They accused the police department of being paid off to ignore loafers and assassins, but to abuse peaceable citizens.[235] The following letter to the editor is representative of the correspondence received in support of the persecuted Army:

Bar-room Loafers Should Move On.

To the Editor of *The Lowell Mail*: Officer Fox has shown very prompt action in regard to having The Salvation Army "move on" and of promptly taking them to the station for not obeying him. Now, he will gain very much in the estimation of all respectable people if he will as effectively cause the loafers on his beat, particularly from the Post Office round to Paige Street, to "move on," and not stand on the sidewalk obstructing the same, so that people can pass without hearing oaths and dirty language from these same bar-room loafers.

While doing this good work let him have an eye to the newsboys, who are scuffling and chasing each other on the sidewalk, rushing into people on the street, and some of them running through the Post Office doors, banging them against anyone who is coming or going without any regard to safety.

If he wishes to show his efficiency and to gain promotion he can look after these things in pursuance of the duties which devolve upon him.

Lowell, Feb. 12, 1894.[236]

Joe led the Salvationists out to march every night, while the rougher elements of Lowell continued to persecute them. One evening, the mob was larger than usual and showered the Salvationists with snowballs and any other object they could find as they followed the group along their route. The Salvationists decided to split into two groups and march in different directions. The mob followed Joe's group and continued to harass and agitate them along the route. When the other group of Salvationists came into sight, Joe attempted to join them. As he marched in their direction, the mob encircled Joe's group and refused to let them pass. Officer John Fox appeared, and when the mob saw him, it quickly dispersed. Joe's group was able to rejoin the others and hastily made its way back to the barracks. The mob was relentless and continued to follow the Sallys, yelling and doing everything it could to provoke and antagonize them.[237]

By this time, Joe had been in Lowell for two months. *The War Cry* lamented that the Salvationists were being mobbed and pelted with stones and snowballs. It pointed out that those who were perpetrating the cowardice acts were not being arrested by the police, and had the shoe been on the other foot, the Salvationists would have quickly been back in jail. The magazine also informed its readers that Joe was continuing the fight and would stay until the matter was resolved. In further commenting on the initial arrest, *The War Cry* printed, "It appears that the officer who arrested him [Joe] had no idea that the bee would sting, but he found out afterward that to stir up Joe was like poking fun at a hornet's nest."[238]

Joe displaying his double-edged sword, shield, and umbrella. The banner behind him is one created to demonstrate the abuse of law enforcement against the Army. Photo courtesy of The Salvation Army National Archives.

On April 30, 1894, *The Lowell Sun* announced the case against Joe and The Salvation Army was over. The city decided it would not prosecute Joe or try the case further. Joe had been in Lowell for three months.

The Turkey had outsmarted the Foxes.

***

Colorado Springs, Colorado, was not an easy appointment for previous officers, as many had suffered abuse at the hands of the law. Prior to Joe's visit, the police arrested the corps officer for conducting an open-air meeting. While in jail, he asked for a cup of water. Instead of a cup, they turned the water hose on him and drenched him so thoroughly that he caught a horrible cold and, within two weeks, was dead. Other jailed Salvationists were sentenced to hard labor on the chain gang to work off their punishment for simply marching in the streets.[239]

Another banner created while in Lowell, Massachusetts and used by Joe across the country to demonstrate the manner in which Salvationists were being treated when they marched or held open-air meetings. Photo courtesy of The Salvation Army National Archives.

When Joe arrived in Colorado Springs, the first evening went smoothly. However, the policeman ordered the corps officer to move to a less crowded area past the alleyway. The crowd was large and attentive, so the corps officer declined.[240]

The next evening, when the group marched to the previous night's location, there was a brass band already playing in that spot. Not wanting to compete, the Salvationists moved half a block away. As they were beginning their meeting, a police officer showed up again and told the group to move along. Joe refused to leave the new spot, pointing out that the other band was playing as well. The open-air continued without issue, and at its conclusion, the onlookers joined the march back to the Army hall where there was an overflow crowd.[241]

After the evening meeting, the police officer found Joe and the corps officer and informed them they needed to appear at the city hall the following morning at 9 a.m. Arriving at the courthouse, it surprised the two to find they were under arrest. When they appeared before the judge, he fined the captain ten dollars. The judge did not try Joe's case but released him and postponed his trial until the following week.

Being free, Joe and the captain continued conducting open-air meetings. As word spread about the arrests and pending trial, larger crowds gathered at the open-air meetings. Because of this, extra police had to be sworn in to manage the throngs of spectators and curiosity-seekers.

The day before Joe's trial, he was arrested again for conducting another open-air meeting. He played the song "Whiter Than the Snow" on his cornet as he was led to jail.[242]

Whiter Than the Snow

1. Tell me what to do to be pure
In the sight of the all-seeing eyes.
Tell me, is there no thorough cure,
No escape from the sins I despise?
Tell me, can I never be free,
From this terrible bondage within?
Is there no deliverance for me,
From the thralldom of indwelling sin?

Chorus:
Whiter than the snow!
Whiter than the snow!
Wash me in the blood of the Lamb,
And I shall be whiter than snow.

2. Will my Savior only pass by,
Only show me how faulty I've been?
Will he not attend to my cry?

Can I not at this moment be clean?
Blessed Lord, almighty to heal,
I know that thy power cannot fail.
Here and now, I know, yes, I feel,
The prayer of my heart does prevail.
– *The Salvation Army Songbook*

Joe signed his own bond for twenty dollars, was released, and immediately joined an open-air in progress.[243] While praying the benediction at the open-air, the police arrested Joe and the corps officer again. Released on bond, Joe was arrested two more times, making a total of five arrests in Colorado Springs.[244]

Upon her arrival in town, Captain Blanche Cox, The Salvation Army's Colorado district officer, faced arrest in the open-air as well. The authorities tried her case with the corps officers but eventually dropped both. The only case carried forward was Joe's. The police continued to arrest Salvationists. However, public opinion soon swayed in favor of the Army. Eventually, all cases pending against the Salvationists, except for Joe's, were dropped. They sent this unusual case up to the county court, where the judge declared Joe not guilty.[245]

He left Colorado Springs with five more notches in his proverbial arrest belt.

***

When police prohibited Salvationists in Malden, Massachusetts from marching with the drum in 1896, Joe joined them in the fight. The entire town turned out to witness the showdown between the Army and the police. On the evening of March 31, as the town clock struck the hour of eight, Joe thrashed the bass drum, and pandemonium broke loose. The police arrested Joe and the Salvationists. They were marched to jail but released after a short imprisonment.[246]

Joe led the march on the streets of Malden the next night, blowing his cornet, while the captain beat the bass drum. They had only processed a short distance when they were both arrested and returned to jail.[247]

The following day, the mayor and board of aldermen voted unanimously to deny the Army's petition to use the bass drum on the march. One of the board members dissented, voting to grant permission to the Salvationists. In the ensuing battle, the Army rallied public sentiment. The authorities were inundated with letters, bad press, and rallies against their decision. The dissenting alderman changed his mind when he felt the case was becoming more about a drum than Christ. He then sided with the original ban against the Army.[248]

During the trial, various community members gave testimony supporting both sides of the case. One of the Salvationists testified against the Army, saying it should not march with the drum because it was against the ordinance. Another person called to give testimony against the Army said the drum had frightened a horse, causing it to throw its female passenger to the ground.[249]

The chairman of the Malden Fire Commission countered by stating it was the crowd, not the drum, that had caused the problem. The corps officer, Captain Faulkner, when placed on the stand, declared the drum was to the Army what steeple bells were to a church.[250]

During the two nights of arrests, law enforcement authorities took twenty-eight people into custody. To keep things from getting too confusing, it was determined to try the cases based on the different nights of their capture. In Joe's first trial, the prosecutor accused The Salvation Army headquarters of intentionally sending Joe to Malden to cause trouble. The defense refuted the accusation arguing that Malden had been on Joe's itinerary for weeks.[251]

The prosecution wanted to resolve the cases quickly because of the high number of police officers called as witnesses. Its rationale was that while the trials were taking place, the streets of Malden were unprotected. By trying the cases based on the different nights of incarceration, the cases would resolve faster. However, they dragged on longer than expected.[252]

No additional evidence was revealed in the second round of trials, but the chief of police stated he was certain the Salvationists would appeal the case to the superior court as they were in the habit of doing.[253]

Two weeks into the trial, the judge charged the defendants with disturbing the peace and imposed fines ranging from ten to twenty-five dollars. Everyone charged appealed to the higher court and declared their intention to go back to jail for their cause. The women were released on their own recognizance; however, the police took the nine men to Cambridge jail. A crowd assembled to see them off to their temporary homes.[254]

When the prisoners arrived at the jail, they took Joe's cornet away from him. He begged for its return, but the police captain refused. The press said of Joe's cornet, "It had been like a baby he'd nursed, his inseparable companion during storms of stones and storms of frowns and hisses— that which could cheer his lonely moments, was gone." Joe was not to be defeated and informed the police captain that if he could not play, he would still lead the vermin in jail to the altar.[255]

To prevent trouble among the other prisoners, the authorities permitted the Sallys five minutes of quiet devotions in the morning. Each morning, the Salvationists knelt on the hard-paved floors and softly sang the songs of early-day Salvationists who had also been persecuted. This practice would last until the June term of court ended.[256] After serving their time, the prisoners were released.

When the freed Salvationists indicated they would march again, the public was in an uproar over the treatment of the Army and pledged to support them. A rumor spread that a hundred men with guns and sticks were ready to confront the police if they tried to arrest The Salvation Army again.[257]

Because of potential riots and danger to the police force, the chief of police made his way to the Army barracks, asking the Salvationists not to march that night. He reasoned marching would result in people getting hurt and possibly killed. In return for not marching, he promised he would see to it that the privileges the Army had asked for were granted. To keep the peace and people out of harm's way, the Sallys did not march.[258]

The leaders of the community called an emergency meeting issuing an order that gave the Army the privilege to parade in an orderly manner on certain main streets between the hours of 7 p.m. and 9 p.m. The police chief returned to the Army hall and presented the document to the Salvationists, who accepted it. Receiving the news, Joe, the officers, and the soldiers stepped outside the corps hall and marched without the drum to the center of town; there, they held an open-air meeting. More than one thousand people followed the march, and nearly three thousand attended the open-air. At the conclusion of the service, the group made its way back to the barracks and held a praise meeting. The public cheered the Salvationists in the streets from start to finish.[259] The following morning, Joe left town for his next appointed location.

***

Joe had previously visited Wilkes-Barre, Pennsylvania, in September 1898, to conduct a ten-day campaign. The visit went smoothly, and the response of the public was positive. He returned a month later to fill in for the corps officer, Ensign Mugford, who was on a short health break. Received by open arms and positive press, Joe returned to Wilkes-Barre. The paper made special mention of his musical prowess and encouraged residents not to miss him on this return visit.[260]

Because of the many open-air meetings conducted throughout the day, it was not long before Joe wore out his welcome. The press, which had once heralded his arrival, began criticizing his music and methods of attracting a crowd.[261]

On Joe's first night in town, he led the open-air march to the public square and held court in front of Featherstone's Saloon. The mayor, passing by, saw the crowd and immediately ordered the arrest of Joe and five other Salvationists for obstructing the sidewalk and beating a drum.[262]

The police led the group to the station house, and before placing them in their cells, the Salvationists fell to their knees and began to sing and pray. This went on for about thirty minutes until the police sergeant arrived and ordered them to stop. They protested because the police would not allow them to bring the drums and American flag into the cell with them. When the mayor arrived and started sorting out the details, he released everyone except Joe and William Hopkins, the soldier who had beaten the drum.[263]

The following morning, the mayor sternly lectured the duo and chided them for the noise and disturbance they had created the previous evening. He warned them that continuing this behavior would have grave consequences. He then released them without imposing a fine or requiring them to post bail.[264]

In that evening's meeting, Joe spoke about what had caused the arrest and imprisonment. He told the group he had been standing on a chair and praying when the police roughly pulled him down and hauled him off to jail. He let the crowd know that while they were in jail, the mayor refused to grant them bail, a public hearing, or breakfast the following morning. Joe concluded his discourse in the usual manner, stating he would appeal the case to a higher court.[265]

Despite this encounter with the law, the Army did not back down from its daily marches and open-air meetings. It increased them so much the press called the Salvationist gatherings a nuisance.[266]

A few days later, a mail carrier lodged a complaint against Joe, the captain (who had returned early from his health break), and his assistant, stating his horse had been scared by the beating of the drum and "the discordant notes upon a croupy cornet."[267] The postal worker jumped from his carriage and grabbed the reins of the horse to keep it from bolting. He told the police commissioner that the Salvationists had caused trouble multiple times, which was why he reported them. With that, the commissioner issued a warrant for the arrests of Joe, Ensign Mugford, and Lieutenant Hillman. Once again, the mayor lectured them about how they were becoming a public nuisance, and, as he had previously done, released them without fine or bail.[268]

The Salvation Army decided it would use this latest arrest as a test case to see whether the city ordinance was legal. The Army's defense lawyer drew up the paperwork and submitted it to one of the county judges for a final decision. The ordinance in question was as follows:

> It shall not be lawful for any person or persons to appear in any of the public streets or places in said city to play any hand organ, hurdy-gurdy, tambourine, or other musical instruments or beat upon a drum, or blow a horn or trumpet, without a permit from the Mayor, and any such permit may be revoked by the Mayor whenever he may deem it expedient. And whoever appears in any of the streets, alleys, or public places to play, beat or blow upon either of such instruments without such permit shall be liable to a fine of not less than $3 nor more than $20.[269]

Now, the press turned against the Army, and the local paper published an article stating that The Salvation Army was a good thing for the saloon men, "It drives people to drink."[270]

The case of The Salvation Army versus the City of Wilkes-Barre came before the judge. The packed courtroom included a large delegation from the Army. The purpose of the trial was to determine the necessity of the bass drum and cornet in religious worship and the legality of the city ordinance banning their use.[271]

The defense argued the Army was abiding by the biblical admonition to go into the highways and byways and compel sinners to repent. The Army's lawyer said the ordinance that had existed for twenty years was only enforced against The Salvation Army:

> Military organizations, shows and concert companies, baseball clubs, ice cream socials, auctioneers, etc., made noise by beating drums without complaint, but when The Salvation Army, a church organization, obeys the Master's call and goes out in the highways and preaches the gospel to people who do not go to any church, they are at once arrested.[272]

The defense continued:

> The return of soldiers; the ringing of bells, playing of bands, firing of cannons, and all noises calculated to celebrate the great victory of the nation [are allowable], [but,] when The Salvation Army attempts to call the people and tell of a greater victory, the victory of Christ over sin and death, their drum is deemed a nuisance.[273]

The prosecution countered:

> The discordant singing, the nerve-destroying notes of the cornets, the constant beating of the bass drum, irritate people and are a menace to public peace. Peter, Paul, and the disciples of Christ had gone into the streets to exhort sinners to repentance, but they had never called in the assistance of a bass drum or the screeching notes of the cornet.[274]

The judge did not rule in favor of The Salvation Army. He decided that beating the drum in public required permission from the mayor.[275]

The Army decided to carry the case to a higher court, even if that meant the Supreme Court of the United States. In speaking to the press, Joe was confident the courts would decide in favor of the Army.[276] After one month in Wilkes-Barre, Joe left for Chicago to continue his fall tour.

It took until July of 1899, ten months, for a decision to be handed down from the State Supreme Court. In a lengthy opinion, the court supported the mayor and local court in their prohibition of The Salvation Army beating the bass drum in public. The judge wrote:

> Laws are made for the government of actions and while they cannot interfere with mere religious belief and opinions, they may with practices. Suppose one believed that human sacrifices were a necessary part of religious worship, would it be seriously contended that the civil government under which we live could not interfere to prevent a sacrifice? Religious liberty does not include the right to introduce and carry out every scheme or purpose which persons see fit to claim as part of their religious system.[277]

In a dissenting opinion, two of the State Supreme Court judges wrote:

> [We] cannot agree with the learned judge ... ordinances must be fair, impartial, general, not oppressive, and consistent with the laws and policy of the State. It is evident that it does not intend to prohibit all playing on musical instruments or beating upon drums in the public streets ... It divides all persons who desire to make music upon the streets into two classes by an arbitrary line, upon one side of which are those who are permitted to play upon instruments or beat upon drums by the mere will and pleasure of the mayor, and upon the other side are those who are not permitted ... by the mere will and pleasure of the mayor. I would reverse the judgment in this case and direct the prisoner to be discharged.[278]

The case of Joe the Turk versus the City of Wilkes-Barre garnered attention far and wide. Periodically, other opinions would pop up in newspapers across the country supporting the side of The Army, such as this one:

> The learned judge of the court does not seem to regard the drum as an instrument of salvation. If he should become familiar with some of the experiences of The Salvation Army, he might change his mind. For instance, they could tell him of a man who had come to desperation, and concluding to end his distress, placed a pistol to his head and attempted to fire a bullet into his brain, but the cartridge failed to explode. As he was preparing to repeat the experiment, The Salvation Army drum attracted his attention, and going to see what it meant, he was awakened to a proper realization of his folly and became a converted man and a useful citizen. It would doubtless be interesting as well as useful to learn how important a part the drum, in some form, has played in sacred service. The Hebrew root *taphaph* signifies 'that which is beaten'—drum or timbrel. It seems to signify anything that is beaten from a tambourine to a kettledrum. That it was very early used in sacred service appears in the tenth chapter of First Samuel, where it is mentioned as one of the instruments of the company of prophets that went to meet Saul. When Moses and the children of Israel sang their song of thanksgiving for their wondrous deliverance at the Red Sea, Miriam, the sister of Moses, led the women responding with timbrels and dances; when David returned with Saul, after the slaying of Goliath, they were likewise met by bands of women with timbrels. When David brought the ark from Kirjath-jearim, this was one of the instruments played in the grand procession.[279]

There was no further mention about the case in *The War Cry* or other newspapers. The Army did not challenge the decision of the State Supreme Court and allowed it to stand. When Joe went back to Wilkes-Barre in 1905 to conduct evangelistic services and lead open-air meetings, he arrived and departed without invoking the ire of the mayor or police department.

***

It was a quiet summer Sunday afternoon in Auburn, New York. Someone playing "The Holy City" on a cornet interrupted the peacefulness. It was, of course, Joe the Turk. The police ordered him to stop playing his horn, and when he stood up on a chair and continued playing, the officer arrested him and marched him off to jail. Joe continued to play as he marched. An estimated crowd of up to two thousand people followed the march. Once in jail, the other Salvationists, who had been at the open-air with Joe, gathered outside his temporary prison and held another open-air meeting.[280]

At his trial, the court charged Joe with blowing a cornet on Sunday. People representing both sides of the conflict filled the courtroom, those who believed in a constitutional principle of religious freedom, and those who believed Sunday should be respectfully observed by peace and quiet. Of course, some just wanted to see a good show, and Joe did not disappoint.[281]

When he entered the courtroom, he was not in his Turkish uniform, but in a plain dark uniform like most Salvationists wore. Upon his head was a gray metal helmet, like a pith helmet but without the spike on the top. Draping diagonally across the helmet was a crimson-colored ribbon with the words, "The Salvation Army" printed in gold. The finishing touch was a Salvation Army eagle crest, symbolizing the Army in America, perched above the ribbon. On his coat was a large metal star, like those worn by sheriffs in the Wild West. He also brought along his constant companion, his double-jointed cornet.[282]

During the trial, the judge asked Joe to describe the circumstances of his arrest. He stood up and began playing the song "The Holy City" to demonstrate how far he had gotten into the song before someone prematurely stopped him and made the arrest. As he reenacted this moment in the open-air, the city attorney and the court recorder demanded he cease playing. There would be no performance in court that day. Joe put his cornet and mute back in its case.[283]

The police officer testified Joe had been playing "some kind of church music ... at least it sounded like church music," and continued to play and defy the officer as he marched him to jail. Joe countered that he only continued to play because he could march better with music than without. He then stepped up onto the witness chair and gave a physical demonstration of how he marched.

When asked to share information about who he was and where he was from, Joe told the crowd he was fifty-one years of age and an Armenian. Although he had been born in Turkey, he was not Turkish, but allowed himself to be called a Turk. He quickly followed with the pronouncement that he had ceased to be a citizen of Turkey thirty-one years prior and was now a proud citizen of the United States. He then shared with the jury about his night in their jail cell, saying it was a "hot night ... with many bedbugs."[284]

Joe's attorney gave his summation and spoke about the historic fight true Americans had waged over the generations for religious liberty. The Salvation Army, he declared, "... went out and saved persons who could be reached in no other way than by the attractions of music and loud exhortations. They alone reach the submerged tenth, and it was the music that attracted those needing the service of the Army workers."[285] As inspiring as the summation was, the jury could not reach a unanimous decision, and a new trial was called for the next day.[286]

The second trial was to take place on Saturday morning. Long before the doors were scheduled to open, an immense crowd had gathered. The public wanted to make sure they had seats for the continued spectacle in the courtroom. Unknown to the public, the attorneys met in private to talk about the case and the jury's failure to reach a verdict.

Before the doors were opened the next morning, the prosecution withdrew the charge against Joe and set him free. The conclusion was a punishment given to him of one night in jail with his noxious bedfellows. They would not prosecute the case further. Joe gathered his things and immediately left Auburn for his next engagement.[287]

The Holy City
Lyrics by Frederic E Weatherly
Music by Michael Maybrick

1. Last night I lay a sleeping,
There came a dream so fair,
I stood in old Jerusalem,
Beside the temple there.
I heard the children singing,
And ever as they sang,
Methought the voice of angels
From Heav'n in answer rang.
Methought the voice of angels
From Heav'n in answer rang.
Jerusalem! Jerusalem!
Lift up your gates and sing,
Hosanna in the highest,
Hosanna to your king!

2. And then methought my dream was changed,
The streets no longer rang,
Hushed were the glad hosannas,
The little children sang.
The sun grew dark with mystery,
The morn was cold and chill,
As the shadow of a cross arose
Upon a lonely hill,
As the shadow of a cross arose
Upon a lonely hill.
Jerusalem! Jerusalem!
Hark! how the angels sing,
Hosanna in the highest,
Hosanna to your king.

3. And once again the scene was changed,
New earth there seemed to be,
I saw the Holy City
Beside the tideless sea.

The light of God was on its streets,
The gates were open wide,
And all who would might enter,
And no one was denied.
No need of moon or stars by night,
Or sun to shine by day,
It was the new Jerusalem,
That would not pass away,
It was the new Jerusalem,
That would not pass away.
Jerusalem! Jerusalem!
Sing, for the night is o'er!
Hosanna in the highest,
Hosanna for evermore!
Hosanna in the highest,
Hosanna for evermore!

CHAPTER 6
THE GREATEST SHOWMAN

In the age of traveling minstrel shows, P.T. Barnum's circus, and Wild West extravaganzas, The Salvation Army had major competition in attracting crowds to its meetings. More than once, Joe arrived in a community only to discover these groups already set up and entertaining the masses. It was not long before the sanctified Salvationist showman took their crowds away and filled the Army halls with people eager to hear and learn more about this mysterious man from Turkey.

Often, The Salvation Army corps would beg him to stay longer, and if it was possible, Joe would give up his day of rest or backtrack and hold meetings in corps he had recently visited. His repertoire of fascinating tales was practically endless, and even if he repeated a story, the crowd loved to hear it again.

***

The length of time Joe stayed in a community varied from two to five days. *The War Cry* records Joe often had to notify corps on his itinerary that he would not make the appointment because he was behind bars.

When Joe came to town, he typically spent three days there and spoke on a set list of topics. The first night, he would give his testimony entitled, "How I Closed Up the Hole in the Wall." Occasionally, if time permitted, he would tell of his imprisonments in East Portland and Portland. He loved to tell of the dramatic conversion of the judge who had sentenced him to jail for twenty-five days.

The second evening, he would share the story of his sister Maritza Yoskatchian's conversion. He never tired of telling about the miraculous way in which she found Christ and her calling to become a missionary in Turkey and Greece. This became a staple of his evangelistic services through the end of his active officership.

Joe's final program consisted of his famous zonophone/saxophone concert. Interspersed with the musical numbers, he would tell the story of how the Ottomans persecuted and killed his people, the Armenians.

Despite his fifty-two arrests, Joe went into hundreds of communities, where he was welcomed with open arms. Most municipalities were overwhelmingly accepting of him, and the press would often give his visit front-page coverage. *The Charlotte Observer* wrote of his arrival:

From *The War Cry, December 1905. Joe in Charlotte, North Carolina with Captain and Mrs. Smith. Photo courtesy of The Salvation Army National Archives.*

Joe the Turk is here, and his cohorts in the city are happy, for he, is as much or even more than they bargained for. He comes well-gowned and in first-class condition; [he] preaches, sings, plays many musical instruments, and entertains in other ways. Joe the Turk is all right. He performed near the square yesterday afternoon and will be out again today. There is no doubt about his being a gen-u-wine Turk, he looks the part. He will preach to a great throng of people today. He is a fine musician and sings well.[288]

The Tribune in Seymour, Indiana, also wrote:

> Joe the Turk is here. The town was thoroughly stirred last night
> on account of the man from Constantinople holding the fort
> at The Salvation Army. A large crowd assembled to hear this
> famous Salvationist and get a glimpse at this terrible Turk. He is
> no imitation but a real Turk. He holds an audience in the most
> miraculous manner.[289]

People appreciated his down-to-earth style and the varied catalog of
stories at his command, which also made him popular with younger audiences. "Joe told many interesting stories … His recital was not difficult to
follow, and his simple style of narrative was pleasing. The children could
not get enough of Joe and had to be literally torn from the front row of
seats, where they had gazed in fascination at his resplendent figure."[290]

During Joe's life, some discounted the depth of his spiritual gifts because
of his showmanship; "surely the two could not coexist." A *War Cry* article
written by a corps officer in Albany, New York, gives a different perspective:

> Great preparations had been made for the visit of Staff-Captain
> Garabed to this famous, historical capital city. Announcements
> had been made from the platform, posters had been put up
> by the bill-plasters free of charge, local papers had heralded
> his coming, and we certainly looked forward to a good time,
> especially in the open-air. We were not disappointed. The
> Staff-Captain was there on time. His glittering Turkish
> costume, including turban and leggings; his first-class musical
> instruments including saxophone, cornet and clarinet, his
> unique Turkish drumstick, his Asiatic cast of features, his
> original style of singing and speaking, all contributed to
> the attractiveness of the meeting. His sound, real salvation
> reasoning and arguments, quickly captivated and convinced
> his most intelligent listeners, and he certainly created a very
> favorable impression.[291]

Opening Night

Joe's testimony was a story he shared until the end of his life. People were fascinated by his adventures in the Wild West and the beginnings of The Salvation Army in California. Equally so, they wanted to hear about his arrests, narrow escapes, and victories over dishonest civil authorities. These were episodes of his life Joe recounted with great relish. He was, however, always careful to give God the honor and glory for releasing him from jail and keeping him alive, though often bruised and battered.

Joe was a pioneer officer. While early Salvationists were trailblazers, Joe's adventures were not the typical experiences of the masses. Limited entertainment opportunities and the ability to personally see individuals from exotic lands only increased the public's interest in Joseph Garabed. Joe's desire to preach and play in as many cities in the United States as possible also made him grow in popularity. Newspaper articles and Salvation Army periodicals reported the massive crowds that attended his meetings. Many were turned away because the venue was at capacity.

In addition to the stories he told on the first night in each town, Joe had an extensive repertoire of musical numbers. To the delight of the audience, he would sing and play in between the stories he told and the sermons he preached.

Newspaper articles mentioned his sense of humor—both intentional and unintentional. He enjoyed interacting with the crowd. One of his favorite things to do was choose an older, staunch-looking member of the audience and teach them a chorus in Armenian or Chinese. He would then have the participant stand up in front of the crowd and attempt to sing it, to the group's delight.[292]

Because of the success of the first night, the crowds would subsequently grow, with additional services added and larger venues secured.

Maritza's Miracle

On the second night of Joe's evangelistic meetings, he would tell his sister's story of conversion. Maritza Yoskatchian lived in Constantinople (modern-day Istanbul) and Smyrna (modern-day Izmir) until the Armenian massacres of 1915–1918. She fled Turkey and relocated to an Armenian refugee settlement in Greece. Her story of accepting Jesus is remarkable, and after her encounter with Christ, she spent the rest of her life serving as a missionary to her fellow Armenians in Turkey and Greece.

The Daily Democrat and Standard newspaper of Coshocton, Ohio, recorded Joe's account of her conversion and printed it in the June 19, 1906, edition:

> When I was converted, I felt so happy right away I must write and tell my sister back in Turkey about it. So, I tell her that I have joined The Salvation Army. When she gets the letter, she thinks I have joined the military, and she runs to the brother, who is a wealthy merchant in Constantinople. When he reads the letter, he sees what it means, and he tells her that I have gone crazy—that I have turned Christian. There, he assembles his friends in the street, and there, with laughter, he reads my letter to them.
>
> But my sister, she ponders over the letter, and she writes back and wants to know more about this Christianity. I write again and again, and she binds my letters into a book, they are so precious to her. But she wants to know more about this religion, so I tell her to go to the Bible publishing house in Constantinople, where the Bible is printed in many languages, and get one of the Turkish Bibles. She does so and she reads and reads. At last, she says, if Christ can save my brother in America, why cannot he save me here. Pretty soon, she locks herself in her room and begins to pray. She prays and prays until all at once, a great light broke in upon her soul, and she sprang up filled with joy for she had found salvation. Wonderful religion! My sister all alone, with no one to teach her and with only a Turkish Bible to guide her, yet Jesus finds her out and brings her into his fold. All who rejoice with me at His wonderful blessings say, amen.

Then, my sister, she is just like me. Right away she must try to save her neighbors. She takes her little book, and she begins to work from house to house. A missionary in her own land and no preparation but her own conversion, and no one to direct her but God. She cannot work as we do, for if she held an open-air meeting in the streets of Constantinople the speaker and all the listeners—it would be the end of them. But she goes among the poor in the slums. She knocks at the humble home, and when the door opens, she crowds in. There it is all dirty and disorder. The unwashed babe lays in the crib. She tells the mother, 'I have come to help you a little,' and she takes the babe up and washes it, then she sets the room in order. But the mother is washing, and she tells her to rest, and she goes to the tub and begins to rub the clothes. Now she begins to sing of Jesus, and then the mother wants to know what it means. My sister now takes out her Bible and reads a little about this wonderful salvation and again, begins to wash and sing. But the mother must know more, and so by steps she is led to the new religion. My sister asks her to kneel and pray, and then she thinks of other members of the family, and by and by, all kneel and maybe the whole house is led to Christ.

So, my sister goes into homes and preaches as she helps the people with their work. Now for fifteen years she has done a wonderful work for Christ so that whole villages are stirred up by her. In one village they say they will surely kill her when she comes again. When it is time for her to make a second trip, a great mob collects stones, and rush after her. She flees and finds an open gate to a garden, but there she finds a babe sleeping in a hammock. She says the innocent shall not suffer, and she rushes back into the face of the mob and there begins to pray, for she knows her time has come. Now, a wonderful thing happens. The great mob falls back and forms a wide circle. It grows silent as she prays and then one by one, all go away until she is left alone, and no harm has come to her. Today, she still lives and is well and everywhere she goes, and all the time, she helps and teaches. Is it not wonderful, this Christ religion?

Now the rich also want to hear about Christ. They say to her, 'Not the poor alone have their trouble. We, too, have our deep sorrow and all our wealth; it cannot help us. Why will you all the time work in the slums? Are not our souls likewise precious?' And now she goes to the rich homes, and they, too, hear her gladly.

For twenty-two years, I have been in the Army, and for fifteen years, my sister has been a missionary. Everywhere and to all peoples it is one religion and one truth. If we gain the victory here, we shall reign with Him.

***

While Joe's double-jointed cornet, saxophone, and command of various languages would draw crowds, there came into his possession another instrument that catapulted him into the arena of popularity unlike anything else he had previously used in warfare. This, he would unveil as a part of his final night's program in a community.

In 1899, the zonophone, or gramophone as it was sometimes called, burst onto the scene. Because of its price, the average home in America, especially rural America, did not own one. When Joe discovered this machine and realized how he could

THE ZON-O-PHONE
The Latest and Best Talking Machine

An advertisement for a zonophone. Joe used this instrument to great effect. He purchased records and was able to play along with them, by ear, on his cornet or saxophone.

incorporate it into ministry and use it to attract crowds, he quickly embraced it.

He purchased several discs of classical, popular, and religious music to fill the repertoire of his concerts. Joe played his instruments by ear, and once he knew the song, he could easily play along with the recording. One might say he was a forerunner of karaoke.

1903 would see the debut of his "Famous Sacred Zonophone/ Saxophone Concert."[293] The local corps would sell tickets to the event, and typically, Joe would perform before a sold-out crowd. Even a decade later, the concert was a popular draw. "On Monday night a zonophone, saxophone sacred concert will be given. This instrument is of the latest and best made in the market. The records are all kinds of sacred band music, songs, and recitations of a spiritual character. Tickets will be sold in advance for ten cents each."[294]

The evening was a special event in the town, and the reviews in the newspapers were always positive. His ability to preach, play, and sing was called impressive. "There was only a single musical performer at the concert and that, Joe. He played six instruments, sang, prayed, and preached."[295]

On one side of the ticket was a picture of Joe, and the holder could keep the ticket as a souvenir of the special evening. Two types of tickets have been found from his concerts. One was the size of a business card and had a picture of Joe wearing his red and gold tunic and holding his saxophone. The second ticket was the size of a postcard and had a larger picture of Joe inside an oval. His name is at the bottom of the photo. An eagle crest, along with Joe's official name and rank, are on the back of the card. "Zon-o-phone Concert for the Benefit of the Local Corps. Don't Fail to Be There. Admittance 10 Cents." There was a space to stamp or write the concert venue's address.

On the third evening, in addition to his famous concert, Joe would tell the story of the murder and displacement of Armenians during the Hamidian/Armenian Massacres (1894–1898). At the end of the nineteenth century, The Salvation Army had one of its finest hours in Europe and North America with its bold response to the crisis. *The War Cry* and newspaper articles vividly depicted the experiences of Armenians and the perpetrators of the atrocities.

The Armenian Holocaust of 1914–1921 would later become the primary focus of Joe's talk on his final evening's presentation. The press would write of his discourse, "His recital of the Turkish atrocities committed upon the defenseless Armenian Christians … is said to be most realistic and impressive."[296] The discussion of the Armenian Holocaust would hit close to Joe, as he had lost members of his own family, particularly his older brother, who had remained in Turkey.[297]

The Hamidian Massacres

Armenians lived in present-day Turkey for around three thousand years, but in 1080 AD, the Seljuk Turks, Mongols, and other groups seized their homeland. Forced to move closer to the Mediterranean Sea, they set up the Armenian Kingdom of Cilicia, which lasted almost two hundred years. The Ottomans then conquered all of Anatolia, including Armenia. The Armenians remained a subjugated people until after World War I.[298] As a race, they came close to annihilation.

Under the Ottoman Empire, Armenians were treated as second-class citizens. They were denied their basic rights because of their adoption of Christianity and refusal to convert to Islam. This has caused great tension between the Armenians, Turks, and Kurds throughout time. Armenian villages were regularly targeted by the Kurds, who took whatever they wanted with no repercussions from the Turkish authorities. Musa Bey, a Turkish tribal leader in the mid-1800s, commented, "The solution of the Armenian question consists in the annihilation of the Armenian race."[299] One cannot help but hear the foreshadowing of future European events in this statement.

Not every Turk felt animosity toward the Armenians. There were periods where Constantinople was a safe and prosperous place for Armenians to live and work. One of Joe's brothers had a thriving business and had become wealthy in the capital city. In writing to his sister's friend, Joe said about his family in Turkey, "When the Turks destroyed the City of Smyrna, my brother was killed and lost all his land and houses, my sister also lost her home, when she reached Greece, she was homeless."[300] This statement was a sign that Joe's brother, whose name we do not know, was a man of means. Joe often referred to him as his "wealthy brother."

Beginning in 1894, Sultan Abdul Hamid II issued an order to kill Christian Armenians when they called for civil reformation. To quell their demands, the Ottomans began murdering Armenians of all ages and genders.[301] The estimate of casualties ranges between 100,000 to 250,000.[302]

This scenario continued to play out for the next four years, until international condemnation forced Turkey to be less aggressive in its approach to the Armenians.[303] At the end of the conflict, approximately three hundred thousand Armenians were dead. The Sultan of Turkey was nicknamed "Bloody Sultan" by the worldwide press.[304]

***

The Ottoman Empire, though multinational, was developing into a Muslim state by 1915. This set it more at odds with its non-Muslim occupants, namely the Armenians.[305] The Turks believed they alone were worthy to rule the empire and were its only trustworthy subjects.[306]

In 1915, the number of Armenians in Ottoman-held lands was around two million, while the Muslim population was between fifteen and seventeen million. Even if the vastly outnumbered Armenians had revolted against the Turks, their impact would have been minimal because of the dichotomy of populations. Most affluent Armenians in Constantinople were highly visible to Turkish leaders and were not involved in any revolutionary activities.[307]

When the Ottomans lost a major battle that year, they attributed the loss to the Armenians, who they believed had undermined them and sided with the enemy. The Armenians became public enemy number one, resulting in another attempt to exterminate the race.[308] Political and educational leaders were the first killed. Women, children, and older men were marched out of their communities through the mountains and valleys of eastern Anatolia. If they survived the treacherous journey, their final resting place was a concentration camp in the desert where they starved to death or were cruelly murdered.[309]

In his memoir, *Armenian Golgotha*, Grigoris Balakian writes:

> Driven to exhaustion, starvation, and suicide, hundreds of
> thousands, perhaps a million or more, would perish; others
> would be forced to emigrate or convert to Islam to save
> their lives. Men died in greater numbers; many women and
> children were taken into families of the local Muslims. Tens
> of thousands of orphans found some refuge in the protection
> of foreign missionaries. It is estimated conservatively that
> between 600,000 and one million were slaughtered or died
> on the marches. Other tens of thousands fled to the north,
> to the relative safety of the Russian Caucasus. Hundreds
> of thousands of women and children, we now know, were
> compelled to convert to Islam and survived in the families of
> Kurds, Turks, and Arabs. By the end of the war ninety percent
> of the Armenians of the Ottoman Empire were gone, a
> culture and civilization wiped out never to return. Those who
> observed the killings, as well as the Allied powers engaged in
> a war against the Ottomans, repeatedly claimed that they had
> never witnessed anything like it. The word for what happened
> had not yet been invented. There was no concept to mark the
> state-targeted killing of a designated ethnoreligious people. At
> the time those who needed a word borrowed from the Bible
> and called it 'holocaust.'[310]

CHAPTER 7

TRUTH IS STRANGER THAN FICTION

People seemed to live vicariously through Joe and the almost unbelievable adventures that were his. The following narratives further assist in understanding who Joe was and what made his ministry so different.

The Salvation Army sponsored an annual camp meeting for its people at Lake Bluff, Illinois, just outside of Chicago. The organizers declared it the largest open-air service in the campground's history, with more than five thousand people in attendance.[311]

Three of the special guests were Lena Hebrandt, whose stage name was "the Hallelujah Midget," Dr. J. Logan, a Delaware Native American, and Joe the Turk.

Lena was a Salvationist from Flint, Michigan. She was thirty-one years old and forty-two inches in height.[312] She wore a conventional black Army dress with a small poke bonnet trimmed with red ribbon.[313] Lena shared her testimony during the meetings but was more widely known for her timbrel playing, as it was said of her, "she could deal powerful blows on it."[314]

Joe the Turk with Lena Hebrandt and Dr. J. Logan (Tom-Ma-He-Kim) at a camp meeting held in Lake Bluff, Illinois. More than five thousand people attended the event. Photo courtesy of The Salvation Army National Archives.

Dr. Logan's native name was Tom-Ma-He-Kim. He dressed in buck-skin clothing, trimmed with feathers and beads. Dr. Logan, a Canadian (First Nations), earned his medical degree from Hellmuth College in London, Ontario. However, he later struggled with alcohol addiction and lost everything. He found Christ at The Salvation Army and became a powerful witness for Jesus. He played salvation songs on his violin and shared his personal testimony at the camp meetings.[315]

The final member of the mesmerizing trio was Joe the Turk, whom the press called the "star of this camp meeting."[316] Joe would sing, play his various instruments, and regale the crowds with daring accounts of his escapades across the country.

The three would sit together on the platform and Joe, who had set up shop on the campgrounds, would sell his goods at the makeshift trade department in between meetings. The Trade tent was described as having circus-like placards on the outside, painted with images, not unlike what one would find at a circus sideshow. One sign showed Joe being arrested by a British-looking police officer, or bobby, and led into a paddy wagon. The wording on the sign read, "Joe the Turk—To Jail for Jesus! This Outrage Must Stop!"[317] The sign was created for Joe during his legal troubles with the law in Lowell, Massachusetts. There was a second sign that depicted the police as they beat and arrested female Salvationists. In the picture, one woman is holding the American flag. The wording on the sign reads, "Stars and Stripes Arrested. We fight for liberty!" Joe carried these banners with him and whenever there was trouble, he would display them to help gain the public's sympathy.

***

The World, a New York City newspaper printed from 1860 to 1931, carried an article about Santas seen on the corners of New York City in their red suits and black boots. This originated when Joe the Turk played the first Santa Claus for The Salvation Army.[318] It was one more incident in which Joe and the Salvationists ran afoul of the law.

On December 19, 1900, Joe dressed up as Santa Claus with a long white beard, red coat featuring a high-peaked hood, and bits of white cotton dabbled on the coat to represent snow. He alternated between playing Christmas carols on his saxophone and on his cornet. He sat on a four-wheeled spring wagon, like a monarch would upon a throne, and was propelled forward by horses through the streets of New York City.[319]

Four Salvation lassies, who wore the latest in clothing technology—transparent plastic raincoats over their uniforms—accompanied Joe. With four collection boxes, they walked next to the wagon, collecting donations for the Madison Square Garden Free Christmas Dinner for the Poor.[320]

To prevent complaints about blocked sidewalks, the wagon driver regularly changed locations. When the wagon stopped on West 14th Street, a police officer, who felt they had lingered longer than they should have, ordered them to move on. Joe protested, trying to help the officer understand why they were collecting funds for a worthy cause, but his eloquence failed him. The police officer arrested the entire group and redirected the wagon to the Fifteenth Precinct Police Station.[321] A group of school-aged boys followed the wagon and ridiculed the Salvation lassies along the way.[322]

When they arrived at the police station and explained the situation to the police sergeant, he released everyone. The sergeant gave Joe instructions to go back out on the streets with the police department's blessings and collect all the money he could for the Madison Square Garden Free Christmas Dinner for the Poor. The sergeant chastised the police officer for interrupting their charitable work and assured Joe no one would hinder him again.[323]

***

In the Fall of 1892, the officers stationed at Macomb, Illinois, Captain Ivings and Lieutenant Stevenson, were arrested for conducting an open-air meeting. The corrupt mayor and law enforcement officers of the town gave the men a sentence of fourteen days in jail. Word on the street was the mayor and his crew were outlaws from Texas and had taken over Macomb with the goal of opening and monopolizing the saloon business in the town.[324]

It was at this point Joe arrived on the scene. Upon hearing Joe was in town, the mayor sent word to him and the other Salvationists that if they marched again, they would all be arrested and thrown into jail with the officers. Not frightened by the threat, Joe organized a march and an open-air meeting for that evening. While the outdoor service was in progress, a group of soldiers went to the jailhouse and serenaded the officers through the barred window.[325]

Forty soldiers and friends of the Army, including the wife of a local judge, marched to the open-air site. The people of Macomb were running back and forth in anticipation of seeing the Salvationists arrested again. Hundreds had gathered, ready to defend the Army against any attack. Joe reckoned that had there been a brawl that night, blood would have been shed.[326]

Before long, the mayor and chief of police made an appearance and ordered the Salvationists to disband. Angered by the gathering, the mayor rough-handled one of the Salvation lassies. The corps sergeant-major stepped in to shield her, and in retaliation, the mayor drew his revolver and declared he would shoot him. He pulled the trigger, but the gun did not fire. He pulled it a second time, and once again, there was no discharge. He swore and cried out that his pistol had never failed him before.[327]

The band of marchers returned to a capacity crowd at the nearby Salvation Army hall and continued with a praise meeting. Because of the pressure on the town's leadership, the mayor announced that the incarcerated officers would be released four days early. Joe organized a grand celebration and told the town the Army would sponsor a gigantic ice cream social in the park. Everyone was invited. Joe even extended an invitation to the mayor and the police department.[328]

A military soldier's reunion was happening on the same day, and as hundreds gathered in the park, Joe solicited the aid of two of their bands for the march. Hundreds of sympathizers joined in the parade, and as they marched that evening, they carried lit torches that illuminated the streets. After returning to the park, hundreds gathered to eat ice cream provided by The Salvation Army. The Salvationists sat down and enjoyed refreshments with "Republicans and sinners, Democrats and aristocrats, Prohibitionists and Salvationists."[329]

Following the ice cream social, several speakers stood on a platform and expressed their support for The Salvation Army. There was so much positivity expressed about the Army that under the cover of darkness, the mayor and his so-called lawmen left town.[330]

Joe stayed in Macomb for five more weeks, during which time the people of Macomb asked him to be their temporary mayor. He pledged he would stay and serve as mayor until they could hold an election to find new leadership. The town was now also in need of a chief of police, so Joe named the Salvation Army captain its temporary police chief until another could be elected.[331]

***

When Joe first encountered The Salvation Army in Liverpool, he witnessed the brutal attacks endured by the Salvationists as they publicly proclaimed the gospel of Jesus Christ, which set the stage for his own personal experience with the Army when he joined them a couple of years later in San Francisco.

Words cannot adequately describe the persecution and punishment the members of Booth's Army endured in those early days. As the unofficial guardian angel of the Army in San Francisco, Joe stood watch at the door of the barracks many nights and endured the ire of the angry mobs who wanted to disturb the meetings inside. "Night after night our comrade (Joe) has kept the door of the barracks with one eye closed up and his legs and body a mass of bruises, inflicted by the roughs of 'The Barbary Coast.' (He) has scarcely missed a meeting, except when too badly bruised through ill-usage."[332]

Three months later, The War Cry would continue to report on the abuse Joe received as he protected the entrance of the Army Hall, "Sergeant Garabed from San Francisco No. 1 (was) struck in the face with a stone. Face all bloody and blood dripping on the floor."[333]

In San Bernardino, California, a man named Richard Hubbard challenged Joe to a duel. After assaulting Joe, he issued a challenge to fight to the finish by the rules of the London Prize Ring or by use of "picks (axe), shovels, knives, pistols, rifles, Gatling guns, torpedoes, or battering rams." Joe immediately filed a complaint with the police, who issued a warrant for the man's arrest. Mr. Hubbard quickly left town.[334]

Upon his appointment as a staff member of the training garrison in San Francisco, Joe and the cadets faced a particularly challenging time dealing with the rabble-raisers on the streets. *The War Cry* reported that someone threatened to stab Joe with a knife, while another promised to shoot him with their gun. The same article reported the Salvationists had come back from the open-air with bruised faces and blackened eyes.[335]

As The Salvation Army marched through the streets to celebrate its fifth anniversary of opening its work in California, an out-of-control boy followed Joe, yelling at him and spitting on his back. The crowd threw stones, bricks, and other missiles at the Salvationists. One stone hit Joe's cheekbone. Despite the injuries and angry mob, the Army held eight open-air meetings that day in San Francisco.[336]

Joe was conducting evangelistic services in Youngstown, Ohio, and as they marched through the town, a group of young boys threw stones and eggs at them. Later that evening, as Joe was leading a congregational song, a stone crashed through a window of the corps building, causing shards of glass to fly everywhere. One piece of glass cut Joe's face, just above his eye, causing profuse bleeding. Joe shared this verse of Scripture in conjunction with the incident: "For I am persuaded, that neither death, nor life, nor angels, nor principalities, nor powers, nor things present, nor things to come, nor height, nor depth, nor any other creature, shall be able to separate us from the love of God, which is in Christ Jesus, our Lord" (Romans 8:38-39).[337]

Joe was arrested five times in Colorado Springs, for continuing to march on the streets with his cornet. The chief of police was so angry with Joe that he threatened to give him a "thumping." Rumors spread that a lynch mob planned to hang Joe. The Salvationists told him to quickly leave town before the crowd could make good on their threat. Joe's response was, "I am not going to run away. I consider it the highest honor that I should be thought worthy to suffer death—death for my Lord and Master, Jesus Christ."[338]

In Malden, Massachusetts, Joe was leading the open-air when the police interrupted the meeting. They cursed at the Salvationists, grabbed them by their throats and shoulders, and hauled them off to jail. The police ordered them to empty their pockets, march to a designated area, take off their clothes, and shower. Afterward, placed in individual cells, they were only allowed to come out of confinement each morning to bathe. Meals consisted of bread, coffee, soup, and water. After two days of confinement, the Salvationists were released on bail.[339]

It was midnight as Joe was making his way to the boarding house he was staying at in Lyons, New York. Along the way, he was severely injured. During the meeting that evening, a group of young men entered and started causing trouble. Joe reprimanded them but to no avail. He sent for a police officer, who forced the boys to exit the barracks. At the conclusion of the meeting, Joe made his way to his room. Near the Geneva Street Canal Bridge, the boys who had been removed from the meeting exacted their revenge and assaulted him. Joe was knocked down, kicked, and beaten, his face receiving several knife gashes. His cornet, which was valued at one hundred dollars ($3,000 in the present day) was smashed and ruined.[340]

In time, news outlets would print similar lines about Joe and his run-ins with those who wanted to harm him:

> He has been stabbed in the back, slashed in the mouth, and battered on the head enough to kill a dozen ordinary men, but he still lives and praises God. The more blood let out of his carcass through stabs and bruises, only gave a chance for more salvation to get in, and the bumps on his head he characterizes as 'bumps of righteousness.'[341]

Frequently, Joe would spend the night in a jail cell infested with bedbugs, or with no bed at all, and sleep on the cold concrete floor.

His final arrest happened in 1917, and the law enforcement officer arresting him treated him brutally. But as the public's attitude toward the Army began to change, Joe was no longer abused, incarcerated, or the object of makeshift missiles. Nevertheless, he carried the battle scars for the rest of his life.

***

Joe had just finished conducting meetings in Chicago when the divisional commander of that area found him. He was in a state of panic and asked Joe to take a detour from his next appointed corps and go with him to Green Bay, Wisconsin. The situation was dire, literally a matter of life and death.

When Joe inquired as to the reason for this sudden change of location, the divisional commander told him The Salvation Army corps officer in Green Bay, Lieutenant Stevenson, was going to be hanged by a blood-thirsty mob.[342]

Leaving immediately, they arrived in Green Bay to find the entire town in an upheaval. The hanging was to take place at the big bridge in town. Thousands of citizens gathered on both sides of the river to watch The Salvation Army officer meet his doom.

Joe quickly assessed the situation and, despite the bloodthirsty mob and personal risk to himself, rushed toward the scene of the would-be crime and began shouting, "Open up, open up in the name of the Lord!"[343]

Whether in shock by the audacity of the Turk or awed by this heroic measure, the crowd parted like the Red Sea to allow Joe through. He set Lieutenant Stevenson free, pulled him through the crowd, and the three officers quickly made their way to the train station. No one in the crowd opposed Joe or tried to stop them from making their getaway.[344]

When General William Booth was conducting an American tour, he visited Milwaukee, Wisconsin. The governor of the state was asked to introduce the General to the great crowd that had gathered. In that introduction he said, "General, you have in your organization one of the most courageous men I have ever met. I refer to Joe the Turk." The Governor then shared the incredible story of how Joe saved a fellow officer from certain death in Green Bay.[345]

Years later, Joe was conducting an evangelistic tour in Montana and found himself in Helena. During his first meeting, a man stood up to share his testimony. He relayed the incredible story of what happened to him in Green Bay years before. It was none other than Stevenson himself. No longer a Salvation Army officer, he had become a very prominent real estate agent and was very much alive.[346]

***

Adjutant Joe received a promotion letter on February 8, 1906 from National Commander Evangeline Booth. Citing his positive contributions to The Salvation Army in the United States, it read as follows:

My dear Adjutant:

I have pleasure in informing you that upon the recommendation of those under whom you work, I have decided to promote you to the rank of Staff-Captain.

I am sure we all appreciate the interest and devotion you have manifested in the past and your earnest endeavors not only to push the Trade in the cities and towns which you have visited, but also the enthusiasm you have shown in assisting the spiritual work of the Corps and stirring up the people to give some thought to their soul's welfare. I assure you that your love for souls is a great cheer to your leaders and makes me feel all the most safe in giving you this added mark of confidence.

Praying that God will help you not only to increase your success in selling the Army goods, but also add numberless souls to the long line of salvation trophies to be laid at the Savior's feet, and with every good wish for your own personal happiness.

Yours in the one Salvation Army,

Evangeline Booth, Commander.

Still, by 1918, Joe had been an officer for more than thirty-one years, and despite the previous glowing letter from the National Commander, he had not been promoted above the rank of staff-captain. Although ranks and promotions were not always given by a schedule in The Salvation Army's early years, this was unusual. By this point in an officer's career, they would have, at the very least, been promoted to the rank of major.

Joe received his long service letter from Commander Evangeline Booth. The letter to Joe was not located among his personal papers. However, based on his style of writing, Joe would always parrot back at the beginning of a letter what had been written to him. Commander Evangeline Booth wrote to him again: "… [I] count it both a joy and a privilege to congratulate [you] for the long years of splendid devotion [you] have given to a worthy cause, which [you] have associated with much sacrifice, nevertheless has brought to [you] the approval of convictions, the smile of Heaven, and approbation of [your] leaders."

Upon the receipt of his long service notification commending him on his faithful and dedicated service, Joe replied to the National Commander with a request for promotion to the rank of major. Though it was a matter he felt strongly about, it never dimmed the light of his service as a Salvation Army officer, nor his enthusiasm for proclaiming the gospel message. Nevertheless, he later wrote again to Commander Evangeline Booth on November 21, 1918:

My dear Commander:

I take great pleasure in writing you a few lines, replying to your most welcome and much appreciated letter of Oct. 9th, received a few days ago, regarding my promotion to the Long Service Order of The Army.

As you say that you count it both a joy and a privilege to congratulate me for the long years of splendid devotion I have given to a worthy cause, which I have associated with much sacrifice, nevertheless has brought to me the approval of convictions, the smile of Heaven, and approbation of my leaders.

I am glad to say that real satisfaction is mine in the recollection of more than 31 years as an Officer, also 3 years as a soldier, totaling, 34 years. When we had only one corps in California, which was in San Francisco #1, and when I got saved those days, it was very bitter persecution days for The Army, police and people were against us, and when we went to open-airs in those days, we never knew whether we would return home alive, where we have been every night mobbed in the open-airs and in the buildings.

Even when I was a soldier for 3 years, where I had my place of business, the mobs have broken in my shop 3 times when I was carrying on the meeting and stolen much goods each time, and many nights I returned from the meeting with broken head, and black eyes, and many knife wounds and stabs and bruises of all kinds. I was fired at with a pistol 5 times. Every day something happened.

I became a soldier in the SA in 1884. After 3 years as a soldier, I sold out my business in three days' notice by Brigadier E. Fielding. I gave the best of my handmade custom shoes to the Army officers for presents and sent all my household goods to The Salvation Army Rescue Home, that was just opened in Oakland, California, and became an officer in The Army, July 24, 1887. Then I was sent to open up the Los Angeles #1 Corps in California.

I was a Cadet under Captain Geo. Rutherford. I am very sorry to say that the Captain left me and ran away. When the police persecution was on there, I was arrested for having meetings on the street. I was waiting for a trial for 7 days. I must say that God was with me, and a great revival broke out with all the prisoners crying for salvation of Jesus. This was the birthplace of the Los Angeles Corps. After 7 days, I was brought before a judge for trial. The power of God fell upon the courtroom, which was crowded with the best people in the city. The judge himself, could not hold back the tears, as well as the people, and I fell upon my knees and prayed for the whole crowd, and the judge arose and said, 'You are a free man. Go on and do all the good you can in our city.'

Los Angeles, at the time, had only 13,000 people. Three days after, the city arose and dismissed the entire police force. Hallelujah! Then I went from the city jail and secured the largest opera house in that city, which was overcrowded nightly, and where many souls were saved. Before I left that city, I had a great victory.

I was also sent to the opening of the San Bernardino, CA, and Pomona, and Santa Ana, CA corps. I was again arrested for having open-airs, etc. Since then, I have been arrested over 52 times in the USA, and once in Smyrna, Turkey. I must say that I have never lost a case, I never gave up the city until the city unconditionally surrendered to our dear Army and Flag. I have fought from New York to San Francisco, CA. Today we do not have much trouble with the police, and they are the best of friends with the SA.

In those days, I was sent by those over me to the hard places where other officers of all rank and file would not go. When I was through with the case, then anyone would follow me. We made it very easy for the officers of today, that is why I have been arrested so many times. I have fought to establish the SA open-air work. I brought the SA from the back alley to the best part of the city.

I well remember days of persecution in this country. Many of the Provincial Officers and Divisional Commanders were so discouraged that they sent someone to close up the Hot Shop, because the police would not give them any chance to hold meetings, even in the worst alley in town.

Some places you could march, but you could not stand one minute. Other places, you could blow a horn, but you could not touch the drum. In other places, it was just the opposite, they allowed the drum, but not the horn. All through this country they have different notions about The Army, to cripple our work. So, I felt if we were to have an Army established in this country, we must fight. So, I made it my business to go to those places where they were closing up as a hard go and reopened many of them where I have had sweeping victory at the court. When

I was through with them, the incoming officers never had any more trouble regarding open-airs. The public opinion changed and removed the mountains of prejudice. Today, you can go back to those cities, and you will find a big citadel with a number of soldiers and a brass band. I must say that God helped me in the most miraculous manner to establish hundreds of corps that would otherwise have been closed. I have been in the front trenches, where the shots and shells were flying the thickest, and in spite of all, I went over the top every time.

Before your administration, I was fighting under your dear brother, Commander Ballington Booth, also Commander Booth-Tucker, and it was that time that I fought my hardest battles to establish The Army's rights. Colonel Cox was the Editor of *The War Cry*, and he knows what I went through in battling against the powers of darkness. All other officers in the field at that time knew also.

I do not desire to take up your valuable time, but I thought I would let you know just a leaf out of my life about past service to God and The Army. I have never lost a case in the court. I have many opinions of the Supreme Court decisions in my favor. My case has become a supreme law of the land. This is why we are not arrested today.

Enclosed please find a copy of a portion of the Supreme Court opinion filed in the Supreme Court at Madison, WI. I have many Supreme Court opinions in other states of the USA. You may know that I am the pioneer man of the USA. I stood for The SA and dear Flag when many great officers of all ranks and files ran away. I also fought the "Major Moore" split, then Commissioner Smith, after that your brother, Mr. Ballington Booth.[347] As you know just as well as myself, that when you came to this country to defend our dear Army, you found great difficulty in the US and other officers, or at least, most of them, were on the fence, many of them went over the fence, so our soldiers did the same; some of the officers returned to the SA after many years of staying away from our dear Army, and did all the harm they could for The Army; some even got drunk and lived all kinds of lives, and as soon as they returned to The Army, they were promoted to Majors and Brigadiers, etc. If not for the few, good, loyal officers and soldiers, like myself, in The Army to fight and keep The Army going, I am sure they would find nothing to come back for.

While others were in and out of our dear Army, I was going on day and night and pushing ahead with The Salvation Army side of things. I must say that even my own people and my countrymen and friends and officers, while I am traveling, say that I have been in The Army all these years and I am not promoted. They threw it in my face.

I can look over the field of the USA today where I have helped to get many souls saved in my meetings, some of them became officers in The Army, and they are being promoted all the time. Some that I used to visit at their corps are now also promoted to be [divisional commanders and provincial commanders], etc. I have the greatest confidence in you.

As I read your very kind letter, you speak so highly of my long and faithful service to God and our dear Army. I appreciate the long service badge which was due me nine years ago. I feel after these 34 years as a loyal Salvationist and 31 years as an officer, 12 years as a Staff-Captain, I am certainly entitled to be promoted to at least Major. I am sure you will give me justice in this matter. God bless you!

I am most faithfully yours,

Joseph Garabed, Staff-Captain[348]

There is no record of Evangeline Booth's response to Joe's request and, as history has proven, he never received a promotion beyond that of staff-captain.

Curious to discover if there might be a reason for this, I looked at Joe's personnel records located at the National Headquarters of The Salvation Army in Alexandria, Virginia, and his personal file held at the Eastern Territorial Headquarters in Nyack, New York. Nothing located gave any reason for why he would not be given a promotion. The fact that Joe was honorably retired, allowed to have his funeral service in the most prestigious facility owned by the Army at that time, and was buried alongside many other Army greats, speaks to his reputation as an officer in excellent standing with the organization. Any further speculation is just that, speculation.

CHAPTER 8
PLAYING IN THE KEY OF ASIA MINOR

During his officership, Joe made three attempts to visit his remaining family in Asia Minor. The first trip back to Turkey was eighteen years after he emigrated. The visit was not a total success, but he tried again eleven years later and was over the moon about the reunion with his family then. Fourteen years later, Joe made his way to Greece to visit his sister and was overjoyed to not only see her, but also to minister to the Armenian refugees she lived among.

Joe often spoke about his family, and during the difficult years in Turkey and Greece, he sent them every spare penny he had. These visits were especially important to him and allowed him to reconnect with his own flesh and blood.

***

During the summer of 1899, International Headquarters hosted a conference in London. Joe was part of an American delegation. They docked at Southampton at midnight on July 19. As the ship dropped anchor into the harbor, everyone on the wharf heard the blast of Joe's cornet. The delegation quickly boarded a train to the capital, and as it passed through the English countryside, the melodious and joyous strains played by Joe on his double-jointed cornet pierced the night air.[349]

Following the gathering, Joe left for Turkey to visit his siblings, whom he had not seen since 1881. Upon arriving and presenting his passport, the Turkish authorities arrested Joe and placed him in jail. He was unaware of a Turkish law that said anyone born in Turkey would always and forever be a citizen of the Empire. Even if they had become naturalized citizens in other countries, Turkish law would not recognize it. The law mandated anyone leaving Turkey without the Sultan's permission would face arrest upon their return.[350]

Joe mistakenly believed that since he had been a US citizen for eighteen years, he could enter Turkey without incident. He also assumed that should there be an issue, the United States Consulate based in Constantinople would be there to assist.[351]

When Joe entered the customs area, the agent told him to surrender his passport, as he had broken the law. Joe refused to let go of his passport, so the agent forcibly took it from him and sent him to jail. Somehow, Joe was able to get word about his predicament to the United States Consul and requested help to get out of jail.

The United States Consul requested that the Turkish government release Joe to them. The Consul gave Joe two options: immediately leave the country or be placed in an American jail, where he would be charged room and board plus a security fee.

Joe accepted the latter offer and stayed in Smyrna, Turkey for only forty-eight hours. One hour before his brother and sister arrived to see him, Joe was forced to leave Smyrna. He bought a ticket for the Port of Piraeus, a part of the Greater Athens, Greece area, and at the last moment, had his passport returned to him.[352]

Joe landed in Greece, and his sister, who was able to get a ticket to Athens, met him there. Joe's older brother could not make the journey, so Joe left without seeing him. He was so distraught by the events in Turkey, that when he returned home, he shared the story with Salvation Army leadership. The Army's attorney took on the case. They were determined to discover the reason Joe was treated so poorly by the United States Consul and his adopted country.

Newspapers across America carried the incident. It quickly became a sensational story. The Salvation Army's national legal representative filed a complaint with the State Department asking for an investigation into the actions of the United States Consul in Turkey.

He wrote in his complaint:

> It is hard to credit the statement that an American citizen
> should be treated in the way in which this citizen had been
> handled, and then to think that we should have a consul who
> has no more regard for his flag and his country than to connive

and to aid in the ill treatment that Garabed was receiving at the hands of the Turks. As a native-born American, I feel that if our flag and country can only give such guarantees as have been given to this citizen, that we have not got much to crow over, after all, as regards the protection which we all thought the Stars and Stripes would always receive and demand.[353]

No record exists regarding the findings of the investigation into the United States Consul's office in Turkey. However, if he had been judged responsible, it would have made headlines again. The absence of further news articles suggests the investigation did not satisfy the United States government's concerns about mistreatment.

One of Joe's great regrets was not seeing his brother, as it would be ten more years before he got another chance to see him.

***

In the late summer of 1910, Joe made his way again to the land of his birth. It took eighteen days by ship to reach his destination. He made effective use of the time he had with his captive audience. Not only did he give daily concerts, but he also had many of the passengers marching as though they were on their way to an open-air meeting.[354]

Joe's arrival in Smyrna was not like his previous visit a decade prior. Things had changed politically, allowing Joe to enter the country without incident. He was able to meet with childhood friends and family. Joe immediately began giving concerts and promoting the work and ministry of the world-wide Salvation Army.[355]

When he presented a concert at the American Protestant Church, the sanctuary was packed, and hundreds were turned away. People sat in the windows and stood in the halls and doorways. Prominent citizens of the community, including two Armenian priests dressed in their luxurious robes, sat at the front of the sanctuary. Joe's topic for the evening was, "The Salvation Army Throughout the World." The crowd was interested, and Joe's stories, especially those of his exploits, kept them engaged. When he played his instruments, the crowd clapped and applauded with enthusiasm all evening.[356] Joe made a point to wear his regulation Salvation Army uniform so the audience could get a feel of what the Army typically looked like around the world. Representatives of the Turkish government were delighted to hear Joe play the cornet, saxophone, and clarinet in a militaristic style.[357]

Turkish security was on standby in case anything got out of hand, but in the end, their presence was unnecessary because Joe thoroughly enthralled his audience. The evening was an immense success for Joe personally. The story of The Salvation Army and its worldwide work was well-received.[358]

Joe stayed at his brother's home in Smyrna and walked out onto the balcony one evening at 10 p.m. and gave a one-hour concert. The response of the neighbors and the local police department was positive. He presented a late-night concert for the duration of his stay.[359]

He spent three months in Turkey and was quick to point out how different things were politically in his homeland. The Turkish government did not require him to show his passport everywhere he went. The people were welcoming and friendly to him as he made his way around the countryside. Joe desperately hoped The Salvation Army would open its work in Turkey, especially in Constantinople, the city where he had spent many of his teenage years.[360]

Joe traveled the country in his Turkish uniforms, which delighted the residents, officials, and even the priests. Wherever he went, he would play salvation music: on a train, a stagecoach, or amid the ruins of the Seven Churches of the Revelation. Joe was so happy to be home again and to be the first Salvationist to blow a horn in Turkey. He did not take the privilege for granted and made sure he took full advantage of every opportunity.

Everywhere he played and preached, he taught his audiences The Salvation Army salute. He stood tall and pointed his right index finger toward heaven. He explained that it meant to "Look up!" When "Uncle Joe," as he was called by the children, walked around the city, the youngsters would stand at attention and point their fingers toward the sky. The kids had truly grown fond of their special guest and treated him as a celebrity.[361]

Joe played music but also preached and prayed without harassment from the authorities. He relished the opportunity to be the first Salvation Army officer seen in the ancient city of Smyrna.[362]

***

During the Armenian Genocide, Joe's sister, Maritza Yoskatchian, fled Turkey to escape the fate of millions of her compatriots. She made her way to Greece, where she found a place to live in an Armenian refugee settlement.[363] It was four years after World War I before Joe would hear from her again. When he did, she shared with him how she had endured much persecution because she refused to deny her Christian faith.[364]

On August 24, 1924, a year before he retired, Joe left for Athens onboard the Greek transatlantic liner, King Alexander. The voyage took seventeen days, and as on previous maritime journeys, Joe wasted no time in evangelizing his captive audience. He conducted meetings, led singing services, gave concerts on his musical instruments, and preached to the seven hundred passengers onboard.[365]

Arriving in Athens, Joe reunited with his sister. With Maritza was her pastor, Reverend Adjamian, who asked Joe if he would present a series of special meetings for the residents of the refugee settlement. Never needing to be asked twice about sharing the gospel, he got settled into his room, then walked out into the middle of the square and began to blow on his double-jointed cornet. The horn and the blast of his cornet was so loud it took only a few minutes for men, women,

Joe and his sister, Maritza Yoskatchian.

and children, Greek and Armenian, to gather around the "Sanctified Salvationist Showman."[366]

Joe conducted an open-air, playing salvation choruses on his saxophone, and then giving a testimony about the hope he possessed in his heart. Interest was so great, he conducted three more open-airs, and as many indoor meetings. While he was so happy to be with his sister again and share the gospel with his people, Joe was shocked by the conditions he witnessed in the refugee camp. There were malnourished children, unemployed men and women, as well as a deep sense of hopelessness experienced by those living in abject poverty.[367]

After five weeks with his sister, Joe left Greece for Marseilles, France. There he met with family and conducted meetings in another Armenian refugee settlement. Ever looking to promote and support The Salvation Army on his international journeys, he held special meetings at the #2 Corps in Marseilles.[368]

After a couple weeks in France, Joe made the journey home to America.

A portrait photo of Joe, dressed in his notable garments, taken during his early officership in Hannibal, Missouri.

Joe's uniform, retrieved from his apartment after his Promotion to Glory. It resides at The Salvation Army Eastern Territorial Headquarters, along with his double-jointed cornet, clarinet, and umbrella.

A close-up picture of Joe's iconic Fez.

Joe's famous clarinet, now kept at The Salvation Army USA Eastern Territory in West Nyack, New York.

A "Joe the Turk" bobblehead created by the USA Eastern Territory.

A one-of-a-kind "Joe the Turk" Funko Pop designed by Captain Ashley Hobgood-Taylor.

A portrait of Joe the Turk, courtesy of The Salvation Army USA Western Territorial Museum & Archives.

Joe posing with his cornet and Turkish garments.

Joe donning his traditional uniform. Joe would wear two stars and stitching around his epaulet (signifying his rank of staff-captain) and the star-shaped badge pinned on his tunic. The five points of the star have the letters S-A-V-E-D on them. Photo courtesy of The Salvation Army National Archives.

*Joe as a young staff-captain in The Salvation Army. Photo courtesy of The
Salvation Army National Archives.*

From The War Cry, November 21, 1896. Caption: "Joe the Eternal Advertiser. Note, the sign is in the shape of a coffin (side view) and on it are drawings of playing cards, smoking pipe, cigarettes, and whiskey. Inside the 'D' is a saloon door that leads to 'Doom.'" Photo courtesy of The Salvation Army National Archives.

A souvenir people could buy from Joe as a memento of his time at a corps. His motto was always, "Jesus is Mighty to Save."

The cover of one of Joe's many songbook pamphlets distributed during his campaigns.

CHAPTER 9

THE WINDS OF CHANGE

Taking a backward glance at history, one often idealizes or romanticizes what it would have been like to live in a particular time. People become larger than life and are designated heroes who did and dared against seemingly impossible odds. But living in that moment themselves, it is highly unlikely that any "hero" actually saw themselves that way. The reality is more mundane and ordinary than ideal and romantic. Heroic deeds are often not recognized and appreciated on that side of history.

Early Salvationists, who are seen today as pioneers and heroes, left a lasting legacy in social reform and religious revival. The Salvation Army went beyond traditional religious practices, becoming a movement focused on compassion and social justice. The Army wasn't just a religious group; it was a force challenging the norms of the mid to late 1800s. Early Salvationists went into the poorest parts of society, offering help to the needy and hope to the downtrodden. Their mission was bold: to bring the message of Jesus Christ to those forgotten by society. These pioneers confronted societal problems directly. They set up shelters for the homeless, soup kitchens for the hungry, and homes for the marginalized long before such services were common. They provided immediate help and also laid the groundwork for modern social services.

From the beginning, The Salvation Army believed in equality and inclusivity. It welcomed everyone, no matter their background, into its community. This was revolutionary in a time marked by strict class divisions. The Sallys challenged social norms and promoted the idea that every individual had worth and dignity.

The early Army also pushed for gender equality. Catherine Booth, co-founder of The Salvation Army, was a key figure in shaping the beliefs of the organization. She strongly supported women's rights to preach and lead, breaking traditional gender roles and paving the way for future female leaders.

Despite facing opposition and persecution, mockery in the press and physical attacks, the early Army remained dedicated to its mission of "soup, soap, and salvation." The resilience of those Christian soldiers only strengthened their supporters and spread their message of hope and redemption. Looking back, early Salvationists were pioneers and heroes for challenging injustice, easing suffering, and demonstrating faith in action. These warriors were leaders in social reform, advocates for the marginalized, and champions of a gospel that sought to reconcile people with God and each other.

For much of his officership, Joe was the darling of the press, and seen by many in the public as a "champion for right." The stories printed by *The War Cry* and other newspapers painted a life of adventure. It was an adventure vicariously shared by many readers. As The Salvation Army moved into the twentieth century, it began to evolve at a rapid pace, but Joe was still living like it was 1892. While he continued to draw great crowds and create exciting press, his "primitive" ways of evangelizing and sensational methods of making headlines were not as welcomed by Salvation Army leadership as they once were.

A New Wind Blowing

As World War I closed, the opinion of the American public toward The Salvation Army began to change. Those who fought in the Great War returned home thinking of the work and ministry of the doughnut girls, resulting in veterans who respected and fell in love with the Salvationist lassies. Consequently, the country began to treat The Salvation Army with great admiration. New songs reminded the public of the yeoman service rendered by the doughnut girls alongside the soldiers on the front lines:

Don't Forget the Salvation Army (My Doughnut Girl)
Music by William Frisch and Robert Brown
Lyrics by James Lucas and Elmore Leggingwell

1. Pennies, nickels, dimes, and quarters, hear them ring.
Oh, what joy and oh what bliss those coins can bring.
For now, our boys are landing at our shores every day.
This is what you're bound to hear them say:

Refrain:
Don't forget The Salvation Army,
always remember my doughnut girl.
She brought them doughnuts and coffee.
Just like an angel, she was their best pal.
As brave as a lion but meek as a lamb,
she carried on beside the sons of Uncle Sam.
So don't forget The Salvation Army, remember my doughnut girl.

2. Glory, Hallelujah, you will hear them shout
Helping any stranger who is down and out.
Humanity uplifting in their most cheerful way.
Is it any wonder that we say?

***

The federal government was grateful for the work and ministry of the Army. It honored Evangeline Booth, presenting her with the Distinguished Service Medal in 1919.[369] The Tournament of Roses Parade committee invited the Army to march in the parade in 1920, and it has continued to do so for more than one hundred years. The Army participated in numerous parades and rallies across the country because of its newfound favor with the American people. As veterans reintegrated into society, joined civic clubs, and became business leaders, they did not forget the Sallys. The Army became accepted, loved, and admired by the American populace.[370]

This was a new sensation for Salvationists, who just a few years earlier, had been mistreated by the mobs, called "crass and vulgar" by some religious leaders, and thrown into jail like common criminals. Americans now saw the Army as a movement whose weapons were love, prayer, and service.

The War Cry reprinted a newspaper editorial that aptly summed up the way the nation now felt about the soldiers and officers of salvation:

> The universal respect with which The Salvation Army workers in France are held is attested by sailors aboard American transports, carrying wounded American soldiers home on furloughs, one of whom made a statement at the headquarters of the United War Work Campaign:

> 'I have talked with scores of American soldiers aboard the transport on which I am stationed,' he said, and I am amazed at their expressions of love and affection for The Salvation Army. One of those boys, who had lost an arm and leg at the Marne, told me that he owes his life to a lassie who gave him a glass of lemonade just as he was attacked with a fever. The surgeon told him that he could not have survived the double amputation had the fever got him.

> Another wounded boy told me that he felt himself slipping into the Great Beyond when he heard a Salvation Army lassie whispering to him to have faith in God. He said that somehow this awakened within him a desire to live, and after she had given him some lemonade, he began to mend immediately. He told me that he had always been a rough guy, but that he would be glad to speak a good word for The Salvation Army wherever he went. He's a hopeless invalid now, half of his lung having been shot away, but if praise of The Salvation Army will widen its influence, then he will prove a valuable auxiliary.

> According to this authority, American officers, without exception, referred admirably to The Salvation Army and were unanimous in saying that its usefulness at the front has been highly beneficial to the cause of humanity and democracy, and

did much to sustain the morale of the troops at a most critical period of the offensive."[371]

With this newfound respectability, the sensational articles and headlines that had been a hallmark of *The War Cry* began to fade and were replaced with more dignified offerings. The Salvation Army's commitment to winning the world for Jesus and its total belief in being a holiness people never wavered, but now there were less startling ways to continue proclaiming that message.

Salvationists marching and playing on the streets became a welcome sight. They were accepted as a benefit, not a nuisance, to communities. Arrests and harassment had all but disappeared. Joe was no longer being incarcerated; his final imprisonment happened in 1917. Joe's *War Cry* articles remained popular, but they no longer contained scandalous accounts of him being chased by mobs, fired upon, or thrown into jails full of cockroaches or bedbugs.

One newspaper reported, "Joe's police record is almost completed. The arrest and prosecution of Salvation Army officers is now a thing of the past. The rugged foreigner whose head and body bear the imprints of the rocks of the rabble now speaks unmolested."[372]

Joe's travel itineraries, which had been published for thirty years in a prominent section of *The War Cry*, decreased in size and regularity. Sometimes, the print on his itineraries was so small that one could hardly read them without the aid of a magnifying glass. His testimony was more than thirty years old and, while exciting, did not seem as relevant as it once was, nor did it reflect the current state of The Salvation Army. He continued to draw crowds to his meetings, but they were not coming by the thousands like before.

Even though Joe would always be seen as a hero in the Army world, leadership's view of him was changing. For example, after Joe borrowed five pounds from someone at International Headquarters on his way from England to Turkey, the American National Commander wrote to International Headquarters: "(I) note the arrangements you have made for his (Joe's) visit to Smyrna. I trust, as you say, that he will be able to get back safely and may not get into any trouble with the authorities

there, though he is not blessed with very much of the bump of caution …
Moreover, he is so fond of sensation that I am afraid if only for the sake
of a good story, he will want to get run in—the temptation will almost be
too great to be resisted. However, there is no knowing. God may even use
him to open the door for us in Turkey, though he is hardly as cautious an
apostle as we should care to choose for this job."[373]

As Joe's retirement date of 1925 grew closer, *War Cry* articles about
him and his campaigns around the United States began to wane. In his
final year of service, his travel itinerary was not listed at all. The last
article printed found Joe off to Europe in search of his sister, Maritza,
who was living in an Armenian refugee settlement in Greece.

CHAPTER 10
RETIRED, BUT NOT TIRED

On January 14, 1925, Joseph Garabed honorably retired from active service as a Salvation Army officer. No officer in his time impacted The Salvation Army in the United States to the degree that Joe did. He conducted nearly four thousand corps visits and received unprecedented newspaper coverage, making him a household name in communities across the country. He was also well-known to the worldwide Salvation Army, as international Salvation Army publications also recorded his adventures.

The War Cry printed the following notification about his retirement:

> In accordance with The Salvation Army's regulations governing the retirement of officers, Staff-Captain Joseph Garabed, widely and well-known as 'Joe the Turk,' has been retired from active service after a period of thirty-eight years of earnest and faithful service to God in The Salvation Army. While officially retired, the Staff-Captain is far too energetic to be laid on the shelf altogether, and will, no doubt, from time to time, be taking an active part conducting meetings, and will give whatever help he can, in pushing the war in every way.[374]

Joe split his time between France and the United States for the next decade. He worked with The Salvation Army in Paris and spent the remainder of his time in Marseilles, where he had family and a lifetime lease on a room in a villa belonging to a cousin.[375]

While in Marseilles, Joe sent a letter to National Headquarters. The French territorial commander had contacted him and requested his help in advancing the work of the Army there. Joe's account of the French Salvation Army mirrored the American Army's past when police would show up and order the Salvationists to leave the streets. If the Sallys wanted to hold a meeting, it could only be inside their building. Joe lamented there would never be a vital expression of The Salvation Army in France until the Salvationists got over their fear of arrest, defied the police, and stood their ground in the open-air.[376]

A few months later, he wrote again to National Headquarters about the difficulty of open-air work in Marseilles:

> I am sure you will agree with me the open-air creates interest in our work and will bring the Army before a large number of people who otherwise would not see our people nor hear our message … The police will not allow the Army to have open-air meetings, even in the alleys. Only a few weeks ago, I was out in the open-air at one of the great parks of the city of Marseilles. I was playing my saxophone [and] how quickly over 1,000 people [were] at the open-air on Sunday at 10:30 a.m. People were coming from all directions. So, the Army in Marseille, France, if they [would] like to have [a] Blood and Fire Corps and have lots of people in open-airs, also crowded buildings, they must fight like I did in [the] USA.[377]

***

After Joe retired, he took out a mortgage and purchased an apartment building located at 120 West 3rd Street in New York City. The five-story building in Greenwich Village was divided into twenty-two rooms, one of which Joe occupied.[378] On his typewriter he prepared a document that each of his tenants had to agree to and sign:

> "This is to certify that (name) have hired and taken from Mr. Joseph Garabed the landlord (room number) building No 120 West Third Street, NYC. _____Dollars payable at 1st of each month.

> Also, no drinking and fighting, no boisterous noise and dancing, and no sporting and gambling for money. Department of Public works, and Police, and Fire Department advising you to not blockade the steps of this building, it must be entirely free passageway to entrance, also not to spit at the steps of this building.

THIS IS THE ORDER OF THE BOARD OF HEALTH

I also agree to give the Landlord 30 days' notice before moving, and never throw any kind of rubbish in any parts of this building. I am most faithfully yours, Joseph Garabed."[379]

The rent ranged from fifteen to twenty-two dollars per month. If everyone paid their rent, Joe would collect four hundred and nine dollars. Doing the math, Joe needed four hundred and thirty-four dollars to cover his mortgage payment. It did not take long for him to start operating in a deficit. One record in Joe's personal file shows a statement sent to a renter who had been allowed to stay in the apartment without paying any rent for one year. Joe's failure to manage his business affairs properly would lead to his financial ruin in days to come.[380]

While he was away in France, his friend, Brigadier Vernon Post, property secretary of The Salvation Army Eastern Territory, managed his business affairs. In correspondence dated June 25, 1926, Post informed Joe there was not enough money to make a full mortgage payment, and the lender was not willing to accept a partial payment. Post indicated he would do what he could to stall the company and prayed they did not make a demand for the full amount. He believed if interest payments were being made, lenders would be hesitant to foreclose on properties, which he thought would prevent the situation from worsening.[381]

Joe incurred heavy expenses to keep his property in compliance with New York City building codes. As a result, collected rent money was used for the cost of correcting code violations, giving Joe less money to pay toward his mortgage on the apartment building.[382]

Later, he received a notice from the New York City Police Department, stating one of Joe's tenants had been arrested for operating a gambling business out of his room. The notice stated Joe, as the building's owner, was also liable, and could face up to two years' imprisonment, one thousand dollars in fines, or both. The outcome of the case is unknown, but it is likely Joe was not punished for the violation. The warm relationship he had built with the New York City Police Department over the years most likely came into play.[383]

Joe also purchased a single-family home in Hastings, New York. While there is no record of the address in Joe's personal file, in a letter dated September 10, 1926, Brigadier Post shared with him news that the realtor had found a new tenant for the property. The potential renter had two young children, and Post described him as responsible. Post did, however, urge Joe to sell the house, as he did not deem it a promising investment. The money gained from the sale of the Hastings property would help Joe pay off the mortgage on the New York City property. Giving Joe another option, he advised him that he could invest the profit from the sale of the house. This would earn interest and give him additional income to supplement his twenty-four dollars a month pension from The Salvation Army.[384]

Post regularly shared his concerns about the apartment building. He told Joe that because it was an old building, it would not continue to draw renters as it had when it was new. Post believed the building could sell for thirty-five thousand dollars. Joe could use the profit to buy a newer property that needed fewer repairs than the building on West 3rd Street. He counseled Joe to sell both properties to gain a profit of twenty-five thousand dollars. Joe could invest the money and earn thirteen hundred dollars a year in interest.[385] Even during those days, New York City was an expensive place to live for anyone who was not a person of means.

Joe told Post he was not interested in selling either property.[386] Records found in Joe's apartment after his death show that Joe eventually had to allow the Hastings property to fall into foreclosure. He also lost the West 3rd Street property but was able to keep his apartment in it by taking on the job of landlord for the new property owner and collecting the monthly rent.

The year before he died, Joe wrote a letter to his niece, Miss M. Kalfa, in Athens, Greece. He reported that hoodlums had beaten and robbed him. He had been in and out of the hospital numerous times during the year. Joe explained that he had not regained his strength and had to undergo two operations on his bladder, from which he had not fully recovered. While hospitalized, he relied on someone to collect the rent. However, they turned out to be dishonest and took all the rent money and many personal items from his apartment.[387]

Before Joe allowed the apartment building to go into foreclosure, he spent a considerable sum of personal money to improve it by adding hot water, steam heat, and a bath. The renovation expenses, the theft of rent money, and the loss of his personal items had put Joe on the wrong side of his creditors; they were coming after him. His financial and physical situation forced Joe to enlist the aid of a real estate company to collect the rent and pay his debts down to avoid a potential lawsuit.

CHAPTER 11

PROMOTED TO GLORY

On October 11, 1937, Nishan Der Garabedian, also known as Joe the Turk, was Promoted to Glory from his apartment. A small slip of paper was found in his personnel folder with the following typed upon it:

Staff Captain Joseph Garabed (R)

Born at Talas, Turkey—January 14, 1860.

He was 77 years of age.

Had been in The United States for 55 years.

An Officer for over 50 years.

Colonel Wm Barrett, Major Erickson and Major Brennecke
have visited him from time to time that year.

Colonel Wm Barrett visited Joe in his apartment at 11:00AM
Monday morning, October 11th. Staff-Captain Joseph
Garabed passed away at 11:30.

The Salvation Army believes that when a person who is in Christ Jesus dies, it is not the end, but the beginning. This is what the phrase "Promoted to Glory" signifies. Joe received his eternal reward on that day. He is basking in the presence of the One who gave His life that all might be saved.

Although written several years prior to Joe's death, the following tribute concerning his upcoming evangelistic meetings in Pensacola, Florida reflects the feelings of many who knew him and experienced his extraordinary ministry:

In securing the services of this particular artist of the Orient,
The Salvation Army people are affording the public an

opportunity of seeing a character who is known throughout the length and breadth of the United States. It is claimed, in fact, that he has accomplished more good, single-handed, and alone, than any other known agent as identified with the Army as a whole.[388]

What the Press Had to Say

THE MORNING HERALD (UNIONTOWN, PA) THURSDAY, OCTOBER 21, 1937

I am saddened by the passing of another in this hamlet's thin gray line of colorful characters. Joe the Turk, who was really an Armenian, and one of the most frenzied crusaders for The Salvation Army, is dead. The first time I saw him he was very much in evidence at a street meeting on Hester Street. And what a sight he was! His uniform was brilliant red, with distinctly Turkish trimming, but his umbrella was his trademark. It was a patchwork of many colors, electric light bulbs which really glowed hanging from the points of each rib and surmounted by a Statue of Liberty and another light bulb. Many stories appear in Joe's obituary notices, but the one I credit most was told to me by a Third Avenue barman, who says Joe used to run a shoe-shine parlor in San Francisco, featured by a hole in the wall. The hole gave into a saloon next door and customers could quaff beer and stronger beverages while having their boots burnished. In 1884 The Salvation Army made him a convert and around the turn of the century Joe came to New York.[389]

READING TIMES (READING, PA), TUESDAY, OCTOBER 12, 1937 "JOE THE TURK" DIES AT AGE 82[sic - 77]

NEW YORK, Oct. 11 (AP) - Joseph Garabed, retired Salvation Army Captain who was widely known as "Joe the Turk" because of an Oriental costume he wore to attract crowds to religious meetings, died today at the age of 82[sic-77].

Garabed, a bachelor, was reported by Army officials to have been arrested more than 150[sic] times early in the century in localities where open-air meetings of all kinds were banned. He was retired 12 years ago from active duty.

He died at his home near The Army headquarters, where funeral services will be held Wednesday.

THE EVENING NEWS (WILKES-BARRE, PA) TUESDAY, OCTOBER 12, 1937, DEATH ENDS THE SANTA ROLE OF "JOE THE TURK"

Salvationist Faced Many Arrests To Collect For The Poor

New York, October 12 - "Joe the Turk," the first man to don a Santa Claus uniform and solicit funds with a tin cup along New York streets, who said he had been arrested fifty times "for being a Christian," is dead at his home, 120 West Third street, at the age of 82[sic][77]. Veteran of many a sidewalk scuffle when New York and 'Frisco streets were lit by gas lights, he will have an elaborate Salvation Army funeral tomorrow morning in the modern headquarters of that religious order, which rescued him from a Barbary Coast "dive" nearly half a century ago.

His real name was Joseph Garabed, but nobody ever called him that. And he was not a Turk. He was an Armenian. But he looked like a Turk, with his gaudy red and gold uniform, his trumpet and his parted white mustache, and everybody called him, "Joe, the Turk." He did not mind.

Ruined as a boot and shoe merchant in a small Turkish city by the Russo-Turkish War, he became a drifter, came to America, and wandered to the West Coast. There he trafficked in boots and shoes and beer, until the thump of an early Salvation Army band converted him to salvation. From then on he devoted himself to the Army, and when he died he was staff-captain, retired of that organization.

THE EVENING REVIEW (EAST LIVERPOOL, OH) SATURDAY, NOVEMBER 13, 1937

THE SUNLIT ROAD by Tom T. Jones

The recent death of Joseph Garabed, a staff-captain in The Salvation Army and better known perhaps as "Joe the Turk," which occurred in New York about a month ago, recalls a visit which he made to East Liverpool many years ago.

Captain Garabed was connected with The Salvation Army for about 38 years, according to his obituary in a recent issue of The War Cry, official organ of the organization in the United States. He traveled from coast to coast in the United States. He suffered indignities, was beaten, and imprisoned, but he adhered constantly to his faith.

It was many years ago that "Joe the Turk" made his visit to East Liverpool. He came to this city by boat, landing at the Broadway wharf. While the boat was being unloaded, Joe, a talented cornetist, climbed to the top of the pile of railroad ties along the riverbank and played a number of hymns. His concert was heard by many persons who had gathered at the wharf to greet him. He spent several days in East Liverpool during which he conducted services in The Salvation Army Citadel here.

Captain Garabed was born in Talas, Turkey, the son of Armenian parents. His father had been a priest and his mother a religious teacher. His father died when Joseph was but three years of age and his mother 11 years later. When he was 17[sic 14] years old Joseph went to Constantinople to start to work.

He had planned to become a shoemaker and was progressing nicely in this trade when Turkey went to war with Russia. He lost everything in this conflict. He decided to come to the United States, settling in San Francisco, where he worked for some time in the white lead mills. He then opened a cobbler's shop.

It was while he was thus working that he experienced conversion and enrolled as a soldier with The Salvation Army. His talents were soon realized, and it was not long until he entered evangelistic work. In an Illinois town, he is said to have driven the mayor and chief of police from the city and ran the municipality himself, until clean, honest officials were placed in charge. He was ofttimes referred to as the "Sanctified Salvationist Showman."

What The War Cry Had to Say

THE SALVATION ARMY WAR CRY/NOVEMBER 13, 1937

The Sanctified Salvationist Showman Gone to Heaven

Who is Staff-Captain Joseph Garabed? The answer is but a faint official echo. But mention "Joe the Turk," and the entire Salvation Army world recognizes a daring, extraordinary Salvationist - a man who has made thrilling Army history, a defender of the faith, a fighter for the ideals of the trip-colored flag, and an evangelist with methods bizarre, startling, and effective.

Among American Salvationists if it's "Joe," then it's "Joe the Turk." Joe has the color of the East, showmanship of the West, passion of the Latins, determination of the Scots, pertinacity of the Norseman, and enthusiasm of the Irish. Years ago, he bet his life on God in The Salvation Army, and from then on did and dared like few others for the salvation of men.

THE SALVATION ARMY WAR CRY / OCTOBER 1937 / A WARRIOR CROWNED

Impressive Funeral Service For Staff-Captain Joseph Garabed (R) "Joe the Turk," Conducted By Commissioner Damon in New York City.

It was a simple service as became a man of simple faith and simple beliefs. Staff-Captain Garabed (R), known to thousands of people in The United States as "Joe the Turk," was called to his eternal reward on Monday, October 11th, and on the following Wednesday morning, a large number of comrades and friends gathered in the New York Temple auditorium to pay their final tribute of esteem and respect to one of the most original and unique characters The Salvation Army has ever known.

Commissioner Alexander M Damon conducted the impressive service and spoke in affectionate remembrance of the life and service of the promoted warrior. "He was an amazing witness to a God who can break the strongest chains of sin," declared the Commissioner. "He triumphed because he lived with Jesus."

Commissioner Edward J Parker, the National Secretary, spoke of his personal contact through many years, with "Joe the Turk." Said the Commissioner, "He was a unique and forceful character whose boundless zeal caused him to break down all barriers for Jesus' sake and helped him to witness in a new way to the power of a living Christ."

The Chief Secretary, Colonel William C Arnold, conducted the opening exercises and Colonel Edward Underwood prayed. The Scriptures were read by Colonel William H Barrett, and Adjutant Evelyn Skinner soloed. Colonel William F Palmer closed in prayer.

The interment service at Kensico Cemetery was conducted by Colonel Barrett. Assisting in the service were Major N Erickson (P), Mr. H Wiseman, and Captain P Harvey, who sounded taps, thus closing a loving tribute to one of the most famous Salvation Army veterans.

The faithful and devoted nurse of Staff-Captain Garabed, Miss Susan Loyal, attended both services.

Order of Service
At the Funeral of
STAFF-CAPTAIN JOSEPH GARABED (R)
Wednesday, October 13, 1937
AT 10:30 am
Conducted by
COMMISSIONER
ALEXANDER M DAMON
New York Temple Corps Auditorium
120 West Fourteenth Street
New York City

Last Will and Testament

In his will, Joe left five hundred dollars to his nephew, Charles Abrahamson, and five hundred dollars to his niece, Selma Abrahamson, who lived in Grand Rapids, Michigan. To his sister Maritza, Joe left one thousand dollars, along with an additional fifteen dollars per month until her death.[390]

Everything else was left to The Salvation Army. Joe asked that half of the remainder be given to The Salvation Army Brooklyn Nursery and Infant's Hospital in Brooklyn, and the other half be given to The Salvation Army Cherry Street Slum Settlement at 94 Cherry Street, New York City.[391]

The sad reality is that when Joe died, he had no estate or money to leave his family or The Salvation Army, only private property and papers found inside his apartment. Those papers, along with his red and gold uniform, world-famous multicolored umbrella, and double-jointed cornet, were taken to the National Headquarters office and placed in the Army's museum. Today those items can be seen at the Heritage Center of The Salvation Army Eastern Territorial Headquarters in West Nyack, New York.

Chapter 12

Where is Joe?

When Joe was Promoted to Glory, he was buried in The Salvation Army section of the Kensico Cemetery, located in Valhalla, New York. Many American Salvation Army greats are buried there, including General Evangeline Booth, General Edward Higgins, Herbert Booth, Commissioner Samuel Logan Brengle, and Commandant Emma Westbrook.[392] All of these plots have large headstones, making it easy to find them. Although he had prepared a will, when Joe died in 1937, there were no funds to carry out his wishes, resulting in his burial in an unmarked grave.

In 1980, a group of Armenians who learned about the Salvation Army officer named Nishan Der Garabedian tried to find his gravesite at the cemetery but were unsuccessful. Approaching a groundskeeper, they inquired as to where Joe was buried. After some research, the groundskeeper located Joe's plot. It surprised the group to discover there was no tombstone or marker to signify the Salvation Army hero buried at that spot.[393]

The Armenians contacted The Salvation Army's Historical Center to ask why there was no monument honoring Nishan Der Garabedian and were told that because Joe had no money or family, they could find no one to fund a headstone.[394] It was

Joseph Garabed's grave in Valhalla, New York.

Joe's tombstone dedication in 1981. The Armenian Church paid for the stone and led the service. Photo courtesy of The Salvation Army National Archives.

explained that at the time he died, the Army did not possess funds to purchase headstones for officers who could not afford them. Daniel Bazikian, a member of the Armenian group, organized the Garabed Memorial Committee. He raised more than a thousand dollars from the Armenian community to pay for the headstone. The School for Officers Training in Suffern, New York received the money left over from the purchase of the headstone.[395]

On May 25, 1981, forty-three years after his interment, Joseph Garabed's tombstone was placed at the head of his grave, allowing everyone who came to Kensico to know his earthly place of rest.[396] The biographical sketch found in the program of dedication included these words:

> We meet here today, members of the Armenian Community
> and Salvation Army friends, to commemorate the life and
> service of Staff-Captain Joseph Garabed whose Armenian
> name was Nishan Der Garabedian. His long life was spent in
> seeking, by all means, to win men and women for Christ.

Deeply aware of his Armenian heritage, nevertheless he allowed himself to be known paradoxically as 'Joe the Turk' in the spirit of St. Paul, who declared, "I have become all things to all men that I might by all means save some."

Caught up in the bitter sorrows of the times in Armenia, he came to America around 1883, and eventually settled at the Barbary Coast of San Francisco. In that wild, notorious environment, through The Salvation Army, he met with Christ, became converted, left the old life, and spent the next fifty years in God's service as an Army officer.

Alone most of the time, and bearing his colorful umbrella covered with texts, his saxophone and trumpet, he marched the streets, held meetings, was ridiculed, beaten, stoned, and imprisoned. He never paid a fine for obstructing the streets, but served out his time again and again, winning the right, unchallenged today, to preach the gospel on the streets.

Untold numbers of men and women were led out of darkness into the light of Christ through his unwearied witness. He died alone in his small flat on New York's East Side in the Fall of 1937.

SERVANT OF GOD—WELL DONE!

Gone but Not Forgotten

The Armenian Reporter shared the exciting news about the service of dedication and celebration of Nishan Der Garabedian, an Armenian and Salvation Army hero:

> The dedication ceremony was an impressive one. Accompanied by a Salvation Army brass ensemble, those attending joined in singing 'Faith of Our Fathers.' Presenting the opening remarks, Colonel G Ernest Murray, The Salvation Army's National Chief

Secretary, said they had gathered to honor a dedicated Salvation Army officer and servant of God. Garabed, once a man of wicked, untempered habits, had been converted to Jesus Christ through the work of The Salvation Army in San Francisco. He was to labor diligently in its work during its trying early years. In those early days, Garabed and other Salvationists were often arrested for parading or holding meetings in the streets. Refusing to pay his fines out of principal, [sic] he spent many a night in jail, but through his persistence he helped The Salvation Army win the right to hold its Gospel meetings in public places. In his work, Garabed constantly sought to point his listeners to the saving power of Jesus Christ. The final inscription on his tombstone, 'Jesus is Mighty to Save,' is a fitting testimony to his faith.

Daniel Bazikian, the Chairman of the Garabed Memorial Committee, stated that they had gathered to honor a faithful servant of God. This gathering also afforded Armenians, however, an opportunity publicly to thank The Salvation Army for the help it had rendered in years past. In 1896, Bazikian pointed out, The Army had aided many Armenian refugees fleeing from the persecutions taking place in their homeland of Turkey.

Miss Aghavni Arsianian, Director of the Christian Education Department of the Prelacy, then led the Armenians present in singing the Hayr Mer, giving the audience a flavor of the Lord's Prayer in Kerapar, classical Armenian. Reverend Karl Avakian, pastor of the Armenian Presbyterian Church of Paramus, New Jersey, gave the prayer of dedication for the tombstone. He offered thanks to God for the life of a Christian servant like Joseph Garabed and called upon those of us today similarly to resolve to follow in the footsteps of Jesus Christ. He also asked God's continued blessings on The Salvation Army. Following his prayer, Paul Almoyan and Paul Vartanian, two members of the Sunday School of the Armenian Brethren Church (Weehawken, New Jersey) placed a beautiful cross-shaped floral arrangement on the tomb.

His Grace, Bishop Mesrob Ashjian, Prelate of the Armenian Apostolic Church of America, offered the final remarks. He compared Garabed's sufferings to those of St Paul, and pointed out to those present the late Captain's connection with the Armenian Apostolic Church. Captain Garabed's own father was a priest in the Armenian Church, and in his early years Garabed was influenced by its teachings. Early in its history, the Bishop pointed out, the Armenian Church was a missionary-minded Church, sending missionaries of the Gospel to different countries, perhaps even as far as Ireland. Through Garabed, the Armenian Church indirectly gave a modern-day missionary to America. The Bishop said he was honored, therefore, to come and take part in this service paying homage to this servant of God.

Those attending this ceremony found it to be a meaningful and moving experience. One suspects that Captain Garabed, though not present in body, felt much the same way. Looking on from the precincts of heaven, in the presence of the Savior he worshipped and served, he must have had a big Armenian smile on his face. After waiting all these years, we think he was entitled to it.[397]

The Salvation Army USA *War Cry*, March 18, 1995

FOR THE SAKE OF THE GOSPEL

by Major Gary Asperschlager

Joe the Turk wasn't a Turk at all. He was Armenian. I knew that all along, but the significance of his nickname and ethnic background escaped me until I attended a memorial service for Joe at New York's Kensico Cemetery.

While waiting for the service to begin, I began talking to an Armenian Orthodox minister. He was there to honor the memory of Joseph Garabed (Joe the Turk's real name) but narrowly missed being there in protest.

He explained to me the history of the Turks and Armenians and the tragic history of hatred between the two groups. Between 1894 and 1896, Turkish mobs massacred Armenians in a series of bloody conflicts. The worst was in 1895 when an estimated 80,000 Armenians were killed. The hatred between Armenians and Turks could be compared to the animosity between today's Bosnians, Serbs, and Croats.

After hearing his story, I began to understand why the minister might have come to protest an Armenian Salvationist being nicknamed "The Turk"! He had been infuriated by the insult to a fellow Armenian and planned to interrupt the service to make his point.

Everything changed, though, when he did a little research about Joe the Turk and his ministry. When he read of Joe's impact for the kingdom of God, the minister began to connect Joe's life with the Apostle Paul's words in 1 Corinthians: "Though I am free and belong to no man, I make myself a slave to everyone, to win as many as possible. To the Jews I became like a Jew, to win the Jews. To those under the law I became like those under the law (though I myself am not under the law) so as to win those under the law. To those not having the law I became like one not having the law (though I am not free from God's law, but am under Christ's law), so as to win those not having the law. To the weak I became weak, to win the weak. I have become all things to all men so that by all possible means I might save some. I do all this for the sake of the gospel, that I may share in its blessings" (1 Corinthians 9:19–23).

The minister understood the pain Joe must have felt when Americans with little historical understanding or sensitivity labeled him Joe the Turk. But instead of protesting, Joe used the mystery and color in the label to become an attention-getting oddity for the Lord. His love for the unsaved allowed him to use even a personal insult to reach others for Jesus.

After that experience in the cemetery, I developed a deeper interest in Joseph Garabed. I eventually spoke with the man who was assigned to go to Joe's apartment after his death and collect Salvation Army memorabilia for posterity.

"Was Joe really aware of all the problems in his native Armenia?" I asked. The man confirmed that he found many newspaper clippings about the massacres among Joe's personal belongings. He believed from the underlining and notes that Joe's own relatives had been killed.

The price for Joe's ministry was personal pain. But he was willing to be all things to all people so he could reach as many as possible for Jesus.

Are we as willing to follow in Paul's - and Joseph Garabed's—footsteps for the sake of the gospel?

EPILOGUE

The Salvation Army held a National Advisory Organizations Conference (NAOC) in Washington, D.C. in 1992. One highlight was a living Salvation Army history museum where people could walk through and experience major events of Salvation Army history. It took fifteen minutes to make the journey through the living exhibits. I received the task of preparing a monologue with music to entertain those who were outside of the exhibit waiting their turn to enter. Major Jake Tritton, then the Southern Territorial Youth Secretary, assigned me to portray Joe the Turk. This was a daunting task since I was nowhere near six feet tall or two hundred and fifty pounds!

I searched high and low for materials about Joe and found precious little. I was surprised to learn no one had ever authored a book about him, only an occasional article here and there. Nevertheless, I was able to present the very abbreviated version of Joe's story more than fifty times during the conference. Because it was lighthearted and had a song attached, it was given positive reviews. After the conference ended, I received numerous invitations to present the monologue at various Salvation Army gatherings.

From that point forward, I took every available opportunity to research the various archive centers of The Salvation Army in Alexandria, Virginia, and West Nyack, New York. In 2004, I was given the opportunity to expand the presentation to a more fully developed representation of Joe's life. The new fifty-minute presentation was unveiled in 2005. I have had the amazing blessing of sharing the story of Joseph Garabed across the United States, Canada, the United Kingdom, the Caribbean, and even South America. It has been my honor to tell his story to new generations and share the incredible contributions he made to The Salvation Army.

The original monologue ended with this song that summarized Joe's life in The Salvation Army. It remains the "closer" of the longer piece even today:

For Freedom!
Eddie Hobgood

1. Now listen to my story and boy is it a tale,
How stones were thrown, and mobs did try
Freedom of speech to quell.
I played my horn in jail was thrown,
And that seemed like the end.
But every time I was set free,
The Army given liberty,
To preach 'gainst Hell and sin!

Chorus:
For freedom! For freedom!
I won't give in 'til justice wins!
Proclaiming the Gospel
Declaring war on sin!

2. One time I was arrested
And thrown into the jail,
A drunken painter and his paints
Were placed inside my cell.
We painted on the walls all night,
"Remember Mother's Prayers", "Get Right!"
The judge was called to see the walls.
He read them and he joined the Cause.
He's in the Army band!

Chorus:
He's marching for freedom!
He's fighting for the King of Kings!
No longer in bondage,
Freedom's sweet song he sings!

3. A desperado gang,
Had taken over the whole town.
The mayor and his outlaws
Tried to put the people down.

They jailed the Captain and his wife,
Then I came on the scene.
The people rallied by my side.
The mayor became petrified.
The outlaws had to flee!

Bridge:
They made me mayor for five weeks!
The Captain was selected ... Chief of Police!

4. And that just goes to show you
What we all know too well
A fool for Jesus is no fool
He's saved from death and Hell!
My hat, my horn, my uniform
Are just a ploy to get,
The dull of sight to see the Light,
The hard of head to hear what's right.
Besides ... I like to dress this way!

For freedom! For freedom!
I won't give in 'til justice wins!
Proclaiming the Gospel
Declaring war on sin!
Proclaiming the Gospel
Declaring war on sin!
Hey!

The monologue's original costume was based on a limited-edition porcelain figurine created in 1991. When the longer piece was being prepared, I decided to look at all his uniform incarnations and recreate two of them as closely as possible. A new song was added to the presentation as an opener, giving the audience a little taste of what was to come.

The Sanctified Salvationist Showman!
Eddie Hobgood

Gather round! Gather round! Gather round!
Gather round! Gather round!
The Sanctified, Salvationist, Showman is in town!

1. You don't know me. You don't know me very well,
But we're going to be very good friends I can tell!
I can see you looking at how I am dressed,
And I can tell that, Oh, I can tell that you're impressed!
My name is Joseph. Joe the Turk is my name!
And my methods drive some people quite insane!
But hear my story, oh, and do not misconstrue,
'Cause it's a story, and every word of it is true!
(Well, most of it! So, go ahead and sue me, okay!)

2. I have traveled this entire country wide
And told of Jesus, how He lived and loved and died,
For all the people, He has come to set them free,
Free from sin and death and pain and poverty!
And I have told this, told this story true and plain,
Even when there were those who sought to cause me pain.
For I have boldly told the truth and it prevailed
Although sometimes, it landed me in jail!
(But I always got out! So, stick that in your pipe and smoke it!)

3. They tried to hang me, tried to hang me from a tree
Because I spoke out, spoke against iniquity.
I preached the gospel, preached it in the open-air
And blew my cornet, blew my cornet loud and clear.
Some came to Jesus, and to them He gave new life.
While there were others, who tried to stab me with a knife!
But I kept preaching and declaring God's own Truth,
And those who fought me, found themselves with one less tooth!
(Well, most of them did not have all of their teeth to begin with!
You know what I am saying?! I think you do!)

The Sanctified Salvationist Showman is in town.
The stories I could tell you are certain to astound!
To many people I seem quite undignified.
They look and stare and sometimes appear mystified.
But that's all part of my great plan,
To spread the Truth throughout the land.
And even if it costs me dearly,
I'll preach and play, because quite sincerely,
It doesn't matter what they try do to me,
As long as I can dress fashionably!
(I look good, don't I? Come on, tell the truth, and shame the devil!)

Gather round! Gather round! Gather round!
Gather round! Gather round!
The Sanctified Salvationist, Sanctified
Salvationist, Sanctified Salvationist
Showman is in town!
The Sanctified Salvationist Showman is in town. Hey!

In addition to the amazing and often funny accounts of Joe's officership, it was important to share his evangelistic heart. A profoundly serious moment in the presentation, culled from various stories and words of Joe, is a challenge to the audience and gives context to Joe's passion and zeal for the gospel. This grounds the piece and makes it far more than a show. Often, the presentation pauses at this point. The audience is asked to personally consider the words Joe has just uttered. They are invited to pray or come forward and kneel should they feel the leading of the Holy Spirit to do so.

Joe's Sermon

From "The Sanctified Salvationist Showman"

I remember one time I was in Colorado Springs, Colorado, and the word on the street was, there was going to be a hanging, and the person being hanged … was me! The Salvationists all said, "Joseph, quick, quick, get out of town before they find you and string you up." "No," I said, "I am not going to run away. I have never been afraid of dying for my faith. Even today, I consider it the highest honor to be thought worthy to suffer for my Lord and Master, Jesus … even to die for Him! When I stop, and I consider the incredible pain and agony that Jesus suffered for me, what is a bruise or a broken bone? What is being stabbed or even shot at? No, I count it all joy to suffer for Him who gave His life for me, and if through my pain, one more person comes to know Jesus Christ as Lord, then everything, everything that has happened to me has been more than worth it.

But I must give you one confession. And that is, there are many days when I am concerned there will come a time in The Salvation Army when officers and soldiers will choose the easier path. They will be afraid of pain. They will be afraid of persecution. They will be afraid of public opinion and will cease to fight. (Holds up the torn and ragged Salvation Army flag) Do you know, do you know what this flag represents? Do you know the number of men and women who have fought beneath this banner and given life and limb to declare its message? O comrades, the world despised our Lord and Master, Jesus. Does it surprise you that the world would despise you as well? Yes, it is easier to retreat; yes, it is easier to blend in with the crowd and to maintain the status quo, but that is not what a soldier is called to do. A soldier is called to fight!

I remember hearing General William Booth speak one time at a great music festival in Madison Square Garden, New York, and he said, "If you are only willing to play your horn in a chapel, you dishonor your heritage." Now, the point is quite clear and has very little to do with music. However, Salvationist musician, if you would only play your instrument for the glory of God in the Army hall and you will not play for his glory in the street, in the open air, in the hard and difficult places, you dishonor your heritage. Salvationist singer, if you would only sing the praises of Heaven in the Army hall and will not sing those praises at home or work or school, in the hard and difficult places, then you dishonor your heritage. If you would only stand up in the Army hall and give your testimony of what Jesus Christ has done in your heart and your life, and you would not give that same testimony to family, to friends, to strangers on the street, in the hard and difficult places, Salvationist, oh, Salvationist, you dishonor your heritage.

Precious blood was spilled to give you the right to proclaim the praises of Him who called you out of darkness into His marvelous light. Will you content yourselves to sit within the four walls of a chapel while countless men, women, boys, and girls die every single day and go into eternity without ever hearing the Good News of Jesus Christ?

If you would honor your heritage, this blood-bought heritage, then you must no longer be silent; you must use every means, every method, every opportunity to declare the Truth of God to this generation.

This is the banner under which I have fought from the very beginning. I have seen brothers and sisters die for what this flag represents. Oh, comrades, I fear the day will come when the flag of The Salvation Army will be nothing, nothing more than a decoration on a table. I fear the day will come when the uniform will be nothing more than a costume on a stage. I fear the day will come when sin will no longer break our hearts, and the deep longing and desire to see the world won to God will no longer burn deep within us.

Oh, God, please never let Your Salvation Army stray from the mission to which You have called it … to win the World for God and to declare the Good News of Jesus Christ, regardless of the cost!

Oh, I know the fighting is hard and that there are days you want to throw up your hands and quit. Oh, but do not quit. For you see, you have been called, you have been chosen to take this banner and everything that it represents to the front lines of the battle and fight. If not you, then who?

There are many days when I stop and ask myself, "Who? Who, when my time is over and my race has been run, who will rise up and take my place?" Is there one who would say, "I will take this banner and everything that it represents— the Blood of Jesus Christ, the Fire of the Holy Spirit, the Purity of God—take this banner to the front lines of the battle and I will fight!" Is there one who would say, "I will carry the light into the dark places!" Is there one who would have the courage to say, "I care not for life nor limb, only that the world would know Jesus is Mighty to Save! "Is there one who would make the prayer of their heart the words of our dear, precious General William Booth who said, "As long as there remains one dark soul without the light of God, I'll fight! I'll fight to the very end!"

O Lord, may we faithful, valiant soldiers of the cross of Jesus Christ be! Amen. Amen and Amen.

Note: The full presentation can be found on YouTube at https://www.youtube.com/watch?v=v94qB2qimgY or at www.tsamusicals.org.

One Final Note

What has sharing Joe's story meant to me? The obvious answer is that had the Army not been born in the streets, and up until the latter part of the last century, continued to celebrate that by "bringing the Church to the people," I would not have found the Army and most assuredly not found salvation. I attended a church that I was not happy in; it was stiff and formal, and very judgmental. And, because of great dysfunction in my family, I definitely did not fit in. Nobody at home forced me to go, and because of that, I was ready to give up on church.

When the Army marched into my neighborhood, I thought the circus had come to town. There was a group of military-looking people on the street corner. One lady was playing an accordion. A gentleman was playing a cornet and another one, beating a big bass drum. There was this other lady who was singing to the top of her lungs, "Have you been to Jesus for the cleansing power? Are you washed in the Blood of the Lamb?" In that moment, I knew I had found my people … or rather, they had found me. There was nothing stiff or formal about them; they were the real deal! They didn't care about my family's dysfunction. In this mess of a kid, they looked past everything that nobody else seemed to care to look past; they saw me, a precious child of God, and became my family and my refuge from all the dysfunction in my life. Eventually, my parents were saved at The Salvation Army, and I believe with all my heart they are in heaven today. My life has been so full and rich, and I have had experiences as a Salvation Army officer that I never dared to dream as a child could be possible. God is faithful. And while this might seem like a bit of a stretch, Joe's faithfulness in proclaiming the Good News of Jesus across the country and winning the right for the Army to hold those street corner services, saved me. For thirty-eight years of Salvation Army officership, the truth is, The Salvation Army owes me nothing. I owe it and God everything. Thank you, Nishan Der Garabedian! Thank you, Salvation Army!

One of the many things I love about the early Army was its full embrace of innovation and creativity. If we, the Army, are not careful, we will regulate innovation and creativity right out of the organization, and we will cease to be a movement and become a museum. Leaders, encourage those under your guidance to be creative and innovative. Make sure they think their ideas through, but please don't let your automatic response be no to something we perhaps haven't done before. If the initial idea isn't there just yet, tell them how they can get to "Yes."

Our world is dealing with problems and issues that didn't even exist in 1865 when our organization started. Charge the young, bright minds that are a part of our movement to dream big, and seek God for fresh new ways to serve. The bottom line is the world needs Jesus, and we cannot shrink from declaring that message. No one expects you to go to jail today for your faith, but too few of us are unwilling to go across the street to share God's love. Let this biography bless you, move you, but most importantly, challenge you to intentionally use your giftings and abilities to tell men and women, boys and girls, about Jesus.

APPENDIX

IMPORTANT DATES AND EVENTS

Date	Event
January 14, 1860	Joe is born in Talas, Turkey of Armenian heritage.
1863	Joe's father, an Armenian priest, dies.
1874	Joe's mother dies in Talas. He moves in with his aunt for a few months and then to Constantinople with one of his brothers.
1877	At the beginning of the Russo-Turkish War, he flees Turkey for Tiflis, Russia (modern-day Tbilisi, Georgia) and lives in an Armenian refugee settlement.
1881	Joe returns to Constantinople for a brief period.
September 1881	Joe takes a ship bound for the United States but has an eight-day layover after missing his connecting ship; he encounters The Salvation Army for the first time.
October 1881	Joe arrives in New York City, then goes to Worcester, MA to live with his brother Simon for a little over a year. After, he begins working his way westward.
November 1882	Joe arrives in San Francisco.
July 1883	The Salvation Army arrives in San Francisco.

June 1884	Joe is converted at The Salvation Army San Francisco #1 Corps.
November 1886	Joe becomes a sergeant at the San Francisco #1 Corps.
April 24, 1887	Joe becomes a cadet.
May 1887	Joe is sent to assist Captain George Rutherford in opening a new corps in Los Angeles as part of his continuing field training.
July 6, 1887	Joe is sent to San Bernardino, CA for a short field training assignment.
July 24, 1887	Joe is sent to Santa Ana, CA to open a new corps—continued field training.
September 15, 1887	Joe is sent to Pomona, CA for continued field training.
October 1, 1887	Joe is sent to San Bernardino, CA and promoted to the rank of lieutenant.
February 4, 1888	Joe is sent to San Francisco #2 Corps as assistant officer and member of the training garrison staff.
March 17, 1888	Joe is appointed to the Sacramento, CA corps.
July 10, 1888	Joe returns to San Francisco Training Garrison.
Aug/Sept/Oct 1888	Joe is appointed as a member of the Summer Campaign Brigade and travels the west coast.
November 1888	Joe returns to San Francisco #2 Corps.
January 1889	Joe is sent to Petaluma, CA as assistant officer.

February 1889	Joe is seconded to the "HQ Warriors" and travels with them through the end of the year.
January 1, 1890	Joe is appointed as a traveling special to the Northwest California division.
April 1, 1890	Joe is appointed to the Northwestern division in Chicago, IL as a traveling special and promoted to rank of captain.
September 1, 1890	Joe is appointed to National Headquarters (New York City) as national traveling special.
April 17, 1891	Joe is naturalized as a citizen of the United States (as per his passport application).
September 1896	Joe is promoted to the rank of ensign and given an additional appointment as trade department special.
December 27, 1900	Joe is promoted to adjutant.
February 8, 1906	Joe is promoted to staff-captain.
November 1918	Joe is admitted to the Order of Long Service.
January 14, 1925	Joe retires from active Salvation Army service.
October 11, 1937	Joe is Promoted to Glory from his apartment in New York, NY at the age of 77.

Joe's Fifty-Two Arrests

The actual number of times Joe spent in jail is not known. Because his imprisonments were so frequent in his early days in San Francisco, they were not recorded in the Pacific Coast Division *War Cry*. Joe claimed fifty-two arrests on his publicity poster, and the fifty-two arrests have been verified. The first arrest occurred when Joe was a cadet, and is included because, while not yet an officer, he was acting in an official capacity on behalf of The Salvation Army Pacific Coast Division.

"The brickbats and stones would fly and often I was arrested."

#	Location	Date	Description
1	Los Angeles, CA	Apr. 1887	**Reported by *The Boston Post*, Boston, MA, December 9, 1923.** Arrested for playing his cornet and converted thirty men in jail. He was released by the judge at trial. (See: "Chapter 5: Arrested Developments.")
2	San Bernardino, CA	Jan. 1888	**Reported by the Pacific Coast *War Cry* and *San Bernardino Times*, January 15, 1888.** Arrested for ejecting a troublemaker from the meeting. Joe was charged with assault and battery. At the trial, the case was dismissed.
3	San Francisco, CA	1888	**Reported by the Pacific Coast *War Cry*, May 24, 1888, and July 1, 1888.** The police marched San Francisco's training garrison and soldiers led by Lt. Joe, who was playing his cornet, to the police station where they were arrested. The case was dismissed the next day.

4	San Francisco, CA	1888	**Reported by the Pacific Coast *War Cry*, July 1, 1888, and May 26, 1888).** Lt. Joe and the cadets were arrested again for marching in the streets; the case went to trial for a second time and again, they were released. (See: "Chapter 5: Arrested Developments.")
5	Petaluma, CA	1889	**Reported by *The Petaluma Daily Morning*, Petaluma, CA, January 25, 1902.** *The Petaluma Daily Morning* reported Joe was arrested in Petaluma when he was stationed there. Joe had not begun writing his travelogue, which explains why it was not listed prior to this news article.
6	East Portland, OR	Oct. 1889	**Reported by the Pacific Coast *War Cry*, October 15, 1889, and November 1, 1889.** (See: "Chapter 5: Arrested Developments.")
7	Portland, OR	Jan. 1890	**Reported by the Pacific Coast Division *War Cry*, January 4, 1890, and January 11, 1890.** (See: "Chapter 5: Arrested Developments.")
8	Portland, OR	Jan. 1890	**Reported January 11, 1890.** (See: "Chapter 5: Arrested Developments.")
9	Los Angeles, CA	Apr. 1890	**Reported by the *Los Angeles Times*, April 18, 1890.** Arrested for disturbing the peace and released on the promise they would not do it again.

10	Los Angeles, CA	Apr. 1890	**Reported by the *Los Angeles Times*, April 19, 1890.** The group went out the next night and was arrested again. The case was dismissed the next day.
11	Madison, WI	May 1891	**Reported by the *Oshkosh Daily Northwestern*, May 13, 1891, and *The Weekly Wisconsin*, May 23, 1891.** The following day Joe was found guilty at court and given fifteen days in jail. His original sentence was ten days, but when he shouted, "Amen," the judge added five more days. He was also fined five dollars plus costs for disorderly conduct. He was in jail nearly one week when he was released on bail, his fine paid by a friend of the Army.
12	Madison, WI	Jun. 6, 1891	**Reported by the American *War Cry*, June 6, 1891.** After being assaulted by an undercover policeman, Joe was told to report to the courthouse the following morning. He did and was placed under arrest. He was taken to the jail and bailed out by a friend of the Army.
13	Northfield, MN	Jun. 1891	**Reported by *The Bismarck Weekly Tribune*, Bismarck, North Dakota, July 3, 1891.** Arrested for parading and disturbing the peace. He was held in jail until the trial, where he was found guilty, but refused to pay the fine. A member of the community paid the fine on his behalf and Joe was released. He marched again but was not arrested the second time.

14	Chicago, IL #9 Corps	Aug. 1891	**Reported by the American *War Cry*, August 29, 1891.** Joe and several others in the open-air meeting were on their knees praying when suddenly, they were forcibly seized by eight policemen and placed inside the patrol wagon. There was no warrant nor were they given due process. They were taken to jail where they were kept overnight. With no bed or pillows, they laid on the floor, but were soon overwhelmed by bed bugs. They spent the rest of the night painting signs on the walls such as, "Jesus will save," and "Eternity; where will you spend it?" The next morning, the police inspector admitted the arrest had been a mistake and let them go.
15	Portage, WI	Mar. 1893	**Reported by *The Wisconsin State Register*, March 25, 1893, and the American *War Cry*, March 25, 1893.** Joe was sentenced to a term of imprisonment for twenty days. His crime was blowing his cornet in the street. The Supreme Court ruled in favor of Joe and the Army. (See: "Chapter 5: Arrested Developments.")
16	Saratoga, NY	Jul. 1893	**Reported by *Poughkeepsie Eagle-News*, Poughkeepsie, NY, July 14, 1893.** On July 7, Joe was convicted of violating the ordinance against holding street meetings and fined fifteen dollars. A friend of the Army paid his bail. (See: "Chapter 5: Arrested Developments.")

17	Saratoga, NY	Jul. 1893	**Reported by *Poughkeepsie Eagle-News*, Poughkeepsie, NY, July 14, 1893.** Two nights later, Joe and two others were arrested for marching and playing instruments in the open-air but were immediately bailed out. (See: "Chapter 5: Arrested Developments.")
18	Saratoga, NY	Jul. 1893	**Reported by the American *War Cry*, September 9, 1893.** Joe and others were arrested a third time and had to sleep in cells covered with bedbugs. They were found guilty, but someone paid bail. The case was appealed to a higher court. (See: "Chapter 5: Arrested Developments.")
19	Binghamton, NY	Jul. 1893	**Reported by the American *War Cry*, July 22, 1893.** Arrested for stopping on the street for two minutes. Joe was released and the Army was given the right to march.
20	Lewiston, ME	Dec. 1893	**Reported by the American *War Cry*, December 30, 1893.** Arrested for stopping too long on the street and obstructing traffic. Witnesses testified that traffic was actually stopped by the rowdy mob throwing snowballs and rocks at the Salvationists. The case was dismissed.
21	Lowell, MA	Feb. 1894	**Reported by *The Lowell Sun*, Lowell, MA, February 5, 1894.** Joe was arrested on February 4 and carried off in a patrol wagon because he was leading the open-air meeting. (See: "Chapter 5: Arrested Developments".)

22	Salem, OH	Apr. 1894	**Reported by *Salem Daily News*, Salem, OH, April 12, 1894.** Joe was locked up for playing his horn in the street on April 11. When he was placed in jail, he played on his cornet, "The Star-Spangled Banner" through a window. A crowd of people gathered to demonstrate against his arrest. The outcome of the case is not listed, but it is assumed the charges were dropped as Joe made his next appointment.
23	Youngstown, OH	May 1894	**Reported by the American *War Cry*, March 12, 1894, and March 19, 1894.** Joe was arrested for obstructing the sidewalk while conducting an open-air meeting. At trial the case was dismissed when it was discovered Joe had not been standing on the sidewalk, thus not breaking the law.
24	Elgin, IL	Jul. 1894	**Reported by the American *War Cry*, July 7, 1894.** Joe and a corps officer, Captain Corliss, were arrested on a violation of city ordinance forbidding music in the square. A friend of the Army posted bail.
25	Elgin, IL	Jul. 1894	**Reported by the American *War Cry*, July 7, 1894, and July 14, 1894.** Joe decided to play his cornet as they marched back to the hall from jail and was quickly arrested again; the same man as before posted his bail.

26	Madison, WI	Aug. 1894	**Reported by *The Evening News*, Wilkes-Barre, PA, August 28, 1911, and the American *War Cry*, September 15, 1894.** Arrested by chief of police for sidewalk obstruction. The fine was paid by an interested citizen, and Joe was released.
27	Madison, WI	Aug. 1894	**Reported by the American *War Cry*, September 15, 1894.** Arrested again on the same charge of obstructing the sidewalk. The fine was paid by an interested citizen, and Joe was released.
28	Colorado Spring, CO	Jun. 1895	**Reported by *The Salt Lake Tribune*, Salt Lake City, UT, June 15, 1895, and the American *War Cry*, July 27, 1895.** Joe and the captain were arrested for obstruction of streets. The captain was found guilty and fined ten dollars. (See: "Chapter 5: Arrested Developments.")
29	Colorado Spring, CO	Jun. 1895	**Reported by *The Salt Lake Tribune*, Salt Lake City, UT, June 15, 1895, and the American *War Cry*, July 27, 1895.** Arrested during a Sunday morning open-air. He played "Whiter Than the Snow" on the way to jail. (See: "Chapter 5: Arrested Developments.")
30	Colorado Spring, CO	Jun. 1895	**Reported by *The Salt Lake Tribune*, Salt Lake City, UT, June 15, 1895, and the American *War Cry*, July 27, 1895.** Arrested with officer for a third time on Sunday night in the open-air. (See: "Chapter 5: Arrested Developments.")

31	Colorado Spring, CO	Jun. 1895	**Reported by *The Salt Lake Tribune*, Salt Lake City, UT, June 15, 1895, and the American *War Cry*, July 27, 1895.** Arrested a fourth time for playing in the open-air. (See: "Chapter 5: Arrested Developments.")
32	Colorado Spring, CO	Jun. 1895	**Reported by *The Salt Lake Tribune*, Salt Lake City, UT, June 15, 1895, and the American *War Cry*, July 27, 1895.** Arrested a fifth time for playing in the open-air. The judge ruled in Joe's favor and all five Colorado Springs cases were dismissed. (See: "Chapter 5: Arrested Developments.")
33	Nebraska City, NE	Jul. 1895	**Reported by the *Omaha Daily Bee*, Omaha, NE, July 30, 1895.** Joe and the captain were arrested for obstructing the street, had trial, and were released. The fire department turned the hoses on the Salvationists, including elderly women and babies. There was public outcry in the local papers and a demand to stop treating the Army in this manner. The case was dismissed.
34	Malden, MA	Mar. 1896	**Reported by *The Boston Post*, Boston, MA, March 31, 1896, and April 4, 1896.** Joe and twelve Salvationists were arrested for marching and beating the bass drum. (See: "Introduction" and "Chapter 5: Arrested Developments.")
35	Malden, MA	Apr. 1896	**Reported by the American *War Cry*, May 2, 1896.** Fifteen Salvationists were arrested the second night. (See: "Introduction" and "Chapter 5: Arrested Developments.")

36	Boston #5—Jamaica Plains	Jun. 1896	**Reported by the American *War Cry*, June 27, 1896.** Police grabbed Joe by the collar and physically moved him off the street. The next day he received a warrant for his arrest. The following night he was arrested and carted off to jail while playing "Shout Aloud Salvation." In the jail cell, Joe wrote on the walls, "Jesus is Mighty to Save." His umbrella was stolen while in court. He was released after three hours.
37	Greenport, Long Island, NY	Nov. 1896	**Reported by the *Brooklyn Daily Eagle*, Brooklyn, NY, November 9, 1896, and November 24, 1896.** Arrested twice in twenty-four hours for holding service in the street and gathering a crowd. The president of the Village Board of Trustees appeared at the trial and ordered the police officer to withdraw his charge; Joe was released.
38	Greenport, Long Island, NY	Nov. 1896	**Reported by the *Brooklyn Daily Eagle*, Brooklyn, NY, November 27, 1896, and the American *War Cry*, January 2, 1897.** Joe went back out to the open-air with a permit the next day, but it was ignored. He was arrested and released again without a fine when it was discovered he had a permit.
39	Greenport, Long Island, NY	Oct. 1898	**Reported by the American *War Cry*, January 2, 1897.** After the corps building was burned to the ground by arsonists, Joe went out on the march and was arrested a third time. The city decided not to prosecute the case as it would look like the Salvationists were being persecuted.

40	Wilkes-Barre, PA	Oct. 1898	**Reported by *Wilkes-Barre Times Leader*, Wilkes-Barre, PA, October 21, 1898.** Arrested for blowing his horn and disturbing the peace. (See: "Chapter 5: Arrested Developments.")
41	Wilkes-Barre, PA	Oct. 1898	**Reported by the *Sunday News*, Wilkes-Barre, PA, October 23, 1898.** Arrested for scaring a mailman's horse and causing it to bolt. It was not the first time it had happened. (See: "Chapter 5: Arrested Developments.")
42	Wilkes-Barre, PA	Oct. 1898	**Reported by the *Wilkes-Barre Record*, Wilkes-Barre, PA, October 28, 1898.** Arrested for a third time and tried to set it up as a test case in the courts. (See: "Chapter 5: Arrested Developments.")
43	Dixon, IL	May 1899	**Reported by the *Dixon Evening Telegraph*, Dixon, IL, May 12, 1899.** Joe was asked to move from the street, refused, and was arrested. To show solidarity with Joe, the entire group of Salvationists refused to leave the open-air spot and were arrested, too. The case was withdrawn.
44	Constantinople, Turkey	Sep. 1899	**Reported by the *Evening Star*, Washington, D.C., October 24, 1899, and numerous papers across the US.** Joe had his passport taken and was placed in jail shortly after arrival. The American Consul told him to leave the country, or he'd be placed in an American jail until they could ship him back home. The *Wilkes-Barre Daily Times* came to his defense.

45	Hyde Park, MA	Oct. 1900	**Reported by the American *War Cry*, October 13, 1900.** The captain was playing the drum, and Joe his cornet, when a group of policemen came up, grabbed them, and took them off to jail. The next day at trial, Joe pled his case and the judge let him go.
46	New York, NY	Dec. 19, 1900	**Reported by the American *War Cry*, January 12, 1901.** Joe was arrested for collecting donations dressed as Santa Claus. He was taken to jail but released by the chief when they discovered he was raising funds for the Great Christmas Dinner.
47	San Jose, CA	Dec. 1901	**Reported by the *Evening Sentinel*, Santa Cruz, CA, December 10, 1901.** While Joe and the corps members were in the open-air, one of the policemen arrested him. The corps officer was also arrested, and the duo was told to report to court on Monday for their trial. When they arrived, the judge told them there was no case and they were dismissed.
48	San Jose, CA	Feb. 1902	**Reported by the American *War Cry*, February 15, 1902.** The next night they marched to the open-air, and while they were praying, the police arrested the whole crowd. They kept the women in jail until 9 p.m. and the men all night. At the trial, they were found not guilty. The judge did not like the decision and sent the jury out again; they returned with a guilty verdict. The case was appealed to the State Supreme Court but was not mentioned again.

49	Albany, NY	Apr. 1906	**Reported by the American *War Cry*, April 1906.** A police officer in civilian clothing rushed into the open-air ring and demanded that Joe move on. Joe hesitated, but then stepped up on a chair to let the group know they were moving. The officer roughly grabbed him, shoved him off the chair, and knocked his cornet and music books into the mud. He then lifted his walking cane over Joe and threatened to smash his head. Joe was dragged to jail but was bailed out. At the trial, the case was dismissed.
50	Stamford, CT	Jun. 1909	**Reported by the American *War Cry*, June 1909, and *The New York Times*, New York, NY, June 13 and 14, 1909.** Joe, along with the officers and soldiers, was arrested for beating the drum and blowing the cornet at an open-air meeting. After being in jail for several hours, he and the others were released. They marched again but were not arrested the second time.
51	Auburn, NY	Jul. 1911	**Reported by the American *War Cry*, July 1911.** Joe was arrested for playing his horn in the street. He was placed in a cell filled with bedbugs. At his trial, the jury could not come up with a verdict. He was sent back to jail and a new trial began the next day. The case was dismissed, as the court felt he had suffered enough the two nights in jail.

52	Athol, MA	Dec. 1917	**Reported by the American *War Cry*, December 1917.** While Joe was holding an open-air meeting, the chief of police clutched him in a brutal manner and walked him off to the police station. After being detained for an hour, he was bailed out by the corps sergeant major. The case was dismissed; the judge also told the chief of police to protect the Salvationists and help them find a good open-air spot.

A Sampler of Songs from Joe's Songbook

The Miner's Song
Tune: "Home, Sweet Home"

1. The hard-working miners, their dangers are great,
And many while working have met their sad fate.
While doing their duty as all miners do,
Shut out from the daylight and darling ones, too.

Chorus
The miner is gone, we will see him no more,
God be with the miners wherever they go.
Oh, may they be ready their call to obey,
Looking unto Jesus, the only true way.

2. He was only a miner killed under the ground,
Only a miner and one more is gone.
Just why he was taken, no one can ever tell,
His mining is over; poor miner, farewell.

3. He leaves a companion and little ones, too,
To earn them a living as all miners, do.
And while he was working for those of his love,
The boulder that crushed him fell down from above.

4. With hearts full of sadness we bid him farewell,
How soon we may follow nobody can tell.
God pity the miners, protect them from harm,
Shield them from all danger with Thy dear strong arm.

Only a Tramp

1. Only a tramp, the night watchman said,
Spurning the form of a body found dead;
Yes, only a tramp the rabble replied,
The coroner said of starvation he died.

Chorus
He's somebody's darling, some mother's son;
Once he was pure; yes, once he was young;
Yes, somebody rocked him a baby to sleep,
Now, he's only a tramp found dead on the street.

2. Only a tramp in the moonbeam's pale light,
With plenty around, he starved last night.
Who closed the door and turned him away,
God will deny some bitter cold day.

3. If Jesus should come and ask at your door
A place to sleep and food from your store,
As once He wandered in poverty's stamp,
Would you turn Him away as only a tramp?

I'm Most Highly Connected
Tune: "The Devil's No Relation at All"

1. I once was badly connected,
I belonged to the family down below,
The devil, too, was my master,
And where he led me there I had to go.
But it's different now, Hallelujah!
A blessed, blessed change to me is given;
I'm now most highly connected,
I belong to the family up in Heaven.

Chorus
Oh! Glory hallelujah! My soul is full of joy,
I'd have you to know it one and all, one and all.
For God is now my Father and Jesus is my Savior,
The devil's no relation at all, none at all,
The devil's no relation at all.

2. I oft look back and wonder
How such a change as this could ever be,
That I, so bound by old Satan,
Could have gained such a blessed liberty.
But it is so, hallelujah! My many sins they are gone;
The devil never more can harm me,
To the family up in Heaven I belong.

3. Should you ever take a ship for Glory,
I tell you what it's likely you will see;
The angels there are quite busy,
Building up a glorious home there for me.
I'm the King's own son, hallelujah!
And very soon He'll summon me away,
To have the rule of a kingdom
In that land that is fairer than the day.

Jim and Me
Tune: "Palms of Victory"

1. The story, sir? Why, really now,
    I haven't much to say;
    If you had called a year ago,
    And then again today,
    No need of any words to tell,
    For your own eyes could see
    Just what God and The Army
    Have done for Jim and me.

2. A year ago I hadn't flour,
    To make a loaf of bread,
    And many a night the little ones
    Went hungry to their bed.
    Just peep into the closet, sir,
    There's sugar, and bread, and tea,
    That's what God and The Army
    Have done for Jim and me.

3. The pail that holds the milk, sir,
    He used to fill with beer;
    He hasn't paid a cent for drink,
    For now, almost a year.
    He pays his debts, he's well and strong,
    He's kind as kind can be;
    That's what God and The Army
    Have done for Jim and me.

4. He used to sneak along the street,
    Feeling so mean and low,
    He looks the world now in the face,
    He steps off bold and free,
    That's what God and The Army
    Have done for Jim and me.

5. Oh, yes, the sad, sad time is past,
   The sorrow and the pain;
   My boy has got his father back,
   And I my man again.
   Do not mind my crying, sir,
   It's just for joy, you see,
   All that God and The Army
   Have done for Jim and me.

6. And mornings when he's gone to work,
   I kneel right down and pray;
   "Father in Heaven, help dear Jim,
   And keep him saved today."
   And every night, before we sleep,
   Thank God on bended knee,
   For what He and Thy Army
   Have done for Jim and me.

Tell Mother I'll be There

1. When I was but a little child,
How well I recollect,
How I would grieve my mother
With my folly and neglect;
And now that she has gone to Heaven,
I'll miss her tender care;
O angels, tell my mother I'll be there!

Chorus
Tell mother I'll be there,
In answer to her prayer;
This message, guardian angels to her bear;
Tell mother I'll be there,
Heaven's joy with her to share;
Yes, tell my darling mother I'll be there!

2. Though I was often wayward,
She was always kind and good –
So patient, gentle, loving,
When I acted rough and rude;
My childhood griefs and sorrows
She would gladly with me share;
O angels, tell my mother I'll be there!

3. When I became a prodigal,
And left the old roof-tree,
She almost broke her loving heart,
In mourning after me;
And day and night she prayed to God,
To take me to His care;
O angels, tell my mother I'll be there!

4. One day a message came to me,
It bade me quickly come,
If I would see my mother,
Ere the Savior took her home;
I promised her before she died,
For Heaven I would prepare;
O angels, tell my mother I'll be there!

THE SALVATION ARMY AND THE ARMENIAN QUESTION

The Salvation Army has historically advocated for those who could not speak or act for themselves. It significantly contributed to raising the age of consent in the United Kingdom and revolutionized the match-making industry by creating a safer method of match production. The Army rescued and continues to rescue people who find themselves trapped in human trafficking. It continues to be a champion for the underdog.

In 1895, the Army played a major role in helping a people group who found themselves on the brink of annihilation. General William Booth called on the worldwide Salvation Army to intervene in the tragic events taking place in Turkey against the Armenian population. Salvationists in Europe were some of the first to receive and assist the refugees. North America was not far behind. In New York City, National Headquarters advocated on behalf of refugees detained at Ellis Island. The United States government would not allow Armenian asylum-seekers to enter the country if they had no family, friends, funds, or jobs. It was genuinely possible that those who experienced unfathomable horrors would be deported back to Turkey and face certain death. When the refugees were finally released, the Army was integral in finding homes and providing practical training for their new life in America.

What follows are excerpts from actual Salvation Army American *War Cry* articles of the Army's involvement and intervention in this humanitarian crisis.

The Salvation Army American *War Cry*/February 9, 1895

"The Armenian Massacre and its Lessons"

Viewed from any standpoint you may choose whether religious, moral, or humanitarian, the recent massacre of several thousands of Armenian Christians, cannot help but produce feelings of sympathy and compassion on the one hand for the Armenians, and on the other, suggest the advisability of something being done to prevent a repetition of this blot upon the civilization of the nineteenth century.

From a humanitarian standpoint it sets on fire in the breast of every true American that spark, which grew to a flame, and determined to burn from the records of America that blight upon our fair country—the slave traffic. It stirs up that inner feeling which makes a man feel indignant when he sees a large boy attack a small one and make him feel for the little fellow. What if they are many miles away? What if they do speak a foreign tongue?

They are our brothers—our fellowmen—and they are being trampled underfoot. The tears of the wives are mingling with the blood of their husbands. Homes are desecrated; loved ones are torn rudely from the hearth that shall know them no more, to be hurried to a cruel death.

Fathers, helplessly bound, see their fair daughters hurried off to death, or worse—at the best—to a life in a harem. Yes, most decidedly, it is of interest to the Salvationist from a humanitarian standpoint ...

The Salvation Army American *War Cry*/October 17, 1896

"Saved From the Bloody Hand of the Crescent"

What are we to do about this fellow? It is clearly evident we cannot pass him. Look! He can hardly stand upon his feet; he totters around as though he were drunk, and his head is in a sling. I guess the only thing we can do is hold him over and deport him. He has no money and apparently no friends, for I'll be hanged if I can understand one word he says, or his motions, either, for that part. Let us find an Armenian interpreter and see what he has to say for himself, anyway.

The conversation may have been a commonplace one, as, no doubt, the immigration officials have a good many peculiar cases to deal with, and during the course of duty have to send a good many poor immigrants back to their native land, because they do not come up to the requirements of the law. In doing so they have to lay aside their sympathetic feelings and act on the law of justice.

It would be folly for me to attempt anything like a detail or even a general outline of the Armenian massacre in 1895, which has stirred the heart's blood of the thinking part of the world. But Mr. FD Greene, Secretary to the National Armenian Relief Committee, New York, in a communication to the Editor-in-Chief (of *The War Cry*), in speaking of that event, says in part:

"This is the race (the Armenians), superior in body, mind, and spirit, that, after having proved its fitness to survive by every test of history and science, is threatened with extinction in our day. From a nation of perhaps 12,000,000, it has been reduced to 4,000,000, of which only about 2,500,000 remain under the Sultan, the rest being in Russia, Persia, and other lands.

"This remnant is having the life crushed out by a system of taxation and misrule that makes it almost impossible to earn anything, and that seizes not less than fifty percent of what is earned. Add to this the continual plundering by Kurds and Turkish officials, the frequent blackmail, imprisonment, exile, and torture, and you have a faint general conception of the condition of the Armenians in normal times of peace. They cannot get justice in court, for no 'infidel,' as they call Christians, can give evidence against their Moslem oppressors in court, because testimony is considered a religious act in which only the faithful can engage. 'Why, then,' you exclaim, 'do not the Armenians defend themselves and strike back?' Because they are not allowed to have a single gun or sword, because they are greatly outnumbered.

The blackest page of the world's history since time was dated, in the year of our Lord, is that written in the blood of Armenian martyrs in 1895. The actual occurrences are indescribably horrifying, and of such colossal magnitude as to stupefy the imagination that tries to grasp them. Fifty thousand murdered. Half a million reduced to beggary by the plunder and destruction of their property. Two hundred and fifty thousand perishing of starvation and disease; a region as large as New England, New York and Pennsylvania swept by a cyclone of blood, fire, and lust!

The question is such a broad one that a person is apt to wander all around. I would like you to skip over, for the time, these horrors and turn for a moment to the latest massacre of five or six months ago in Constantinople. Thousands of men, women and children were cruelly attacked, and in some instances whole families were annihilated. Among those who suffered from this onslaught was a bright, intelligent young man. His entire circle of relatives was cut or shot down. He had his head battered and laid open to the skull by the butt of a soldier's gun, his shoulder was fearfully slashed by a sword, he was dragged off to a prison, along with thousands of others, where the wounded, dead and dying were hurled into a helpless heap, plundered of any valuables they may have had, clothes nearly all taken from them. They were left to fester, die and decay without help of any kind. After four days in this living tomb, the guard purposely allowed him to drag his uncared-for body into the fresh air of liberty to seek safety in some foreign land. After much suffering and wandering, he found friends who helped bind up his wounds. Having a brother in America, he resolved to go to him, and, receiving necessary assistance, started. Thus, at the opening of our story we find Arshag Hovesphson unable to speak a word of English or make himself understood. His brother was soon found, and he was allowed to step upon free soil.

He must see how they did it in the new country, and accordingly went to the famous Bowery, in company with some new-found Armenian friends. During their travels they ran across the open-air meeting of the Bowery corps. The rest is easily told. As hundreds of others have done, he followed to the hall, on the first Sunday night in the country, and was captured by the spirit of conviction, went to the mercy-seat, and found Jesus, although unable to speak or understand a word of English. God met with him and saved his soul. I might add that his native home is only two miles from that of Ensign Garabed, or better known as Joe the Turk. Arshag is a soldier of the Bowery corps.

The Salvation Army American *War Cry*/October 17, 1896

"Armenia: A Call to Prayer" by The General (William Booth)

A series of atrocities of the most painful character have, during the last few months, been continuously inflicted upon the inhabitants of a province in the Turkish Empire, known as Armenia. The story of these horrible persecutions has horrified the people of Europe and America—indeed, has called out the commiseration and condemnation of the whole of the civilized world. These sufferings are continued, and may, at any moment, break out in still further terrible malignity and to a still greater extent.

The Powers and peoples of Europe and America have, together and separately, expostulated with the Turkish Government, and entreated it to stay these sufferings, and to insist upon the protection of its poor, helpless subjects, but that Government has, up to the present hour, been either unwilling or unable to comply with this reasonable request.

This agony has been again and again pushed upon our attention. Some of our dearest friends are in absolute anguish on the subject. An Armenian—a Salvation soldier—reached this country recently, having worked his way from New York on a cattle-boat, and is now on his way to Erzeroum, the scene of some of the most terrible massacres that have taken place. He seeks his two little sisters at the risk of his life, their father and mother having been murdered.

The cries of these distracted, bleeding, wronged and down-trodden thousands, plead to us to do something that will prevent the perpetuation of these ghastly calamities; nay, wailing voices come from the very graves where murdered thousands lie waiting for the Resurrection Morning, appealing to our hearts and saying piteously, "Help! Help! For humanity's sake—for God's sake, help us!"

The Spirit of God, which is the Spirit of Compassion, pleads within our hearts to help these people, who have so long professed the Christian faith, and who have done nothing to deserve this terrible visitation.

Where the great nations, with their powerful governments and influential churches, have tried to stay these rivers of blood and failed, what can we hope to be able to accomplish? So far as earthly influence is concerned, perchance we cannot do very much, but there is one thing we can do—

WE CAN PRAY.

Therefore, I have selected and appointed a day when my dear Army soldiers and friends shall, throughout the world, earnestly and believingly cry to the Living God to come out of His place, as in the days of old, and stretch forth His mighty arm for the deliverance of this people.

PRAYER MUST BE OFFERED.

I. That the heart of the Sultan of Turkey, and the hearts of ministers and advisers may be moved to show mercy to the suffering Armenians, and to all the subjects in his dominion who are in similarly painful circumstances.

II. That, should deliverance fail to come to Armenia through the Sultan, the Europeans, and American nations, rising superior to all selfish considerations, and laying aside all fears and rivalries, may combine and insist that these inhuman butcheries and atrocities shall at once be put an end to.

III. That if deliverance to these poor sufferers is not accomplished in this manner, that God will in some other way interpose to accomplish the work of mercy.

IN ORDER TO HAVE EFFECTIVE INTERCESSION

1. Let every friend of the Army be entreated to join with us in this intercession, either in their own homes, churches, or by combining with us in our barracks.

2. Let earnest petition go up to God from the early morning to the close of the day mentioned, in the dwellings of our soldiers, both at the family altar and in private.

3. In order that our people's minds may be instructed on the subject and their hearts moved to tender and earnest pleading, let the purpose for which prayer is offered be explained and extracts read from *The War Cry*, or other authentic reports, concerning the sufferings the Armenians have had to undergo, at each meeting in the barracks, and then let prayer by publicly offered, as above set forth.

THE METHOD OF PRAYER.

1. Let every prayer be presented in true sincerity and deep earnestness, all present, being invited to join in spirit, and, according to the Scriptural injunction and our own usage, let all the people say "Amen."

2. Let every officer and soldier remember while he prays that God must be pleased with the intercession for such a benevolent purpose and let everyone strive to believe that not only is God listening to him while he prays, but that He will effectually answer the petitions offered and undertake for these poor people, although it may not be done exactly at the time and in the manner asked for.

"Whatsoever things ye desire when ye pray, believe that ye receive them, and ye shall have them" (Jesus Christ).

The Salvation Army USA *War Cry*, October 24, 1896

"The Armenian Horror

Relief For The Helpless

Departure of Colonel Still to Marseilles

The Army Hoists the Red Cross Flag"

The Armenian question is no nearer settlement. The massacre

of 600 more Armenians in the provinces has been confirmed. The tension of feeling in Constantinople is still at high pressure, and the public exhibition by the chief of police of bombs alleged to have been made by Armenian revolutionaries has inflamed the racial and religious spirit of the city. An enterprising London, England daily came out with the sensational announcement that a new European triple alliance had been formed for upholding the existing form of Turkish government. On the other hand, the tone of the continental press has altered to a more friendly recognition of the sincere wish of England, that something should be done to prevent the further massacre of Armenians, some even going so far as to hint that this may be the outcome of the Balmoral visitor. At any rate, Lord Salisbury is now there, and in a few days we ought to know whether the circumstance is about to make for peace. God grant it!

Fresh cruisers, belonging to the French and Italian fleets, have been ordered on the Levant, and other signs of diplomatic and active precautions have been reported day by day. The deportation of Armenians from Constantinople has been forbidden by the Porte, but a large number succeed in making their escape from a country where the prospects of further disorder and outrage are so sadly certain.

Perhaps the event of the week, the influence of which is impossible for us to estimate, has been the speech of Mr. WE Gladstone, at Liverpool, England. The gathering which assembled in Hengler's Circus was unique to political history. Lord Darby occupied the chair, and the resolution which the veteran statesman moved was seconded by Sir AB Forward, MP, Secretary to the Admiralty, so that the meeting was of a non-party character. The resolution reads as follows:

"That this meeting trusts that Her Majesty's ministers, realizing to the fullest extent the terrible conditions in which their fellow

Christians are placed, will do everything possible to obtain for them full security and protection: and this meeting assures Her Majesty's ministers that they may rely on the citizens of Liverpool in whatever steps they may feel it necessary to take for that purpose."

Mr. Gladstone spoke for over an hour, and while he deprecated war, advocated the withdrawal of the British Ambassador from Constantinople and the dismissal of the Turkish Minister from London, believed that coercion of this order need not and would not lead to war.

In the meantime, the distress among the weaker race has assumed alarming proportions. Their choice lies between the sword and starvation. Those who have succeeded in finding exile in other lands, especially in France, are also in dire straits.

On learning of the sad lot of Armenian refugees at Marseilles, the General [William Booth] dispatched Staff-Captain Hodler, hither, with the object of ascertaining whether the Army could do anything to mitigate the distress. Staff-Captain Hodler happily found that two ladies, well-known for their benevolence, were already on the scene, and were, in conjunction with the authorities, assisting the Armenians with food and shelter.

One of these ladies telegraphed the General, on learning Staff-Captain Hodler's object, imploring the cooperation of the Army in the work already started. The General, at once cordially responded to the appeal. Staff-Captain Hodler was ordered to remain at Marseilles, and on Thursday night, Colonel Stitt, the Secretary for our International Social affairs, took the continental express for the South of France. We learned this morning that everything possible is being done for the housing and feeding of these poor Armenians, and arrangements are being made for their transfer to other countries.

The Armenian Refugees

We sincerely trust that there may be no difficulty in landing the Armenian refugees, who are now on their way to New York. There appears to be no doubt as to their probable suitability to make good American citizens. Our present plan is to receive them, as soon as they are landed, at our Farm Colony in Ramsey, NJ, and forward them as quickly as possible to their various destinations in different parts of the country. They will be scattered as much as possible, so as to avoid conflicting with the labor market in any particular locality. Until suitable positions have been found for them, they will be kept busy on our Farm Colony, and it is hoped that permanent settlements of them may be made in various suitable county districts. It is possible that a number of the refugees may be forwarded to our Social farm in California.

How To Help the Refugees

We shall be glad to hear from officers, soldiers, or friends, who will undertake to care and provide for one or more Armenians, stating how far they can assume responsibility as to:

a. Car-fares.

b. Temporary home and support till employment has been found.

c. Kind of employment available and amount of wages payable.

It must be remembered that most of these refugees have left behind families, relations, and friends, who are reduced to the point of starvation by the cruelties of the Turks, and that they are anxious to earn some money as soon as possible after their arrival with a view to sending help.

The language will be a difficulty, but the Armenians are good linguists, and will quickly pick up English. A certain proportion of those who are coming will doubtless know English or French.

In regard to their trades or professions, it is believed that some will be suitable for clerks, while others will make good servants, farm-hands, or artisans ...

The Salvation Army USA *War Cry*, November 7, 1896

"Refugees on the Farm"

The Armenians are Happy and Contented on the Farm at Ramsey, NJ—Well Cared for—Clean and Comfortable Quarters—Never Enjoyed as Much Liberty in Their Lives— Town Folks Receive Them with Open Arms—A Doctor Volunteers His Service Gratis.

To one accustomed to city life, the prospect of a short time in the country, under ordinary circumstances is cheery indeed, but my visit to The Salvation Army Farm at Ramsey, NJ, was under extraordinary circumstances, yet it was cheery and interesting. Who has not heard of the Armenian refugees, whom The Salvation Army has undertaken to provide for? A number of them had been around Headquarters the best part of the day, and about 5:30 pm, the writer saw a number start, with what few belongings they had, for the train, which was to carry them to the only place of shelter they knew of in this world—The Salvation Army Farm ...

There are forty acres in the plot, and on this there are about 100 fruit trees—apples, pears, and cherry—besides grape vines. About thirty acres have been cleared and is under cultivation; the remainder is woodland, which will supply firewood. There is a neat two-story house containing eight light, cheery rooms, each having an entrance from a hallway, which no doubt will be used in case of families. The men's apartments were in the "converted barn," and were well-fitted up. As one entered, they found themselves in the dining room, which has three rows of long tables. Off this was another room, similarly equipped, from this room a door leads into the first dormitory, which is supplied, as all the rest are, with berths or bunks, similar to those of a vessel, and have a woven wire-spring mattress, upon which they have a soft mattress like those of our Food and Shelter Depots, which are covered with soft leather or Morocco. Each has a soft feather pillow and blanket. The other rooms on the ground floor are the kitchen, with its large range, and a store-room leading off it.

The floor upstairs is divided into sleeping apartments and fitted like the one described. There is a stairway at the end of the building. One lands in the dining-room near the entrance, the other is at the opposite end, and lands in the yard. The rooms are large, light and well ventilated. Several large wood stoves give ample heat for the entire building.

The large chicken-house, with cement floor, has been turned into a lavatory, and is fitted up with a long row of washboards. Outside of this is a thirty-foot well, with a large bucket pump. The superintendent informed me that they would be able to take care of about 150 men at one time.

The men who are there are very interesting indeed. One of their number speaks eight languages and is mastering English very nicely. They all seem to talk French fluently. They appear to want to do something continually and are very happy when they have the privilege of doing some little chores or in helping to fix up the place for their incoming comrades. They told us they were quite comfortable, and never enjoyed as much freedom in all their lives. One of the party carries a deep, ugly-looking scar upon his cheek, received from a Turkish sword. They looked upon Major Glen as their father, and one can easily detect the loving looks which are bestowed upon him as he does anything towards making them comfortable. Everything in and around the buildings is as clean as a new pin, while the rough walls have been covered and look cheerful. They seem to relish the air of the township of Ho-Ho-Kus, and are delighted with their environments, and are looking forward to the arrival of their comrades who are detained at Ellis Island.

"Armenian Gleanings"

From The Refugees

"Can you tell me anything of your experience in Turkey," I said to a well-dressed, intelligent-looking young man of twenty-two. His face saddened as he said, in broken English: "Yes, I saw 200 persons killed. The crowd came rushing through our streets, entering our houses, robbing, and killing. I ran to a well in the back yard and descended to the water's edge. The sound of voices above told me they were seeking my life. It was dark. I got in the water. A dog was dropped down but was killed in the fall. A lantern was lowered, but I hid beneath the water [and] they soon went away, leaving me in my fearful fright. I remained in the well two days and nights. Among the slain was my uncle, whose blood flowed into the well.

Looking into the face of a fine young man of nineteen years, I detected a look of extreme solemnity and sadness. He could not speak English. Turning to the interpreter, I instructed him to say to him: "You are looking very sad. You must look up and be cheerful," to which he smiled a sad smile. In asking him for information, he said: "I saw twenty-five killed with my own eyes. I was a clerk in a carpet house. It was during the terrible massacre of Constantinople. The many businessmen had left their offices in the large office building. Clerks and under-officers were finishing their daily duties. Hearing a tumult outside, we discovered the Turks were upon us. Locking our doors, we tried to escape out. Twenty-five of us found it impossible. The doors were burst open. In the confusion, I managed to get away, and after the soldiers had done their deadly work and had left the building, I escaped. Four days after I sought shelter and help at the French embassy and was shipped to Marseilles. From there I came on to New York," "You are a clerk. I want three young men for light farm work and gardening to go down to Long Island. Would you like to go?" "Yes, gladly."

Another refugee finds himself at the National Headquarters of The Salvation Army. As he sits in that fifth-floor office, on Fourteenth Street, New York, he tells his tale of sorrow; but now rejoices that, by God's help, he has escaped, and, by the aid of The Salvation Army, will find employment.

"What is your name, my friend?" "_____" "Where did you sail from?" "Smyrna. I met The Salvation Army at Marseilles, who provided food, shelter, and clothing, besides showing every kindness, and talking and praying with us." "What did you see during the massacre?" "I saw bodies lying on the street, being eaten by dogs. I saw a friend nearby shot down, the ball entering his breast and passing through his body. My uncle was also killed. I also heard of a man who was a shoemaker, a member of the Presbyterian Church; he was sitting with his family reading the Bible. When the Kurds entered, the family fled, but he remained. As the frenzied murderers entered his room, they found him perusing the pages of the Holy Book. They had no mercy, and when he was found by his family he was lying upon the blood-stained Bible."

The Salvation Army American *War Cry*/November 14, 1896

"Special Armenian Songs"

Armenia
Tune: "My Country 'Tis of Thee"

1. Armenia's refugee!
Gladly we welcome thee,
'Neath Star and Stripe!
Here rest thy weary feet,
Find thou a safe retreat,
While eager hands compete
Thy tears to wipe!

2. Welcome for Jesus' sake!
He knows thy sad heartache,
Numbers each tear!
Gathers thy martyr flock,
'Neath Everlasting Rock
Safe from tormentor's shock
From tyrant's fear!

3. Ye who prefer to die,
Rather than Christ deny,
Welcome once more!
Welcome, heroic band!
Nation of martyrs grand!
Welcome to Freedom's Land
Through wide flung door!

4. Freshly life's journey start!
Linked with us hand and heart,
Follow thy Lord!
Here without fear of foe
Serve thou thy God below,
Till He on thee bestow
Martyr's reward.

–Commander Booth-Tucker

Welcome, Armenians
Tune: "Just Tell Her That You Saw Me"

We've heard the voice of weeping and the fearful tale of woe,
The awful cries have echoed in our ears,
Of children torn from mothers' breasts,
and killed with murd'rous blow,
Of blood that mingled with the widow's tears.
No mercy or compassion ever moved those hearts of stone,
The streaming blood but filled them with delight;
With everything that men count dear so rudely from them torn,
Armenia's day has turned to darkest night.

Chorus
Just tell those dear Armenians their troubles soon are o'er,
Just tell them that our God will answer prayer;
Just tell them there are welcome hands to greet them to our shore,
And we're praying for their kinsmen over there.

They've dared to stand for Jesus, when standing meant to fall,
They gave up all for sake of Christ, their Lord;
And when they gave them choice to die or on Mahomet call,
They said they'd rather perish by the sword.
They knew that on the Cross of old the Savior shed His Blood,
For His dear sake they suffered pain and loss;

And braving death's most horrid forms, true to their Lord they stood,
They died for Him who died upon the Cross.

—Ensign Kupfer

The Salvation Army USA *War Cry*, **November 14, 1896**

"Great Armenian Meeting in Carnegie Hall"

Utmost Enthusiasm Displayed over the Landing of the
Refugees—The Unanimous Opinion was: "They Must Be
Allowed to Land!" And They Have Been Allowed to Land.

The eyes of the entire Christian world are turned towards
Armenia. One hundred thousand corpses strew its hills and
valleys. Twenty thousand homes are reduced to ashes. Three
hundred thousand widows and orphans pierce Heaven with
their wail of woe. A million trembling creatures are waiting
and wondering whose turn shall come next, before the hand of
slaughter and rapine shall be turned aside.

What wonder, then, that from the first information we received
that some 333 Armenian refugees were sailing for our shores,
every effort was put forth by the Commander and Consul on
their behalf! All ordinary work (if Army operations can ever be
classified as ordinary) seemed to pale before our anxious desire
concerning this handful of persecuted people, who were fleeing
from the cruel sword and looking longingly towards our country
as a refuge from the storm.

And day by day fresh revelations of the unspeakable horrors
witnessed in Armenia poured in upon us, and it seemed to us
who stood nearest to her that we could trace upon the Consul's
face the effect of sleepless nights and agony of soul involved.

Indeed, it seemed as though a heavy cloud had settled down upon our bright Headquarters, and as though we were walking The Valley of Shadow with our suffering Armenian comrades.

Shortly before the Carnegie meeting the Commander abruptly entered the Consul's office and burst into tears as he recorded the contents of a heartrending letter, just placed in his hands by an Armenian gentleman, all of whose male relatives had recently been killed in a terrible massacre.

Then too, there were the appealing faces and soul-stirring stories of the Armenian refugees at Ellis Island, and the dark, sad background to the picture which they represented—the tens of thousands still standing in the gateway of destruction on Turkey's soil, and the one ever-recurring question that burnt itself upon our souls with increasing intensity was, what is to be the outcome of the Armenian meeting?

But the eventful hour has arrived, and with agitated hearts; aye, and somewhat heavier footsteps than of yore, we ascended the stairs leading to Carnegie Hall.

Something in the very atmosphere seemed to say that there were interests at stake that night, fraught with extraordinary possibilities. It was as though a funeral pall overshadowed us. And it seemed as though we must breathe softly before the Lord. The issues of life and death appeared to hang upon that meeting! Even now, at the latest moment, news comes to hand telling of the recent tragedy at Ageen. Ah, what might not even then be taking place in Turkey whilst we were assembled to see how best we could help the martyrs there!

Meanwhile, in the anteroom, the Commander and Consul were conferring with the speakers of the evening on the latest phase of the situation.

In another room a group of Armenians were eagerly gathering, and presently the signal was given that all was ready for the meeting to commence. Enthusiastic cheers were given as the procession of speakers filed on to the platform, the Consul leading by the hand a dear little Armenian boy in native dress. They were scarcely seated before another procession, the sight of which was extremely stirring, and which aroused deafening cheers, made its appearance. Under the leadership of Colonel Holland and Major and Mrs. Glen, some fifty or sixty Armenians filed in from the top of the great platform to the seats allotted them. Truly a melting, indescribable picture they presented as waving the Army and American colors and with an immense banner, "God help Armenia!" floating over them, their faces lighted up with gratitude, they stood, looking the thanks they were unable to utter.

Truly at that moment the Carnegie Hall presented a marvelous appearance. From floor to ceiling it was an unbroken sea of glowing, interested, sympathetic faces, whilst the platform showed by the variety of its occupants how uniting a bond between Christians of all denominations is this Armenian question ...

Without a moment's loss of time, the Commander gave out a verse alternately of "America" and of his latest song, "Armenia," and as the great audience joined in the words, a wonderful influence stole over the meeting.

And then upon our knees our hearts responded to the Rev. Cuthbert Hall's petition on behalf of Armenia's claim upon the sacrifice of Jesus, and our souls laid hold as never before upon the truths expressed in those glorious words, "Rock of Ages," as with closed eyes the vast throng voiced in song the united petition.

It goes without saying that when the Commander rose to give the opening address, he received a hearty welcome such as threatened to lift the roof, and which certainly must have lifted his heart by the abundant appreciation and hearty sympathy it expressed. His remarks were frequently broken in upon by enthusiastic applause as in terse and telling language he brought before us the Army's attitude regarding Armenia's need, and its prayer and faith for Armenia's sufferers ...

Then with kindly words of appreciation the Commander introduced Dr. Grace Kimball, "The heroine of Van."

In vivid language she portrayed the horrors witnessed there and the distresses of these heroic people, her address being summed up under three heads:

1. Why these Armenians are leaving their homes.

2. Why they turned their eyes to this country.

3. What hopes could be entertained regarding them in this country?

We determined, by the grace of God, to do all that lay within the power of the world-wide Salvation Army, to uphold at every cost, the sacred and eternal interests of Jesus Christ.

Dr. Kimball told us of villages that have been swept off the face of the earth, of once prosperous cities reduced to starvation, of the terror seizing the people.

May God help us to pray down the light and liberty to these sufferers.

Mr. Ira D Sankey was warmly received, and his song, "Throw out the life-line," was singularly appropriate to the occasion.

Then the Armenians rose to their feet and in their own language, with uplifted faces and clasped hands, recited together the Lord's Prayer. It was a moment difficult to describe, and perhaps few scenes so effective have ever been witnessed under our Blood-and-Fire Flag. Testimonies followed from two

Armenians, who spoke of the horrors they were themselves witnesses of and from which they had escaped as by miracle. They told us of men and women being indiscriminately and wantonly tortured, whose anguish only terminated with death.

In her address the Consul reminded us of the adage, "One touch of nature makes the whole world kin.'" "But what," she cried, "will one touch of grace accomplish? I tell you it will light such a fire in the heart of Christendom that the world has never yet seen, such as will stir this vast continent from ocean to ocean before which even the inspiring glow of pioneer Christianity will fall into the shade!'" "Let your response to His appeal be definite! Pray, but rest not satisfied in prayer. Let your heart and life be purged from all that would interfere with your prayer reaching the heart of God and availing much."

"But let us go even further; let us spring into the arena of action; let us rise superior to selfish considerations and be prepared to suffer personally, politically, or even nationally, if that be necessary, rather than Christ shall be crucified again in our midst and His Blood be found upon our garments."

The moment had come for a collection. It was to be dedicated to the needs of the Refugees, and whilst that was being generously given, a large number of cables and wires, representing various nationalities and denominations, were read by Dr. Louis Klopsch, of *The Christian Herald*, whose hearty cooperation in all that touches the interests of Armenia is already well known to the readers of *The War Cry*.

Among the donations announced was one of $1,000 from *The Christian Herald*, $1,000 from London, and $500 from a friend, and $95 (the savings of a servant-girl), together with lesser sums, for which there was not time for specific announcement.

The Rev. B. Fay Mills, the well-known evangelist, made some

forcible remarks, after which Dr. Josiah Strong, whose presence is ever-welcome upon our Army platform, proposed the following resolution:

Resolved that this meeting desires:

1. To express its uttermost detestation of the unspeakable horrors through which the Armenian nation has been called to pass, and its deepest sympathy with the sufferers.

2. To extend the right hand of welcome to the Refugees who have sought the shelter of our shores.

3. To protest against classifying as ordinary immigrants the Armenians who have fled to our shores to escape from slaughter, and to urge the Government to give the most liberal possible interpretation to the law regulating the landing of immigrants and to exercise the discretion therein allowed by accepting the "oral guarantee" of the responsible societies and friends who have pledged themselves to see that the refugees shall not become a public charge.

4. And further, that this meeting, without desiring to dictate to the Government, earnestly implores it to use every peaceful method within its reach to bring about such accord among the Christian powers as shall compel the Turkish Government to put an immediate end to the terrible massacres and bloodshed of the past few years.

Then the Rev. Dr. Burrell rose to second the same, taking for his text the words (in allusion to the Armenians detained at Ellis Island), "Let them come in." The doctor, in eloquently pleading for their admission, said, "Their faces tell us, their history tells us, their heroic patience shows us they are the stuff Americans are made of, and that they are "what America needs." Later he added, "We have been crying, 'Poor Armenians!' so long that it is time we touched the magic chord of sympathy and showed our suffering comrades that we mean it."

The Commander then put the resolution to the audience, asking that to testify their unqualified approval, they should rise and clap their hands. Truly that crowning sight and sound carried all before it, for from the ceiling to floor the huge congregation rose and joined in.

It was nearing eleven o'clock when the Consul concluded the meeting with prayer, and thus closed one of the most memorable meetings in Army history, a meeting destined to stand out among the long record of memorable meetings. The huge crowd, despite the short four days' notice, the burning subject, the heart-rendering stories, the soul-thrilling scenes, the sympathy, the cooperation, the enthusiasm, all combined to make it a unique occasion, even in the unique history of the unique Salvation Army.

Brigadier Alice Lewis.

The Salvation Army American *War Cry*/November 14, 1896

"Sweet Freedom"

The Armenian Refugees are Released from Ellis Island

The Consul's Love—All are Comfortable.

One can best sympathize with those in affliction when their sympathy arises from a kindred suffering. Yet it seems to me that the American public will fall far short of that kind of sympathy when the case of the Refugee Armenians, who have sought refuge upon our shores is considered. Yet, the American sympathy had not been withheld in this case, as had been shown by the liberation of some 300 of these dear, persecuted people from Ellis Island, NY, where they have been held by the immigration authorities.

For some time, the Commander, Consul, Colonel Holland, in cooperation with others, have been working almost day and night to secure their right of admission to this country. Mass meetings have been held, interviews conducted, letters written, telegrams exchanged, bonds offered, etc., and thank God, their efforts have not been in vain, for on Friday, October 30th, they were passed and stepped upon free soil. Free—oh, how much that means to them! ...

We who had the privilege of welcoming these dear people, as they landed at the Battery Park, NY, will never forget that scene. The National Staff Band had drawn up inside the gates, and as they sent out the strains of America, the refugees filed out, headed by the Consul, the Chief Secretary and Brigadier Lewis, whose joy knew no bounds. It would be utterly impossible to describe it as it was. There were a number of men and women, with their families of little ones, carrying in their hands their only worldly possessions in the shape of baggage. These were followed by younger men, all of whom looked strong and stalwart, and unlikely to become a burden to anyone.

In passing the band, each man doffed his cap and bowed, while the expression worn was one of gratitude and wonder.

The Salvation Army American *War Cry*/December 1895

"Christmas in Turkey"

By Captain J Garabed (Joe the Turk)

The end of the year is drawing nigh, and Christmas-time is again with us. A time in which our hearts rejoice that our Savior was born on Christmas Day, and that He came into this world to redeem us from all sin.

Nineteen hundred years ago our Heavenly Father, seeing the sinfulness of man and realizing the necessity of a Savior, in His infinite mercy gave unto us His only begotten Son, who suffered all manner of persecution for our sake. We rejoice in the name of Jesus Christ, and welcome the day of His birth a thousand, yea, ten thousand times.

I remember the time when I was in total darkness concerning Jesus and His love, and where I was born and raised, namely, Turkey, in Asia, where ignorance is dense, each Christmas it has for generations been the custom for families to send each other a candle about two feet long, to be burnt on that day. The receiver, having gotten one from some relative, even at a distance, reciprocates by sending back one in return. By doing so, every man, woman and child is supplied. They are burnt both at home and at church on Christmas Day and Night, on which occasion an all-night meeting is held in most of the churches. In the middle of the night the populace of a town or city can be seen going and coming from their homes to the churches with their candles in their hands. The light given out by the candles signifies the birth of Christ and the light He brought with Him when He came to the world.

When I was a small boy, my mother used to pull all us children out of bed in the middle of the night and make us carry our candles to and from the church—that day being a great confessional day, when all men and women confess their sins. To illustrate how people are kept in ignorance, and their need of the true light that comes from Christ alone, I will say we are taught a certain form of prayer from early childhood, which lasts us through life, the meaning of which we know nothing, because people talk nothing but the Turkish language. The priest goes on with his preaching in some unknown tongue. He himself, being brought up in the same ignorant manner as ourselves, comprehends but very little of what he says.

Our churches have no seats. The floors are carpeted all over, and no one, male or female, is allowed to enter in with their shoes on, but must take them off at the door.

On account of the absence of seats, most people carry cushions from their homes to the church to sit or kneel upon during service, especially at the festivals, as everyone is expected to stay all night.

All that is required of the congregation to do is to repeat a formal prayer. When this is over, they become weary and sleepy, not being interested in the meeting, as they do not understand what is said by the priest. About 2 or 3 o'clock in the morning the people, being tired out for the want of sleep, fall off their cushions promiscuously all over the church and go to sleep. The priest, however, continues with the ceremony, regardless of the actions of his people, as he must continue in order to keep awake himself.

It is customary for mischievous boys who attend church to carry a large needle about six inches long, with a strong thread, such as is used by sail-makers. When the people fell asleep, we boys would sew the coat-tails and pants-legs of the worshipers to the carpet on the floor, and where two or more were lying close to each other, we would sew them together, continuing on in this manner all over the church, until many were united, but were not all of one mind.

We would then go to some man and tell him to get up, as he had slept long enough. When he tried to rise, however, he found himself fastened, either to the carpet or some person, who in turn would wake up, and thus confusion would ensue.

Gossip went around town the next day about those who were sewed together. Those fortunate enough to escape would have the laugh on the others.

This is the way my boyhood days were spent, so you see the light shed from the candles left me and my people in darkness as much as ever.

After the [Russo-Turkish] War I started for Russia, to learn what I could about this great salvation; but, alas, when I got there I found people living in just as much ignorance as in my own country, for Christmas, instead of being referenced and given over to the praises of the blessed Redeemer, was kept as a day for drinking, carousing and merry-making generally. The people said the day came but once a year, and they would make the best of it and gratify their own desires. As I at that time thought as they did, I naturally fell in line with the crowd.

Not being satisfied with what I saw and heard in Russia, I retraced my steps and returned to Constantinople. After sojourning in the latter city, I made up my mind to emigrate to America, hearing it was a Christian country, which I was seeking after. Alas, how soon my hopes were blighted after arriving here! I soon learned that Christmas Day was not much different here from what I found it to be in all other countries I had been in. This caused me great disappointment, as I expected to find it a holy day instead of a gala day. A day I discovered it to be when friends and relatives meet to have a merry time in a worldly way, instead of holding the day sacred to the worship of our Lord and Savior Jesus Christ, after whom, bless His Name, the day is called.

I continued to live in sin and darkness, however, until I met The Salvation Army in the streets of San Francisco where I heard the sound of the drum and saw a torchlight procession, which appeared to me as though the Judgement Day was nigh at hand.

I followed the procession to the hall, and what I saw and heard there soon convinced me that the soldiers had something in a spiritual way that I knew nothing of. Their bright testimonies and their happy faces convinced me that their hearts were running over with joy.

I soon found a change in my heart. As the light dawned in my soul, darkness began to disappear, and I was made a new creature in Christ Jesus, thus making me able to worship the same light the wise men were directed to by the Star of Bethlehem, by which they found the Savior of the World in that humble manger. I could soon say with my lips from the bottom of my heart: "Praise God for sending us such a Redeemer!"

So, we welcome Christmas-time once more, and I thank God for sparing me to see eleven years as a Salvationist. They have been the best eleven years of my life. I am sorry that I did not hear of my precious Savior sooner, for ever since I consecrated my life to God and got the blessing of a clean heart, I realize more than ever the beauty of Christmas Day, and my only ambition in life is now to carry the message of salvation (like my master) to those who are living in the same condition Jesus found me in when He spoke peace to my soul.

People in this country whom I knew last Christmas are not with us now, for God has called them away, and the world knows them no more. We who are living today ought to be thankful, saved, or unsaved, for God's tender mercies towards us. Therefore, Christians who are serving God in a formal way only, I beg you to put aside all formality and buckle on the whole armor of righteousness. Give God your heart, and worship Him in spirit and truth, and let this Christmas be the best in all your lives.

John Milsaps—A Sketch

"Highlights in History, A Western Pioneer, Major John Milsaps"
The War Cry, November 2021
By Major Jason Swain

In the 1880s, a battered and well-read copy of *The War Cry* arrived in San Francisco. It landed in the hands of a few members of the West Coast Holiness Association. At their next meeting, the holiness men unanimously decided to change their name to The Salvation Army and elected George Newman as their first commander.

One of their members was John Milsaps. Milsaps was a Texan, but decided at an early age to go to California. After his conversion, he began attending meetings and volunteered to sweep up after they were over. He was made a sergeant and assisted Commander Newton. When the official representative, Major Alfred Wells, came from London to take over the operation, he found that most of the original holiness men, including Commander Newton, had quit or moved on to other ventures. However, Sergeant Milsaps was there.

Milsaps was an ascetic, as many early-day Salvationists were, and remained a life-long bachelor. He lived simply and often wore shabby, ill-fitting uniforms. He instructed the finance department to give much of his allowance to "officers with families, who need it more than I." He often slept in his office to save on rent.

Milsaps edited the West Coast *War Cry* for many years. He went on the expedition to Hawaii and assisted in the first meetings there. He would lead the Hawaii division for a few years before retirement. During the Spanish-American War in 1898, Milsaps sought for permission to be a chaplain to the United States military that was gathering near San Francisco. He also briefly joined the Salvationists sent to France in 1917, though he was retired by that time. Major Milsaps was Promoted to Glory in 1932. He lived in a small cottage but had amassed a large collection of books by the end of his life. His books and papers were given to the Houston Museum.

SUGGESTED READING

Armenian History:

Grigoris Balakian, *Armenian Golgotha, A Memoir of the Armenian Genocide, 1915-1918*. Published by Vintage Books, a division of Random House, Inc., New York. March 2010. ISBN: 978-1-4000-9677-0.

Ronald Gregor Suny, *"They Can Live in the Desert but Nowhere Else": A History of the Armenian Genocide*. Published by Princeton University Press, Princeton, and Oxford. 2015. ISBN: 978-691-14730-7.

Charles River Editors, *The Rise and Fall of the Ottoman Empire: The History of the Turkish Empire's Creation and Its Destruction Over 600 Years Later*. Published by Charles River Editors, Columbia, South Carolina. January 4, 2020. ISBN: 9781984061027.

Quinton Barry, *War in the East: A Military History of the Russo-Turkish War 1877-1878*. Published by Helion & Company Limited, West Midlands, England. 2012. ISBN: 978-1-911096-69-6.

Salvation Army History:

Edward H. McKinley, *Marching to Glory: The History of The Salvation Army in the United States,1880-1980*. Published by Harper & Row Publishers, San Francisco, CA. 1980. ISBN: 978-0-8028-6468-0

Judy Vaughn, *The Bells of San Francisco: The Salvation Army with Its Sleeves Rolled Up*. Published by RDR Books, Berkeley, CA. 2005. ISBN: 1-57143-150-0.

Major Jason R Swain, *Under Two Flags: The Rise, Rebellion, and Rebuilding of The Salvation Army in America 1870-1913*. Published by The Salvation Army Crest Books, Alexandria, VA. 2021. ISBN: 978-1-946709-37-0.

DISCUSSION GUIDE

Chapter One—Let's Start From the Very Beginning

Overview: This chapter details the early life of Nishan Der Garabedian in Talas, Turkey: his education, early tragedies, and his initial journey to America.

Discussion Questions

1. How did Turkish educational policies influence Nishan's early life in Talas? What trait(s) did he exhibit?

2. How might living in a multicultural environment have impacted Nishan's worldview?

3. Nishan forgave the man who shot him. What does this reveal about his early character and values? How might this trait have influenced his later life? Have you ever had to forgive someone for something they did to you?

4. Discuss Nishan's experience with The Salvation Army in Liverpool. What did he witness and how did he respond?

5. What challenges did Nishan encounter when he arrived in America? How might these experiences mirror modern immigrant experiences?

Dig a Little Deeper

The Bible emphasizes forgiveness as a fundamental aspect of Christian faith. In both the Old and New Testaments, God is portrayed as merciful and forgiving, encouraging believers to seek forgiveness and extend it to others. In the New Testament, Jesus teaches the importance of forgiving others, as seen in the Lord's Prayer (Matthew 6:12). We ask for forgiveness in response to the forgiveness we have given to those who have sinned against us. Forgiveness has a reciprocal nature. As believers, we are to show mercy to others just as we have received mercy from God. We often gloss over this part of the Lord's Prayer. If we don't give forgiveness, how can we expect to receive it? Forgiveness is central to the biblical message, promoting reconciliation, compassion, and the transformative power of God's grace.

> "Be kind to one another, tenderhearted, forgiving one another, as God in Christ forgave you" (Ephesians 4:32 ESV).

> Show mercy. No soul was every made poor by loving too much or injured by forgiving too often. – Catherine Bramwell Booth

Discuss the role of forgiveness in the life of a Christian.

Chapter 2—West Coast Calling

Overview: This chapter explores John Garabed's transformation into "Joe the Turk," his initial struggles, and his eventual conversion in San Francisco. This chapter provides a vivid description of San Francisco's lawlessness during the late nineteenth century, Joe's integration into this chaotic environment, his encounters with The Salvation Army, and his gradual path to conversion and service.

Discussion Questions

1. How do the various incarnations of Joe's name represent the journey he has been on? Joe received the nickname of "Turk" before he met The Salvation Army. Why might he have allowed it to become his nickname even before he realized the ministry potential it held?

2. How did the chaotic environment of San Francisco shape Joe's early experiences? In what ways did it contribute to his eventual conversion?

3. Reflect on John Milsaps' role in Joe's journey to faith. How does Milsaps's consistent behavior and dedication influence Joe?

4. How did Joe's physical strength and presence initially serve as tools for violence, but later become assets in his protective role for The Salvation Army.

5. What do the lyrics of "Joe's Song" say to you? What's the significance of the "light" and the "drum?"

Dig a Little Deeper

Jesus said in Matthew 5:10-12 "Blessed are those who are persecuted because of righteousness, for theirs is the kingdom of heaven. Blessed are you when people insult you, persecute you and falsely say all kinds of evil against you because of me. Rejoice and be glad, because great is your reward in heaven, for in the same way they persecuted the prophets who were before you."

The Salvation Army, which today serves in more than one hundred and thirty countries around the world, ministers to those who have been persecuted for their faith. Do some research and discover how your group can pray for the oppressed and, through The Salvation Army's World Services office (or your denomination's missionary department), support those who have been displaced and in need of the basic necessities of life.

1. Reflect on your own experience of transformation and redemption. How do personal struggles and environments shape one's faith journey?

2. What lessons can be learned about persistence, faith, and public testimony in the face of adversity?

Must we give in? Must we decline to tread in the blood-stained footsteps of the Captain of our salvation? Must we decline the honor of being in the advance guard of the Lamb's army because of the pain, because of the conflict, because of the persecution? – Catherine Booth, Co-Founder of the Army

In what ways do Christians experience persecution today?

Chapter 3—Marching Orders

Overview: This chapter follows Joe as he embarks on his journey with The Salvation Army across the Pacific Coast Division. It details his various assignments, arrests, and the establishment of Salvation Army outposts in different cities. This chapter highlights Joe's perseverance, faith, and unique approach to spreading The Salvation Army's mission despite challenges and opposition.

Discussion Questions

1. How does Joe demonstrate resilience in the face of adversity throughout this chapter?

2. Compare and contrast the responses Joe receives in different towns. What factors contribute to the varying levels of acceptance or hostility?

3. Discuss the significance of the Los Angeles judge's reaction to Joe's courtroom prayer.

4. What does the reaction of the mob in Los Angeles and other hostile encounters reveal about societal attitudes toward The Salvation Army during this period?

5. What do you think Joe's prayer in the Los Angeles courtroom sounded like?

Reflection

1. Share personal experiences where you faced adversity and how you overcame it.

2. Reflect on the broader implications of Joe's story for mission work today. Don't just think outside your country. How can we apply Joe's principles of resilience and faith in our own lives?

Dig a Little Deeper

What does this passage say to you about overcoming adversity?

> *God is our refuge and strength, an ever-present help in trouble. Therefore, we will not fear, though the earth give way and the mountains fall into the heart of the sea, though its waters roar and foam and the mountains quake with their surging ... The Lord Almighty is with us; the God of Jacob is our fortress (Psalm 46: 1-3,11 NIV).*

Lt. Colonel Richard Slater (1854–1938), the father of Salvation Army music, penned these lyrics:

> *When the road we tread is rough, let us bear in mind,*
> *In our Savior strength enough, we may always find;*
> *Though the fighting may be tough, let our motto be:*
> *Go on, go on to victory!*

How does this "fighting song" give us a glimpse of the mind of a Salvationist in the late 1800s?

Chapter 4—Tools of the Trade

Overview: This chapter highlights Joe's growing notoriety, his evangelistic efforts across the United States, and the unique tools and strategies he employed to draw crowds and spread the gospel message. His adoption of the moniker "Joe the Turk" and the distinctive cultural and musical elements he incorporated into his ministry are discussed in detail.

Discussion Questions

1. How did Joe's unique background and appearance contribute to his popularity both within and outside The Salvation Army?

2. What do you think were the most effective tools or strategies Joe used in his evangelistic work? How did his approach differ or align with other evangelists of his time?

3. Discuss the effectiveness of Joe's creative methods, such as the gospel umbrella, in attracting and engaging audiences. What can we learn from his approach? Can you think of any modern parallels?

4. How did Joe's personal experiences, including the Armenian massacres, shape his ministry and message? How did he use his platform to address this injustice?

Dig a Little Deeper

How can we apply the lessons from Joe's story to our own lives? Whether through creative evangelism, advocacy work, or supporting marginalized communities, do you feel inspired to build on Joe's legacy, and how?

Steve Green penned the following words. Discuss how it applies to this chapter and this present day in which we live.

Find Us Faithful

We're pilgrims on the journey of the narrow road,
and those who've gone before us line the way;
Cheering on the faithful, encouraging the weary, their
lives a stirring testament to God's sustaining grace.
Surrounded by so great a cloud of witnesses, let us run the race
not only for the prize, but as those who've gone before us.
Let us leave to those behind us, the heritage of
faithfulness passed on through godly lives.
O may all who come behind us find us faithful,
may the fire of our devotion light their way.
May the footprints that we leave, lead them to believe,
and the lives we live inspire them to obey.
O may all who come behind us find us faithful.
After all our hopes and dreams have come and gone,
and our children sift thru all we've left behind,
May the clues that they discover, and the mem'ries they uncover,
Become the light that leads them, to the road we each must find.

Describe how this song speaks to you.

Chapter 5—Arrested Developments

Overview: This chapter details the numerous arrests and subsequent trials of Joe the Turk. This chapter highlights Joe's dedication to the Army's right to evangelize in public spaces and his unwavering commitment despite frequent incarcerations. It explores the harsh treatment Joe faced, his public and legal challenges, and broader implications for religious freedom.

Discussion Questions

1. What do you think motivated Joe to persist in his public evangelism despite the frequent arrests and harsh treatments he faced?

2. How did the public's perception of The Salvation Army often change in the communities where Joe was arrested?

3. Many newspapers covered Joe's arrests; some stories were positive and others negative. What was the impact of both supportive and critical media coverage? How is Christianity often portrayed by secular media today?

4. Why was the use of instruments like the drum and cornet so contentious, and what significance did those instruments hold for the Salvationists?

Dig a Little Deeper

Consider organizing a mock trial or debate based on one of Joe's court cases to gain a deeper understanding of the legal and ethical issues involved. Have two people represent the defense and the two others, the prosecution. Select a judge and have the remaining people serve as the jury. If you choose the debate option, divide into two groups, and let one group represent the Army and the other, the prosecution.

Discuss the meaning of these statements? What could be this generation's open-air ministry?

It is in the interest of the service to be in the columns of the newspapers as often as possible. – General William Booth

I would advocate the insertion of [Salvation Army] advertisement in every Sunday paper, in every sporting page, in every vile print that is largely read by the people, where sinner's eyes go on a Sunday or any day. – George Scott Railton

The Salvation Army would slowly die were our open-air meetings to cease; they are not merely one of our activities but are our life. Ours is religion with an outward thrust. To deny that is to die by slow paralysis. – General Albert Osborne

The Army's Cathedral is the open-air! – General William Booth

Discuss what a modern-day open-air meeting might look like? Outdoors? Indoors? Online?

Conduct a modern-day twist on an open-air. Think about Joe's methods as you plan.

Chapter 6—The Greatest Showman

Overview: This chapter explores Joe the Turk's flamboyant style and evangelistic fervor. The chapter delves into his ability to draw and captivate crowds despite competition from various entertainment forms of the time, such as traveling minstrel shows, circuses, and Wild West spectacles. Joe's captivating storytelling, musical talents, and the dramatic accounts of his and his sister's conversions played a central role in his evangelistic endeavors.

Discussion Questions

1. How did Joe's theatrical approach help him attract and retain audiences? Do you think his showmanship detracted from or enhanced his spiritual message?

2. How did Joe use storytelling to convey his message effectively? Discuss the role of personal narratives/testimonies in engaging an audience.

3. How did Joe's Armenian heritage and the historical context of the Armenian massacres influence his ministry and message?

4. Discuss Maritza's conversion and parallel it to early-day Salvation Army slum sisters. [www.thewarcry.org/articles/the-slum-sisters/]

Dig a Little Deeper

The Salvation Army has a rich and vibrant history of integrating the arts into its ministry. The Army's brass bands have become iconic, performing at worship services, community events, and parades. Alongside the brass bands, singing groups play a significant role, filling the air with hymns, contemporary Christian music, and original compositions that convey messages of faith and hope.

Visual arts have also found a place within the Army. Art exhibitions showcase works by artists from within its ranks, often reflecting themes of spirituality, social justice, and community.

Drama and theatre have long been used by The Salvation Army to engage with the public. Historically, street theatre has been a dynamic method for capturing the attention of passersby, presenting dramatic performances that highlight social issues and deliver spiritual messages. Beyond the streets, the Army produces plays and musicals that focus on moral lessons, biblical stories, and contemporary social issues. Dance, too, has become an integral part of ministry as dance groups use movement to express faith and inspire others at worship services and events.

Literature and writing also have their place within The Salvation Army's artistic endeavors. The Army publishes a variety of books, magazines, and newsletters that feature poetry, stories, and essays related to faith and social issues. Youth programs within The Salvation Army often include creative arts camps, where young people can explore and develop their talents in music, drama, dance, and visual arts in a supportive environment.

Trust God with your creativity – He has
more ideas than you do. – Cendia

How have you used storytelling, drama, or the arts in your Christian walk?

Chapter 7—Truth is Stranger Than Fiction

Overview: In this chapter we are introduced to the extraordinary and almost unbelievable experiences of Joseph Garabed. The narratives showcase his unique contributions to The Salvation Army's ministry and highlight his daring and adventurous spirit.

Discussion Questions

1. How does the account of "The Unusual Trio" speak to diversity in the early Salvation Army? How does The Army (or your church) celebrate diversity in your faith community?

2. Were you surprised to learn that Joe was the first Santa on the streets of New York? This method of collecting funds predates Salvation Army red kettles. Does it appear to you that early-day Salvationists were more creative than today? Why?

3. Joe was asked to be the temporary mayor of Macomb. How might this event have benefitted The Army in future days?

4. Joe experienced a great amount of bodily harm and persecution over the years. What would cause a person to endure such things and not walk away? What do you hope your response would be if you were persecuted for your faith?

5. What does Joe's experience with not being promoted reveal about his character? How would you respond if this were you?

Dig a Little Deeper

The Night Before Christmas was written in 1823 by Clement Clarke Moore. This poem is said to be responsible for many of our modern-day notions of Santa Claus. By 1900, it was already a part of popular culture. Nevertheless, it took great imagination to make the leap from Santa bringing gifts to good little boys and girls to collecting donations to provide a special meal for the poor on Christmas Day.

Our imagination is a remarkable gift from God, enabling us to create, envision new possibilities, and look beyond the present. As beings created in the image of a creative God (Genesis 1:27), we possess the ability to imagine and conceptualize ideas that are yet to come into existence.

This capability is expressed through various creative endeavors such as art, music, writing, and innovation. Our imagination allows us to picture better futures, devise unique solutions to problems, and discover new ways to glorify God.

We are blessed with the significant ability to perceive how God might want us to fulfill His purposes on earth. By prayerfully engaging our imagination to align more closely with God's intentions, we open ourselves to the Holy Spirit's guidance, leading our thoughts toward divine inspiration rather than aimless fancy.

What modern cultural personalities, events, or symbols can you think of that might be reimagined to help draw attention to the need that exists today in your community?

Chapter 8—Playing in the Key of Asia Minor

Overview: This chapter covers Joe's three attempts to visit his family in Asia Minor and Greece, the challenges he faced due to geopolitical issues, and his contributions to the Armenian community and The Salvation Army during his travels.

Discussion Questions

1. How did the political climate of Turkey in the late nineteenth and early twentieth centuries impact Joe's travels and efforts to reconnect with his family?

2. What challenges did Joe face in balancing his American identity with his Armenian roots? How did this affect his interactions with authorities in Turkey?

3. How did Joe use music as a tool for connection and ministry during his travels? What impact did his performances have on the communities he visited?

4. Reflect on Joe's observations and actions in the Armenian refugee settlement in Greece. How did his experiences there shape his perspective on humanitarian aid and social justice?

Dig a Little Deeper

The Salvation Army has a position statement on serving refugees and asylum seekers. Read it in your group and discuss how this statement is being carried out in your faith community. [https://www.salvation-ist.org.uk/faith/social-justice-peacemaking/positional-statements/social-justice-peacemaking/Refugees-Asylum-Seekers]

Talk about the conditions in the refugee settlement and the broader implications of Joe's observations on current refugee crises.

Chapter 9—The Winds of Change

Overview: This chapter delves into the transformation of The Salvation Army's image from a controversial group to a respected and beloved institution, highlighting the impact of World War I and the contributions of the doughnut girls. It also provides a nuanced perspective on heroism and the passage of time, showing how Joe's once-celebrated methods and persona gradually fell out of favor as the organization evolved.

Discussion Questions

1. How does the chapter attempt to balance the common romanticized view of historical figures and events?

2. The Army went beyond traditional religious practices, becoming a movement focused on compassion and social justice. According to the first section of this chapter, in what ways did the Army exhibit these traits?

3. How did World War I impact the relationship between The Salvation Army and the American public?

4. Do you sense any change in Joe's attitude toward evangelism, even when The Salvation Army was moving away from traditional forms of evangelism?

5. How does the chapter illustrate the broader theme of change and adaptation within movements and institutions?

Dig a Little Deeper

Use Joe's story as a case study to explore broader themes of change, adaptation, and the tension between tradition and modernization in organizations. Break into groups and discuss the following, then come back and share your thoughts.

1. Innovative Evangelism: Joe's unconventional methods, such as parading through towns in flamboyant outfits and using

theatrical techniques, exemplify how embracing change and innovation can attract attention and engage new audiences. This approach was a departure from traditional evangelism and highlighted the need for adaptability in reaching diverse populations.

2. Resourcefulness: Joe's creative use of available resources, such as music and performance, underscores the necessity of resourcefulness in adapting to changing circumstances. Organizations must be willing to leverage their unique assets and strengths to remain relevant.

3. Balancing Tradition with Innovation: Organizations must find ways to honor their traditions while embracing necessary changes. This balance can be achieved through open dialogue, inclusive decision-making, and a clear vision that integrates both historical values and modern needs.

Have someone in your group research The Salvation Army doughnut girls and give a brief report.

There are numerous articles and photographs on the internet; here are two good ones.

https://www.worldwar1centennial.org/index.php/communicate/press-media/wwi-centennial-news/3929-doughnut-girls-the-women-who-fried-donuts-and-dodged-bombs-on-the-front-lines-of-world-war-i.html

https://www.smithsonianmag.com/history/donut-girls-wwi-helped-fill-soldiers-bellies-and-get-women-vote-180962864/

Chapter 10—Retired, but not Tired

Overview: This chapter chronicles the post-retirement life of Joseph Garabed, who remained active and impactful despite his official retirement from The Salvation Army. The chapter explores Joe's continued involvement with the organization in both France and the US, his ventures into real estate, and the financial and personal challenges he faced in his later years.

Discussion Questions

1. What were the main challenges Joe faced in France, and how did they compare to his experiences in the US?

2. How did Joe's entrepreneurial efforts impact his financial stability and overall well-being in his later years?

3. Why do you think Joe was so hesitant to sell his properties?

Chapter 11—Promoted to Glory

Overview: This chapter details the final years and passing of Joseph Garabed. It captures his death, the reflections of those who knew him, and the legacy he left behind.

Discussion Questions

1. What does the term "Promoted to Glory" signify in the context of The Salvation Army, and how does it reflect its beliefs about death?

2. Reflect on the various tributes and obituaries. What do they reveal about Joe's impact on those who knew him and the wider community?

3. Discuss the significance of Joe's funeral and the presence of high-ranking officials from The Salvation Army. What does this indicate about his standing within the organization?

4. In what ways can Joe the Turk's story inspire us and future members of The Salvation Army, churches, or other service organizations?

Dig a Little Deeper

The *War Cry* article about Joe's funeral called him "one of the most original and unique characters The Salvation Army has ever known." Based on all you have learned about Joe in the previous chapters, write a short obituary about him.

Reflect on the importance of preserving Joe's personal effects and how they serve as tangible reminders of his contributions. Discuss how physical artifacts/archives/museums can help keep memories and legacies alive.

Chapter 12—Where is Joe?

Overview: This chapter discusses the posthumous recognition and commemoration of Joseph Garabed, highlighting the Armenian community's efforts to honor his legacy. It explores the significance of his unmarked grave and the eventual installation of a headstone in recognition of his contributions to The Salvation Army and his Armenian heritage.

Discussion Questions

1. How does the story of Joseph Garabed's unmarked grave and subsequent recognition reflect on the importance of remembering and honoring individuals' contributions to their communities?

2. What does the Armenian community's effort to fund and install a headstone for Joe indicate about the value they place on one's heritage?

3. How does Joseph Garabed's life and ministry illustrate the concept of personal sacrifice for a greater cause? Compare his actions to those of the Apostle Paul as described in 1 Corinthians 9:19-23.

4. How did the historical context of Armenian-Turkish relations impact the perception of Joe's nickname and his legacy within the Armenian community?

Dig a Little Deeper

Invite members to reflect on their own willingness to embrace challenges and sacrifices for the sake of a greater good, drawing parallels to Joe's and Paul's examples.

Though I am free and belong to no one, I have made myself a slave to everyone, to win as many as possible. To the Jews I became like a Jew, to win the Jews. To those under the law I became like one under the law (though I myself am not under the law), so as to win those under the law. To those not having the law I became like one not having the law (though I am not free from God's law but am under Christ's law), so as to win those not having the law. To the weak I became weak, to win the weak. I have become all things to all people so that by all possible means I might save some. I do all this for the sake of the gospel, that I may share in its blessings (1 Corinthians 9: 19-23 NIV).

How does Paul's statement "I do all this for the sake of the gospel" influence our understanding of his motivations and goals?

How can we align our own motivations similarly?

Endnotes

1. Salvation Army officers are those who have completed a course of study at a Salvation Army school/seminary/Bible college and have been ordained as ministers and commissioned as officers. A person in training is called a cadet, while commissioned officers hold the ranks of lieutenant, captain, major, lt. colonel, colonel, and commissioner. The international leader of The Salvation Army holds the rank of General.

2. Doughnut girls were Salvation Army officers and soldiers who served during WWI by providing the men fighting on the front lines with home-cooked meals.

3. Until we reach the point in the story where Joe arrives in America and changes his name, to honor his heritage, I will use his given Armenian name, Nishan Der Garabedian.

4. The Salvation Army American *War Cry*, July 1908. "Turkish Characteristics: A Mission Field that Religiously Presents Many Obstacles" (11).

5. ibid (11).

6. ibid (11).

7. The Salvation Army American *War Cry*, January 15, 1887. "Liberty Lighting the World, God's Liberty Column or Testimonies of Poor Sinners Set Free, From California 'Cry'" (7).

8. The Salvation Army American *War Cry*, December 30, 1933. "Joe the Turk, The Gripping Story of a Famous Salvationist Pioneer" by Adjutant William G. Harris (4).

9. ibid (4).

10. ibid (4).

11. ibid (4).

12. ibid (4).

13. ibid (4).

14. *The Springfield Democrat*, Springfield, MO, February 12, 1892, "About the Salvationists, Joe the Turk Draws Big Crowd Last Sunday, and Tells of His Conversion, Once a Drunkard and a Wanderer, But now Clothed and in His Right Mind. Through the Labors of The Salvation Army" (3).

15. The Salvation Army Pacific Coast Division *War Cry*, November

1886, "Notes of a Life," (1).

16. *The Springfield Democrat*, Springfield, MO, February 12, 1892, "About the Salvationists, Joe the Turk Draws Big Crowd Last Sunday, and Tells of His Conversion, Once a Drunkard and a Wanderer, But now Clothed and in His Right Mind. Through the Labors of The Salvation Army" (3).

17. ibid (3).

18. ibid (3).

19. The Salvation Army, *The Conqueror Magazine*, September 1893, "Joe the Turk" (337).

20. The Salvation Army American *War Cry*, July 12, 1890, "Joe the Turk, an Interview" (15).

21. ibid (15).

22. ibid (15).

23. ibid (15).

24. ibid (15).

25. ibid (15).

26. ibid (15).

27. ibid (15).

28. *The Boston Traveler*, Boston, MA, December 11, 1923, "Joe the Turk, Sally Strong-Man, Champion of Tolerance in Hub Again."

29. ibid (unknown).

30. ibid (unknown).

31. The Armenian Museum of America, Watertown, MA; and Reverend Joseph Garabedian, Paramus, New Jersey, Armenian Presbyterian Church. (Reverend Garabedian is an Armenian language scholar.)

32. "The Barbary Coast," Morgan Palumbo, November 8, 2016, www.theculturetrip.com.

33. ibid.

34. The Salvation Army Pacific Coast Division *War Cry*, June 7, 1890, "Joe the Turk, Captain Nishan Garabedian" (3).

35. The Iola Register, January 27, 1919, "Joe the Turk is in Town, Celebrated Salvation Army Leader Spent Sunday Here and Will Remain Over Tonight."

36. The Salvation Army American *War Cry*, July 12, 1890, "Joe the Turk, An Interview" (15).

37. ibid (15).

38. ibid (15).

39. The Salvation Army Pacific Coast Division *War Cry*, November 1886, "Notes on a Life" (1).
40. The Salvation Army American *War Cry*, July 12, 1890, "Joe the Turk, an Interview" (15).
41. ibid (15).
42. ibid (15).
43. *The Boston Post*, Boston, MA, December 9, 1923, "Joe the Turk Tells of Battles Under Salvation Banner."
44. *The Springfield Democrat*, Springfield, MO, February 12, 1892, "About the Salvationists, Joe the Turk Draws a Big Crowd and Tells of His Conversion" (3).
45. "The Barbary Coast," Morgan Palumbo, November 8, 2016, www.theculturetrip.com.
46. *The Boston Post*, Boston, MA, December 9, 1923, "Joe the Turk Tells of Battles Under Salvation Banner."
47. ibid.
48. ibid.
49. ibid.
50. ibid.
51. ibid.
52. ibid.
53. Collier, Richard. *The General Next to God*. HarperCollins, London, UK, 1965, (170).
54. The Salvation Army Pacific Coast Division *War Cry*, June 7, 1890, "Joe the Turk, or Captain Nishan Garabedian" (3).
55. "Letter to San Francisco Corps on the Occasion of its 50th Anniversary." Written by Joseph Garabed, found in National Headquarters Archives.
56. ibid.
57. *New York Times*, New York City, NY, December 12, 1923, "A Turk Salvation Army Leader, Marion R. Glenn."
58. The Salvation Army Pacific Coast Division *War Cry*, November 1886, "Notes on a Life" (1).
59. The Salvation Army American *War Cry*, October 20, 1894, "Captain Garabed, Better Known as Joe the Turk, All the Way from Constantinople—His Early Life—An Amateur Policeman—Jesus is Mighty to Save" (3).
60. The Salvation Army Pacific Coast Division *War Cry*, November

1886, "Notes on a Life" (1).

61. ibid (1).

62. ibid (1).

63. The Salvation Army Pacific Coast Division *War Cry*, April 15, 1887, "Small Shot."

64. *The Pittsburg Press*, Pittsburg, PA, October 20, 1890, "With Fife and Drum, Grand Rally of Salvation Hosts at Brooklyn, Sketches of Some of the Peculiar, Yet Famous Leaders—Booth's Big Army" (1).

65. *Detroit Free Press*, Detroit, MI, March 13, 1891, "A Son of the Orient, Joe the Turk Causes a Rally of Salvation Army Soldiers" (2).

66. The Salvation Army American *War Cry*, "Joe the Turk: The Gripping Story of a Salvation Army Pioneer" by Adjutant W. G. Harris (4).

67. *The Boston Post*, Boston, MA, December 9, 1923, "Joe the Turk—Hard to Kill—Tells of Battles Under Salvation Banner."

68. ibid.

69. ibid.

70. The Salvation Army Pacific Coast Division *War Cry*, April 30, 1887.

71. The Salvation Army Pacific Coast Division *War Cry*, May 1, 1887, "Small Shot."

72. The Los Angeles Almanac, % US Census Bureau, www.laalmanac.com.

73. ibid.

74. *New York Times*, New York City, NY, December 12, 1923, "A Turk Salvation Army Leader."

75. ibid.

76. ibid.

77. ibid.

78. ibid.

79. ibid.

80. The Salvation Army Pacific Coast Division *War Cry*, May 15, 1887, "Los Angeles Opened! 'Shoot the Tent' A New Battlefield in the Land of the Oranges" (1).

81. ibid (1).

82. ibid (1).

83. ibid (1).

84. ibid (1).

85. ibid (1).

86. The Salvation Army Pacific Coast Division *War Cry*, June 15, 1887, Los Angeles California, "Four Souls, Thunderstorm Around the Tent, but the Angel of Mercy Inside and Tow Souls Saved."
87. The Salvation Army American *War Cry*, October 20, 1894, "Captain Garabed, Better Known as 'Joe the Turk,' All the Way from Constantinople" (3).
88. The Salvation Army Pacific Coast Division *War Cry*, June 15, 1887, Los Angeles, California, "Four Souls, Thunderstorm Around the Tent, but the Angel of Mercy Inside and Tow Souls Saved."
89. The Salvation Army Pacific Coast Division *War Cry*, August 15, 1887, Santa Ana, "New Officers."
90. The Salvation Army Pacific Coast Division *War Cry*, November 1, 1887, San Bernardino.
91. *The Daily Courier*, San Bernardino, CA, November 1, 1887 (5); *The Daily Courier*, San Bernardino, CA, November 2, 1887, "A Bad Man" (5).
92. The "White House" referenced was a home built in San Bernardino in 1850. It is a large white house that sits high upon a hill.
93. The Salvation Army Pacific Coast Division *War Cry*, January 15, 1888 (no headline).
94. The Salvation Army Pacific Coast Division *War Cry* (reprinted article from The San Bernardino Times, January 15, 1888.
95. The Salvation Army Pacific Coast Division *War Cry*, August 15, 1888, "Small Shots" (5).
96. The Salvation Army Pacific Coast Division *War Cry*, September 1, 1888, "The Summer Campaign" (4,5,6).
97. ibid (4,5,6).
98. ibid (4,5,6).
99. The Salvation Army Pacific Coast Division *War Cry*, September 15, 1888, "The Summer Campaign" (1,2,3).
100. ibid, (1,2,3).
101. ibid, (1,2,3).
102. The Salvation Army Pacific Coast Division *War Cry*, October 1, 1888, "The Summer Campaign" (1).
103. The Salvation Army Pacific Coast Division *War Cry*, October 15, 1888, "The Summer Campaign" (4,5,6).
104. ibid (4,5,6).
105. The Salvation Army Pacific Coast Division *War Cry*, November

1, 1888, "The Summer Campaign: Close of the Summer Campaign, Farewell Shots, Big Meetings" by Captain Wray Hurt.

106. *The Petaluma Weekly Argus*, January 5, 1889, (5).

107. *The Petaluma Weekly Argus*, January 12, 1889, "A Sensible Method" (3).

108. The Salvation Army Pacific Coast Division *War Cry*, February 15, 1889, "Adjutant Halpin's First View of Central California District" (4).

109. The Salvation Army Pacific Coast Division *War Cry*, October 1, 1889, East Portland, (7,8).

110. *Daily Arkansas Gazette*, Little Rock, AR, January 2, 1909, "Joe the Turk is Coming, Famous Salvation Army Character Will Spend Three Days Here" (1).

111. The Armenian Museum of America, Worcester, MA, 65 Main St, Watertown, MA, 02472.

112. The Salvation Army American *War Cry*, March 12, 1892, "Joe in Missouri" (10).

113. *The Cincinnati Enquirer*, Cincinnati, OH, April 30, 1894, "Joe the Tamed Turk" (8).

114. "The Life and Death of The Terrible Turk," Graham Noble, May 23, 2003, Eurozone, (18-30).

115. The Salvation Army American *War Cry*, October 18, 1902, "Joe the Turk."

116. ibid.

117. *The Boston Post*, Boston, MA, December 9, 1923, "Joe the Turk—Hard to Kill—Tells of Battles Under Salvation Banner."

118. *The Pioneer*, Bemidji, MN, June 21, 1913, "Joe the Turk to Lecture, Has Traveled Much and Will Tell of Treatment Received by Christians" (1).

119. *Sacramento Daily Record-Union*, Sacramento, CA, May 9, 1889, "Joe the Turk" (3).

120. *Detroit Free Press*, Detroit, MI, March 13, 1891, "A Son of the Orient: Joe the Turk Causes a Rally of Salvation Army Soldiers, He Addressed a Largely Attended Meeting at Fraternity Hall Last Night" (2).

121. *The Tennessean*, Nashville, TN, January 20, 1896, "Captain Joe the Turk: Interesting Talks by an Original Member of The Salvation Army" (5).

122. *Arizona Daily Star*, Tucson, AZ, April 6, 1902, "Joe the Turk: A Unique Specimen of the Genus Evangelist" (5).

123. The Salvation Army American *War Cry*, July 1917, "Joe the Turk at Danbury, CT" (7).

124. *Daily Arkansas Gazette*, Little Rock, AR, January 10, 1909, "Joe the Turk is on the Job, Salvation Warrior, Who Has an Extensive Police Record is Here on a Mission Campaign" (7).

125. *Abilene Semi Weekly Farm Reporter*, Abilene, TX, December 15, 1908, (3) and December 18, 1908, "Character That is Interesting, Joe the Turk's an Eccentric Salvationist, Coming to Abilene" (2).

126. *The Calumet News*, Calumet, MI, May 26, 1913, "Joe the Turk Here" (3).

127. *Fort Scott Daily Tribune* and *Fort Scott Daily Monitor*, Fort Scott, KS, January 24, 1919, "Visited People's College, Joe the Turk Gave an Impromptu Concert Yesterday Afternoon—At Salvation Army Hall Tonight" (1).

128. The Salvation Army Pacific Coast Division *War Cry*, October 1886, San Francisco, Second California Corps, 632 Commercial Street, "Out on Stormy Nights."

129. The Salvation Army Pacific Coast Division *War Cry*, April 12, 1890, "Farewelling, Joe Gives His East Portland Jail Experience" (4).

130. *The Charlotte Observer*, Charlotte, North Carolina, October 30, 1905, "Mr. Joe, the Turk, As He Is, Visitor in the City."

131. ibid.

132. The Salvation Army American *War Cry*, July 1917, "Joe the Turk at Danbury" (7).

133. The Salvation Army Pacific Coast Division *War Cry*, March 29, 1890 and April 5, 1890, "San Francisco III" (6) and "Central California Collection" (5).

134. *Fort Scott Daily Tribune* and *Fort Scott Daily Monitor*, Fort Scott, KS, January 24, 1919, "Visited People's College, Joe the Turk Gave an Impromptu Concert Yesterday Afternoon—At Salvation Army Hall Tonight" (1).

135. *Asheville Citizen-Times*, Asheville, NC, June 11, 1916, "Joe the Turk Draws Big Crowd on Square" (10).

136. *The Iola Register*, Iola, KS, January 27, 1919, "Joe the Turk is in Town."

137. *The Scranton Republican*, Scranton, PA, September 2, 1911, "Joe the Turk Ends His Pilgrimage Here, Famous Salvationist Gives Concert and Sermon at the Barracks" (6).

138. *Reno Gazette-Journal*, Reno, Nevada, August 12, 1914, "He Sings in Eight Tongues" (5).

139. *Alpena Argus*, Alpena, MI, March 4, 1891, "Joe the Turk Was in this City" (3).

140. *The Salt Lake Herald*, Salt Lake City, UT, November 9, 1901, "Joe the Turk Visits Utah, Famous Salvation Army Leader Who Has Been Mobbed in America and Imprisoned in Turkey Will Preach in Salt Lake, Speaks Six Languages" (8).

141. Aramco World, July/August 2011, Volume 62, Number 4, Stewart Gordon: archive.aramcoworld.com.

142. ibid.

143. ibid.

144. The Salvation Army American *War Cry*, November 1891, "What He Thought, If The Lord Can Save Me" (4).

145. The Salvation Army American *War Cry*, September 10, 1892, "Joe, and His Umbrella in Illinois" (7).

146. *The Evening World*, New York City, NY, November 19, 1892, "Salvation Soldiers Gather, Fully 5,000 Coming to the Grand Continental Congress" (1).

147. *The World*, New York, NY, November 20, 1892, "Joe the Turk, and His Famous Multi-colored Umbrella" (24).

148. The Salvation Army American *War Cry*, June 27, 1896, "Joe the Turk: 'Following Jesus,' He Says, 'Is No Child's Play.'" (2).

149. The Salvation Army American *War Cry*, August 15, 1896, "Joe the Turk Has Police protection, Captures a Bottle of Rum, Wonderful Case of Conversion" (10).

150. She became famous as the heroine of the 1863 poem, "Barbara Frietchie," by John Greenleaf Whittier, in which she pleads with an occupying Confederate general, "Shoot if you must this old gray head, but spare your country's flag."

151. *Los Angeles Herald*, Los Angeles, CA, November 11, 1896, "The Salvation Army War, Perils of a Friendly Call at Rival Headquarters" (7).

152. The Salvation Army American *War Cry*, August 6, 1898, "Joe the Turk at the Capital" (11).

153. *Logansport Pharos-Tribune*, Logansport, IN, January 3, 1916, "Joe the Turk is Coming Here." (10).

154. *The Sun*, New York City, NY, April 19, 1914, (4). Also carried in: *The Pensacola Journal*, November 3, 1906; and *Arkansas Democrat*,

January 11, 1909.

155. *The Wilmington Dispatch*, Wilmington, NC, August 10, 1912, "Unique Character, Joe the Turk Will Close Visit Tomorrow" (2). Also carried in: *Petaluma Daily Morning Courier*, August 28, 1914; and The Salvation Army American *War Cry*, January 9, 1915.

156. *The Wilmington Dispatch*, Wilmington, NC, August 9, 1912, "Joe the Turk Here, Prominent Salvation Army Worker in Wilmington for Visit" (8). Also carried in: *The Washington Herald*, February 4, 1912; *The Oregon Daily Journal*, July 13, 1914; and *The Ward County Independent*, July 15, 1915.

157. *The Cincinnati Enquirer*, Cincinnati, OH, October 21, 1937, "Central Press Association" (4).

158. *The Courier-News*, Bridgewater, NJ, March 13, 1911, "Joe the Turk Speaks Here Tonight, This Will Be the Concluding Meeting in a Series He Held at Salvation Army" (9).

159. *Press and Sun-Bulletin*, Binghamton, NY, April 21, 1911, "Armenian Women at Sight of Turk's Sword Tremble, Refugees See Again Husbands and Brothers Cut Down with Terrible Two-edged Weapon Which Joe Wields" (13).

160. The Salvation Army American *War Cry*, May 1911, "Joe the Turk, Brigadier Kimball's Missionary Work—Thrilling Scene at Binghamton with Adana Refugees" (10).

161. The Salvation Army American *War Cry*, July 22, 1893, "Joe the Turk on the Warpath, Previous to His Jailings by the New York State Authorities" (10).

162. The Salvation Army *Officer Magazine*, December 1893, (359).

163. ibid, (359).

164. The Salvation Army American *War Cry*, January 20, 1894, "Lord Ratna Pala's Midwinter Tour of New England, Accompanied by the Irrepressible Joe the Turk, Blood and Fire Times Amid Snow and Ice" (13).

165. "Trade News" (published by The Salvation Army), written by Major Hodges, NHQ Trade Secretary, date unknown).

166. Blood and fire are the two elements of The Salvation Army's flag. Blood represents salvation through the blood of Jesus Christ and fire represent the Holy Spirit's power to sanctify and make whole.

167. The Salvation Army American *War Cry*, August 15, 1896, "Joe the Turk Has Police Protection, Captures a Bottle of Rum, Wonderful Case of Conversion" (10).

168. *The Baltimore Sun*, Baltimore, MD, August 29, 1904, "Throngs at

Glyndon, Interesting Services at The Salvation Army Camp" (6).

169. Ervine, St. John. *God's Soldier: General William Booth*. Volume I, pg 444-446.The MacMillan Company, New York, 1935.

170. Ervine, St. John. *God's Soldier: General William Booth*. Volume II. Page 619. The MacMillan Company, New York, 1935.

171. McKinley, Edward H. *Marching to Glory: The History of The Salvation Army in the United States 1880-1980*, pg 5-7. Harper & Row Publishers, San Francisco, CA.

172. ibid. *Pg* 62-65.

173. The Salvation Army Pacific Coast Division *War Cry*, July 1, 1888, "Jailed for Jesus: The Training Garrison (San Francisco No. 2) Arrested and Imprisoned, Acquitted Twice in One Week, Victory for the Army!" (1).

174. ibid (1).

175. ibid (1).

176. The Salvation Army Pacific Coast Division *War Cry*, July 15, 1888, "Small Shots."

177. *The Los Angeles Times*, Los Angeles, CA, April 19, 1890, "The Salvationists: The "Army" Capitulates to the Police, The Soldiers Again Taken to the City Prison" (5).

178. *The Los Angeles Times*, Los Angeles, CA, April 21, 1890, "The Salvationists: They Parade, but Without the Drum and Fish-horn" (2).

179. *The Los Angeles Times*, Los Angeles, CA, April 27, 1890, "The Salvationists: The Noisy Nuisance Again Out in Full Force" (3).

180. The Salvation Army Pacific Coast Division *War Cry*, May 17, 1890, "Small Shots" (5).

181. The Salvation Army Pacific Coast Division *War Cry*, October 15, 1889, "Jail and Court: East Portland, OR, Another Bad Ordinance" (2).

182. The Salvation Army Pacific Coast Division *War Cry*, November 1, 1889, "In the Toils: East Portland, Arrest and Imprisonment of Seven Salvationists" (5).

183. ibid, (5).

184. ibid, (5).

185. ibid, (5).

186. ibid, (5).

187. The Salvation Army Pacific Coast Division *War Cry*, November 15, 1889, "In the Toils and out Again: East Portland, Oregon, A Poor Rule That Won't Work Two Ways" (4).

188. ibid, (4).

189. ibid, (4).

190. *The Saint Louis Dispatch*, St Louis, MO, March 2, 1895, "Joe and the Judge: A Salvation Army Turk Tells of a Conversion" (4).

191. The Salvation Army Pacific Coast Division *War Cry*, November 15, 1889, "In the Toils: East Portland, Arrest and Imprisonment of Seven Salvationists" (5).

192. ibid, (4).

193. The Salvation Army Pacific Coast Division *War Cry*, December 1, 1889, "Scenes in the War" (1).

194. The Salvation Army Pacific Coast Division *War Cry*, January 4, 1890, "In Jail Again: Hundreds of Cockroaches Running in Every Direction" (5).

195. ibid, (5).

196. The Salvation Army Pacific Coast Division *War Cry*, January 11, 1890, Portland, (7).

197. *The Saint Louis Dispatch*, St Louis, MO, March 2, 1895, "Joe and the Judge: A Salvation Army Turk Tells of a Conversion" (4).

198. *The Evening Review*, East Liverpool, OH, April 7, 1905, "Salvation Army Worker Who Has a Remarkable and Interesting History, Joe the Turk, Who is Speaking in This City Has Been Arrested More than Forty Times in 25 Years" (14).

199. The Salvation Army American *War Cry*, March 25, 1893, "Joe Barred In, The Sound of the cornet is Heard in Prison—article reprinted from *Wisconsin State Register*" (15).

200. The Salvation Army American *War Cry*, April 1, 1893, "The Portage Arrest, Joe Not the Skipping Kind" (8).

201. ibid, (8).

202. ibid, (8).

203. ibid, (8).

204. ibid, (8).

205. ibid, (8).

206. ibid, (8).

207. ibid, (8).

208. ibid, (8).

209. ibid, (8).

210. ibid, (8).

211. The Salvation Army American *War Cry*, July 7, 1893 and July

29, 1893, "In Jail for Jesus, Joe the Turk and Five Comrades Arrested for Marching at Saratoga, NY, Insisting Upon Their Rights, They Are Sent to Jail, The Crowd Cries: Outrage! Shame! Ballston Jail" (4).

212. ibid, (4).
213. ibid, (4).
214. ibid, (4).
215. ibid, (4).
216. ibid, (4).
217. The Salvation Army American *War Cry*, September 9, 1893, "Joe the Turk: He Tells of His Arrests, Persecutions, Victories, and Hopes" (3).
218. ibid, (3).
219. ibid, (3).
220. *The Lowell Sun*, Lowell, MA, February 5, 1894, "Unfortunate Incident in His Crusade Against Sin, Charged With Obstructing the Street" (1).
221. *The Akron Beacon Journal*, Akron, OH, February 5, 1894, "Members of Salvation Army Arrested" (2).
222. *The Lowell Sun*, Lowell, MA, February 5, 1894, "Unfortunate Incident in His Crusade Against Sin, Charged With Obstructing the Street" (1).
223. *Abilene Daily Reflector*, Abilene, TX, February 6, 1894, "Joe the Turk, and Two Army Musicians Arrested at Lowell" (1). Also carried by *The Kansas City Gazette, Ottawa Daily Republic, Columbus Weekly Advocate, Iola Register, Kiowa County Signal, Times-Democrat*, and *The Onaga Herald*.
224. *The Lowell Sun*, Lowell, MA, February 6, 1894, "The Army, It Turns Out to the Trial in Court Today, Joe the Turk was Ably Defended by Mr. Burke, Army was Charged with Obstructing Middle Street" (1).
225. *Wilkes-Barre Times*, Wilkes-Barre, PA, February 24, 1894, Lowell, MA, "The Time Case Appealed, Salvationists Fined" (2).
226. *The Lowell Sun*, Lowell, MA, February 8, 1894, "Who Were Responsible? Salvation Army Gets a Reception From Curious People, Joe the Turk Cracks a Joke at the Expense of Officer Fox" (1).
227. ibid, (1).
228. *The Times*, Philadelphia, PA, February 11, 1894, "Police Guard Salvationists, the Army Ridicules the Arrest of One of Their Number" (8).
229. The Salvation Army American *War Cry*, April 7, 1894, "Inquisitional Tyranny in New England, Salvationists Repeatedly Arrested

and Persecuted on Puritan Soil. Shall it Continue?" (1).

230. *The Lowell Sun*, Lowell, MA, February 12, 1894, "The Salvation Army Appeals to the Governor for State Protection" (1).

231. ibid, (1).

232. ibid, (1).

233. *The Lowell Sun*, Lowell, MA, February 17, 1894, "Cracks a Joke" (16).

234. The Salvation Army American *War Cry*, March 3, 1894, "Lowell Arrests, Excitement and Sympathy, Good Men and True Rally to the Army's Support" (2).

235. ibid, (2).

236. ibid, (2).

237. The Salvation Army American *War Cry*, March 17, 1894," The Rabble in Power, The Salvation Army Pelted with Snow and Dirt and Crowded by the Mob of Hoodlums" (5).

238. The Salvation Army American *War Cry*, April 17, 1894, "Inquisitional Tyranny in New England, Salvationists Repeatedly Arrested and Persecuted on Puritan Soil. Shall it Continue?" (1).

239. The Salvation Army American *War Cry*, September 7, 1895, "In Prison Oft, Joe Jailed Again—Waylaid by Hoodlums—Wanted to Crucify Joe—a Shower Bath" (13).

240. The Salvation Army American *War Cry*, July 27, 1895, "The Colorado Arrests, Joe the Turk Arrested Five Times—Allowed a Brass Band—He Paid His Debts" (15).

241. ibid, (15).

242. ibid, (15).

243. ibid, (15).

244. ibid, (15).

245. ibid, (15).

246. *The Boston Traveler*, Boston, MA, March 30, 1896, (see Introduction for more detail).

247. *Boston Post*, Boston, MA, April 4, 1896, "Drum vs. Bell, Malden Salvationists Putting Up a Fight, Churches Alike Guilty, One witness Testifies Seeing a Woman Thrown From Her Horse, Which Was Terrified by Army's Loud Music" (14).

248. *Boston Post*, Boston, MA, April 1, 1896, "Big Drums to God, Salvation Army in Malden Receive a Setback, Unanimous Action Taken, If an Attempt is Made to Defy Law, Look Out, Joe the Turk Attacked" (1).

249. *Boston Post*, Boston, MA, April 4, 1896, "Drum vs. Bell, Malden Salvationists Putting Up a Fight, Churches Alike Guilty, One witness Testifies Seeing a Woman Thrown From Her Horse, Which Was Terrified by Army's Loud Music" (14).

250. ibid, (14).

251. ibid, (14).

252. *Boston Post*, Boston, MA, April 8, 1896, "No New Facts, Malden Salvationists Still in Clutch of Law" (2).

253. ibid, (2).

254. *Boston Post*, Boston, MA, April 15, 1896, "Army in Jail, Malden's Salvationists Fined for Disturbing the Peace" (2).

255. *Boston Post*, Poston, MA, April 16, 1896, "Joe the Turk Mourns, His Cornet is Taken Away From Him. Have Morning Prayers Daily" (5).

256. ibid, (5).

257. The Salvation Army American *War Cry*, May 2, 1896, "The Malden Difficulty, Arrest of Salvationists—Drums Taken Away—Savage Treatment of Salvationists—a Great Crowd" (1, 4).

258. ibid, (1, 4).

259. ibid, (1, 4).

260. *Wilkes-Barre Times*, Wilkes, Barre, PA, October 20, 1898, "Joe the Turk Returns" (8).

261. *Wilkes-Barre Times Leader*, "The Evening News," Wilkes-Barre, PA, October 21, 1898, "Must Observe the Law, Joe the Turk and Other Salvationists Must Conform to the Ordinances" (1).

262. ibid, (1).

263. *Sunday News*, Wilkes-Barre, PA, October 23, 1898, "Joe the Turk Arrested For Beating the Drum and Blocking the Sidewalk, An Exciting Time at the Lock-up, He and a Companion Given 10 Hours in the Lock-up—the Female Members Cry and Weep" (16).

264. *Wilkes-Barre Times Leader*, "The Evening News," Wilkes-Barre, PA, October 21, 1898, "Must Observe the Law, Joe the Turk and Other Salvationists Must Conform to the Ordinances" (1).

265. ibid, (1).

266. *Sunday News*, Wilkes-Barre, PA, October 23, 1898, "Joe the Turk Arrested For Beating the Drum and Blocking the Sidewalk, An Exciting Time at the Lock-up, He and a Companion Given 10 Hours in the Lock-up—the Female Members Cry and Weep" (16).

267. ibid, (16).

268. *The Scranton Republican*, Scranton, PA, October 29, 1898, "In Trouble Again, Three of The Salvation Army People Placed Under Arrest" (12).

269. *The Wilkes-Barre Times*, Wilkes-Barre, PA, November 2, 1898, "To Test An Ordinance, Salvation Army Say It Is Not a Nuisance to Play a Drum" (5).

270. *Wilkes-Barre Times Leader*, "The Evening News," Wilkes-Barre, PA, November 7, 1898, "Mayor Nichols, and Joe the Turk" (4).

271. *The Wilkes-Barre Record*, Wilkes-Barre, PA, November 15, 1898, "Salvation Army Case Before the Court—Arguments For and Against The Bass Drum and Cornet" (5).

272. ibid, (5).

273. ibid, (5).

274. ibid, (5).

275. *The Wilkes-Barre Record*, Wilkes-Barre, PA, November 21, 1898, "Says the Case Will Be Carried Up" (5).

276. *Sunday News*, Wilkes-Barre, PA, November 20, 1898, "Salvationists Interviewed, What They Have to Say in Regard to the Decision of Judge Woodward" (1).

277. *The Wilkes-Barre Record*, Wilkes-Barre, PA, July 29, 1899, "The Salvation Army Case is Decided. The Mayor Sustained by the Superior Court in His Order Regarding the Beating of Drums" (2).

278. *Wilkes-Barre Semi-Weekly Record*, Wilkes-Barre, PA, August 11, 1899, "Dissenting Opinion in The Salvation Army Drum Case, Judges Beeber and William W Porter Do Not Concur with a Majority of the Court in Deciding in Favor of the Mayor—The Case Will be Appealed to the Supreme Court" (2).

279. *Morning Tribune*, Altoona, PA, November 11, 1899, "The Drum from a Scriptural Standpoint" (6).

280. The Salvation Army American *War Cry*, July 1911, "Joe the Turk's Arrest, Auburn Jury Disagreed—Dismissed at Second Trial" (12).

281. ibid, (12).

282. ibid, (12).

283. ibid, (12).

284. ibid, (12).

285. William Booth's book, *In Darkest England and the Way Out*, declared there was a submerged tenth of the population that lived in poverty and without salvation. His goal was to reach that tenth and

change their fate through the work and ministry of The Salvation Army.

286. The Salvation Army American *War Cry*, July 1911, "Joe the Turk's Arrest, Auburn Jury Disagreed—Dismissed at Second Trial" (12).

287. ibid, (12).

288. *The Charlotte Observer*, Charlotte, NC, October 29, 1905, "Joe the Turk Has Arrived."

289. *The Tribune, Seymour*, IN, July 11, 1907, "Joe the Turk, Man From Constantinople Heard by Big Crowd" (1).

290. *Democrat and Chronicle*, Rochester, NY, October 1, 1906, "This Army Hero Battle-Scarred, Joe the Turk Bears the Marks of Warfare, Under Arrest No End of Times, Famous Salvation Army Worker Attracts Large Audiences to Meetings in the Street and the Citadel— Real Turk Converted to Christianity" (10).

291. The Salvation Army American *War Cry*, April 1906, "Joe the Turk, Albany, NY, Particulars of the Arrest" (13).

292. *The Courier-Journal*, Louisville, KY, August 7, 1905, "Joe the Turk is Versatile Salvation Army Worker, Sings and Plays and Amuses the Audience While Preaching—A Man of Varied Experience" (3).

293. The Salvation Army American *War Cry*, February 14, 1903, "From Joe the Turk."

294. *The Junction City Daily Union*, Junction City, KS, January 17, 1914, "Joe the Turk Here, Noted Salvation Army Worker is in the City" (1).

295. *The Scranton Republican*, Scranton, PA, September 2, 1911, "Joe the Turk Ends His Pilgrimage Here, Famous Salvationist Gives Concert and Sermon at the Barracks" (6).

296. *The Richmond Item*, Richmond, IN, January 15, 1913, "Truth About Turks From Captain Joe, Convert Will Describe Atrocities Practiced by Moslems on Christians" (6).

297. *New Castle News*, New Castle, PA, June 13, 1924, "Sacred Concert to be Given Tonight, Joe the Turk Will Play Several Numbers— Will Describe Turkish Massacre" (20).

298. The Armenian Museum of America, Watertown, MA, is an institution that has the largest collection of Armenian artifacts in North America. It is a 501 (c) 3 charitable organization dedicated to the preservation of Armenian culture and history.

299. Musa Bey, "The Story of Turkey and Armenia, Chapter 2: The

Evil of the Turk—Written by an Eyewitness, but Kept Anonymous for Personal Safety" (31).

300. "Letter to Lucy H. Marred," December 1, 1931. From Joseph Garabed's personal files found in his apartment after his death. The Salvation Army Historical Archives, West Nyack, NY.

301. Cleveland, William L. *A History of the Modern Middle East*, (2nd ed.). Boulder, CO: Westview. 2000. (119).

302. Bartrop, Paul R, and Totten, Samuel. *Dictionary of Genocide*. Greenwood Publishing Group: Westport, CT. 2007. (23).

303. Cleveland, William L. *A History of the Modern Middle East*, (2nd ed.). Boulder, CO: Westview. 2000. (119).

304. Balakian, Grigoris. *Armenian Golgotha: A Memoir of the Armenian Genocide, 1915-1918*. Vintage Books, A division of Random House, inc., New York. 2010. "Chronology."

305. ibid, Introduction, page xiv.

306. ibid, Introduction, page xv.

307. ibid, Introduction, page xviii.

308. ibid, Introduction, page xix.

309. ibid, (19).

310. ibid, Introduction, pages xx & xxi.

311. *Chicago Daily Tribune*, Chicago, IL, July 23, 2894. "Opens With a Rush, Salvation Army Encampment Draws a Crowd to Lake bluff, Hallelujah Midget, Tom-Ma-He-Kum, Joe the Turk Among the Special Workers, Biggest outdoor Meeting in the History of the Grounds" (3).

312. *Chicago Daily Tribune*, Chicago, IL, July 23, 2894. "Opens With a Rush, Salvation Army Encampment Draws a Crowd to Lake bluff, Hallelujah Midget, Tom-Ma-He-Kum, Joe the Turk Among the Special Workers, Biggest outdoor Meeting in the History of the Grounds" (3).

313. *Harper's Weekly: Journal of Civilization*, Volume 38, New York, Saturday, August 11, 1894, "Three Odd Salvation Soldiers, The Indian, The Midget, and The Turk" (759).

314. *Harper's Weekly: Journal of Civilization*, Volume 38, New York, Saturday, August 11, 1894, "Three Odd Salvation Soldiers, The Indian, The Midget, and The Turk" (759).

315. *Chicago Daily Tribune*, Chicago, IL, July 29, 1894, "Joe the Turk's a Star" (26).

316. ibid, (26).

317. ibid, (26).

318. *The World*, New York, New York ,1924, "Joe the Turk Has Spent 40 Years in Saving Souls, Picturesque Salvation Army Captain is Big Drawing Card."

319. The Salvation Army American *War Cry*, January 12, 1901, "Joe's Christmas Adventures in New York City, Joe the Turk (Ensign Garabed) has had another collision with a fractional part of the 'powers that be.' Time: about 8pm. Date: December 19th, 1900" (16).

320. ibid, (16).

321. ibid, (16).

322. ibid, (16).

323. ibid, (16).

324. The Salvation Army, *The Conqueror Magazine*, November 1892, "Exciting Time at Macomb" (343).

325. ibid, (343).

326. The Salvation Army American *War Cry*, October 29, 1892, "Macomb Wonderfully Stirred—Jottings by Joe the Turk" (7).

327. The Salvation Army, *The Conqueror Magazine*, November 1892, "Exciting Time at Macomb" (343).

328. ibid, (7).

329. ibid, (7).

330. *The World*, New York, New York, November 20, 1892, "Coming to Congress, Salvationists Pouring Into the City from All Parts of the Country. Joe the Turk and his Famous Many-Colored Umbrella" (24).

331. The Salvation Army American *War Cry*, December 3, 1892, "Joe the Turk in Chicago, and Vicinity" (13); and December 17, 1892, "Hallelujah Hosts, Report on the Continental Congress of The Salvation Army led by Commissioner Ballington Booth at Carnegie Hall" (2-5).

332. The Salvation Army Pacific Coast Division *War Cry*, November 1886, "Sergeant John Garabed, 2D Cal. Corps" (1).

333. The Salvation Army Pacific Coast Division *War Cry*, January 15, 1887, "San Francisco, A Real Battlefield, Terrible Scene of Blood."

334. *The Daily Courier*, San Bernardino, CA, November 2, 1887, "A Bad Man" (5).

335. The Salvation Army Pacific Coast Division *War Cry*, June 1, 1888, "Small Shots" (6).

336. The Salvation Army Pacific Coast Division *War Cry*, July 15, 1888, "5th Anniversary of the Pacific Coast Division, Seven Glorious Days—Big Marches and Big Crowds" (4).

337. The Salvation Army American *War Cry*, May 5, 1894, "Joe the Turk in Ohio with His Little Foxes, In Prisons Oft, Youngstown Gobbles Him Up" (6).

338. The Salvation Army *Officer Magazine*, October 1896, "In Prison Oft, Joe the Turk Still Moves Around. A Leaf from His Diary" (298-299).

339. The Salvation Army American *War Cry*, May 2, 1896, "The Malden Difficulty, Arrest of Salvationists—Drums Taken Away—Savage Treatment of Salvationists—a Great Crowd" (1).

340. *Democrat and Chronicle*, Rochester, NY, January 3, 1898, "A Salvation Army Soldier Brutally Assaulted at Lyons" (7).

341. *Arizona Daily Start*, Tucson, AR, April 6, 1902, "Joe the Turk, A Unique Specimen of the Genus Evangelist" (5); and *The Oklahoman*, Oklahoma City, OK, May 13, 1903, "Interesting Evangelist."

342. The Salvation Army American *War Cry*, February 3, 1934, "Joe the Turk, the Gripping Story of a Famous Salvationist Pioneer" (4, 5).

343. Ibid, (4, 5).

344. Ibid, (4, 5).

345. Ibid, (4, 5).

346. Ibid, (4, 5).

347. Major Thomas Moore, a British officer, led a separation of The American Salvation Army from the International Army. Eventually, The Salvation Army of America, which was later called American Rescue Workers, rejoined the International Movement. Major Jason Swain's book, *Under Two Flags: The Rise, Rebellion, and Rebuilding of The Salvation Army in America, 1870–1913*, gives a detailed account of the incident.

348. "Letter written to Commander Evangeline Booth," 132 West 14th St., New York City, NY, November 21, 1918. Found in Joseph Garabed's personal papers after his death. Letter can be found at The Salvation Army Historical Archives, West Nyack, New York.

349. The Salvation Army American *War Cry*, August 19, 1899, "The American Contingent at International Exhibition."

350. *New York Times*, New York, October 26, 1899, "Joe the Turk" (6).

351. *The Tennessean*, Nashville, TN, October 24, 1899, "Joe the Turk, Salvation Army Complains of Treatment He Receives in Native Lands" (1).

352. ibid, (1).

353. *Wilkes-Barre Times Leader*, "The Evening News," Wilkes-Barre, PA, October 30, 1899, "Joe Garabed Was Imprisoned and He Charges the US Consul at Smyrna With Not Treating Him as an American Citizen" (2).

354. The Salvation Army American *War Cry*, September 1910, "Joe on Shipboard" (11).

355. ibid, (11).

356. The Salvation Army American *War Cry*, September 1910, "Joe the Turk in Smyrna, Conducts Meeting in Land of the Sultan" (11).

357. ibid, (11).

358. ibid, (11).

359. ibid, (11).

360. The Salvation Army American *War Cry*, January 1911, (7).

361. ibid, (7).

362. ibid, (7).

363. *The Anniston Star*, Anniston, AL, August 6, 1920, "Special Series of Meetings to Close, Joe the Turk Will Tell Tonight of the Armenian Massacres" (7).

364. *Fort Scott Daily Tribune* and *Fort Scott Daily Monitor*, Fort Scott, KS, January 24, 1919, "Visited People's College, Joe the Turk Gave Impromptu Concert Yesterday Afternoon, At Salvation Army Hall Tonight" (1).

365. The Salvation Army American *War Cry*, December 27, 1924, "the Army in Greece, Salvation Meetings Conducted by Staff-Captain Garabed With the Armenian Refugees in Athens—Personal Work Aboard Ship, Joe the Turk and His Sister With Her Pastor" (5).

366. ibid, (5).

367. ibid, (5).

368. ibid, (5).

369. McKinley, Edward H. *Marching to Glory: A History of The Salvation Army in The United States, 1914-1929.* Harper & Row Publishers, (135).

370. ibid, (135).

371. The Salvation Army American *War Cry*, November 1918, "Salvation Army Respected, Editorial from Washington, PA, The Weekly Recorder" (11).

372. *The Bremen Enquirer*, Bremen, IN, May 13, 1920, "Joe the Turk Tours Country for SA Appeal, Meets Great Enthusiasm, His Story Illustrates Change of Attitude Toward Army in Last Ten Years" (6).

373. "Letter written to Colonel McAlena." The Salvation Army International Headquarters, London. England, September 14, 1899, by The Commander, Frederick Booth-Tucker. Personal correspondence from National Headquarters, found in National Archives.

374. The Salvation Army American *War Cry*, January 31, 1925, "Retirement: Retired From Active Service."

375. "Notice to Public," January 19, 1925. Lifetime lease discovered in the personal file of Joseph Garabed, and kept at The Salvation Army Eastern Territorial Archives, West Nyack, New York.

376. Personal correspondence to Lt. Commissioner Ernest Holz, January 24, 1927. Discovered in the personal file of Joseph Garabed, and kept at The Salvation Army Eastern Territorial Archives, West Nyack, New York.

377. Private correspondence to Lt. Colonel William F. Palmer, March 24, 1927. Discovered in the personal file of Joseph Garabed, and kept at The Salvation Army Eastern Territorial Archives, West Nyack, New York.

378. From Joseph Garabed's personal papers recovered in his apartment after his death, which lists all the apartments in the building he was living in. Discovered in the personal file of Joseph Garabed, and kept at The Salvation Army Eastern Territorial Archives, West Nyack, New York.

379. ibid.

380. ibid.

381. Letter to Joseph Garabed in Marseille, France from Brigadier Vernon R. Post, dated June 26, 1926. Discovered in the personal file of Joseph Garabed, and kept at The Salvation Army Eastern Territorial Archives, West Nyack, New York.

382. Letter from Joseph to Brigadier Vernon R. Post, parroting back the contents of the original letter, February 8, 1926.

383. Liability Notice, Common Gambler, March 18, 1935. Discovered in the personal file of Joseph Garabed, and kept at The Salvation Army Eastern Territorial Archives, West Nyack, New York.

384. Letter to Joseph Garabed while staying in Marseille, France from Brigadier Vernon R. Post, September 10, 1926. Discovered in the personal file of Joseph Garabed, and kept at The Salvation Army Eastern Territorial Archives, West Nyack, New York.

385. ibid.

386. Letter to Brigadier Vernon R. Post in New York City, from Joseph Garabed while in Marseille, France. Discovered in the personal file of Joseph Garabed, and kept at The Salvation Army Eastern Territorial Archives, West Nyack, New York.

387. Letter to M. Kalfa, Joe's niece, August 56, 1936. Discovered in the personal file of Joseph Garabed, and kept at The Salvation Army Eastern Territorial Archives, West Nyack, New York.

388. *The Pensacola Journal*, Pensacola, FL, October 27, 1908, "Joe the Turk to Begin Lecture Series on Next Saturday Night" (8).

389. *The Cincinnati Enquirer*, Cincinnati, OH, October 21, 1937, "Central Press Association" (4). Also found in various other periodicals.

390. Last will and testament of Joseph Garabed, dated November 30, 1926, New York City, New York. Discovered in the personal file of Joseph Garabed, and kept at The Salvation Army Eastern Territorial Archives, West Nyack, New York.

391. ibid.

392. Rob Jeffrey, archivist at The Salvation Army Eastern Territorial Headquarters Archives, West Nyack, New York.

393. *The Southern Spirit*, Territorial Periodical of The Salvation Army, USA Southern Territory, February 24, 1992, "Remember the Soldier's Courage" by Mary Strain.

394. ibid.

395. ibid.

396. *Outreach, A Publication of the Prelacy of the Armenian Apostolic Church of America*, Volume IV, Number 3 and 4, July and August 1981, "Salvation Army Veteran's Grave Marked in Winchester."

397. *The Armenian Reporter*, 1967-1991.

INDEX

A

accused, 45, 69, 95, 100

addiction, 26, 32, 69, 124

Adjutant, 82, 84, 131, 171, 275, 278, 280

adventurous, 265

Akron, 286

Alameda, 45

Albanians, 15

Albany, 113, 208, 290

alcohol, 17, 27, 34, 69, 79, 124

Anatolia, 119–120

Angeles, 12–13, 34, 37, 39–40, 48, 62, 78, 133, 194, 197–199, 257, 278–279, 282, 284

Apostle, 178, 272

appeal, 87, 101, 103, 228, 240

appealed, 90, 93, 101, 201, 207

appearance, 51, 59, 61, 126, 238, 259

appointed, 12, 29, 40, 102, 130, 194–195, 225

appointment, 12, 43, 47–48, 51, 76, 97, 111, 128, 195, 202

Arabia, 58

Arabs, 15, 121

Argentina, 6

Arizona, 280, 293

Arkansas, 76, 280–282

Armenia, 1, 7, 11, 13, 15, 52, 119, 175, 179, 223, 225, 234–236, 238–240, 290

Armenian, iii, vii, 7, 11, 13, 16–18, 20, 24, 31, 44–45, 52, 54, 58, 66, 108, 114–115, 118–119, 121, 139, 141, 143–144, 158, 166–167, 169, 174–178, 193, 219–224, 226–230, 232, 234, 236–238, 241–242, 251, 259, 263, 267, 272, 275–276, 280, 283, 290–291, 294, 296

Armenians, 11, 15, 19, 24, 51–53, 65–66, 112, 115, 118–121, 173, 176, 178, 220–222, 225–230, 235, 237–242

Army, ii–iii, v–vii, 1, 4–7, 9–14, 18–20, 24, 26, 28, 30–34, 37–45, 47–49, 51–56, 58–59, 61–64, 67–72, 74–87, 89–108, 111–115, 117–118, 123–124, 126–137, 140–142, 144, 146–151, 153–157, 159–162, 165–177, 179, 181–182, 186–189, 193–195, 197, 199–202, 204, 214–215, 219–221, 223, 225–231, 233–239, 241–243, 245–247, 249, 251–253, 255–259, 261–265, 267–272, 275–296

arrest, 38, 41–43, 69, 75, 78, 82–83, 86, 91–96, 98–99, 101–103, 107–108, 127, 129, 139, 157, 160, 197, 199–200, 202, 205